Felonism: Hating in Plain Sight

FELONISM

Hating in Plain Sight

ANDY AND LINDA POLK

Printed in the United States of America

ISBN: 978-15227876-9-3

Library of Congress Control Number: 2016901915

PUBLISHER: ANDY AND LINDA POLK
P.O. Box 128071
Nashville, TN 37212
www.felonism.com

An error does not become truth by reason of multiplied propagation, nor does truth become error because nobody sees it. Truth stands, even if there be no public support. It is self sustained.

—MAHATMA GANDHI

Contents

Thanks

No human being survives in this world without help from others, starting with the parents who conceive us. Along with our wonderful parents we want to thank Geo Geller for planting the seed that grew into this book and connecting us to a network of people who were willing to help us along the way. Among those are Lauren Ruiz who helped us see our many errors, Issa Ibrahim who masterfully painted Lady Justice griev-ing over felonism's destructive forces in today's criminal court system, Jennifer Welker who created the powerful cover for this book, and Angela Shelton who has joyfully provided us the professional advice, contacts, and wisdom we desperately needed.

Our sincere thanks goes out to each person in this book who demonstrated great courage by honestly talking about the most vulnerable parts of their lives. We pray each contributor will be accepted as the wonderful person he/she is, and we hope they will be greatly rewarded for unselfishly exposing themselves in hopes of helping others.

Even though they are no longer living on this earth, we thank the spirits of Harriet Tubman, Henry David Thoreau, Mahatma Gandhi, Dr. Martin Luther King, Jr, Nelson Mandela and countless others who have faced great danger, even death, to bring about equality for all humans.

Hoping to tell the truth ahead of time, we thank you, the readers, who use what influence you have in your own piece of the world to shine a light on felonism, stop its destructive pattern, and heal our nation.

Our final word of thanks (for the moment) goes to Charlie and Pauline Sullivan and their supporters. Forty years ago, they recognized the problems being created by felonism and founded what is now an international organization, CURE (Citizens United for the Rehabilitation of Errant). Pauline and Charlie have dedicated their lives to the elimination of felonism from public policies wherever it exists. We invite you to support their efforts. Their address is P. O. Box 2310, Washington, DC 20013–2310.

Introduction

Within these pages are real stories about real people who have endured oppression. Some realize that this oppression has altered the way they relate to themselves and the world, as if they had received plastic surgery on their souls. Others seem to have little awareness of the felonism in their own lives, but they plainly see it in those of others. As you read each story, we hope you will recognize their humanity and their struggles to overcome persecution and make a positive place for themselves in this world, because understanding is how we connect to each other.

Just like you, each contributor has their own set of biases based on their experiences, so we have tried to present this issue of felonism from several different directions. Our stories come from people who have lived in prison, lived with prisoners, and worked in prisons. Two of our contributors worked as prison staff before they became prison residents. Desiring to show all sides of the issue, we invited judges, law-enforcement officials, and politicians to make their own contributions to this book, tell their side of the story, but all declined. While these professionals declined to explain their decisions, we know that speaking out against felonism can generate political suicide. We honor those individuals for taking care of themselves.

If you have never had an encounter with the American criminal "justice" system, it may seem that felonism does not affect you or your family, but it does. If you have interacted with police, attorneys, judges, and all the accompanying players, you may think there is nothing more for you to learn, but we hope these pages will provide new insight for all readers.

Felonism is a tool. Just as slavery, racism, sexism, and all other isms have been employed as tools for those willing to abuse power, felonism is being used to manipulate society and increase the power of a few. Although the term is new, the concept is historic.

Felonism has the potential to seriously weaken our society, not just today but throughout our children and grandchildren's future. It is like a hidden cancer in America, metastasizing into every segment of our nation. Just like cancer, felonism may become fatal if we allow its continued growth. No matter what your station in life, we implore you to increase your awareness of felonism and become part of the solution.

We offer some solutions in the last chapter of our book, but first we ask you to join us in a verbal autopsy of this American dis-ease. Witness for yourself how felonism has contaminated the lives of just about every citizen in America, and join us in our outrage at the devastation it is imposing. As a nation, we have always been successful when we unite around a common cause. As individuals, every citizen, whether abiding in a prison cell or mansion, can make a meaningful contribution toward the elimination of felonism. We hope this book is just the beginning of that transformation for our readers and our country.

Authors' Note:

*Words in **bold print** are prison slang. Their definitions can be found in the glossary. Many names and locations have been changed or omitted to protect the innocent and the guilty. Some changes have been identified, but some have not.*

Opinions vary regarding the use of capital letters when identifying racial and ethnic groups. Because the term "white" can include people from all seven continents, we do not capitalize it. When the term "black" refers to people of African descent, we use a capital letter to identify it as a more specific group. We see both groups as equal in value.

Felonism: Hating in Plain Sight

Chapter 1

An Overview of Felonism

For if you suffer your people to be ill-educated, and their manners to be corrupted from their infancy, and then punish them for those crimes to which their first education disposed them, what else is to be concluded from this, but that you first make thieves and then punish them?

—Thomas More, *Utopia*

Oppression of various social groups in America has always sprung from a pattern. People in authority propagate fear and disdain against certain groups with the intent of amassing and maintaining power and wealth. While this pattern may not be conscious, organized, or clearly articulated, it was, and is, implemented by people who are willing to employ treachery to dominate and extract resources from others. Evidence that this pattern is real can be seen in the historic dominance of Native Americans, Africans, women, and others.

These identified segments of society have been segregated and abused physically, financially, socially, and politically—not because they are inferior or deserve to be oppressed by mainstream society, but because it profited the dominant, contemporary Abusers of Power.

A major strategy for these Abusers of Power is propaganda that has just enough truth mixed with lies to create fearful messages acceptable to the uneducated, poor, and/or less powerful. These manipulative directives are often coupled with religious "truths" to extract greater reverence and

3

obedience among the general population. When ignored or confronted with resistance, Abusers of Power aggressively proclaim that their opponents are unpatriotic, worthy of God's wrath, or both.

Yet the pawns of these dishonorable schemes rarely receive the benefits they are promised: favor from the "upper class" (or God), or protection for themselves and family members from the fictitious Monster of the Moment.

The Progression of Oppression Leading to Felonism

Oppression of Indigenous People

Even before the founding of America, European explorers practiced this pattern of tyranny with the indigenous cultures they encountered. Peaceful tribes were maligned and attacked for the benefit of those in control of the colonists. Dominating the very people who helped the settlers survive, those who would amass political favor and wealth enslaved, tortured, and murdered the people they discovered in their newfound territories. They justified the theft of land and enslavement of human beings by claiming it to be "God's will."

A specific example of this pattern is evident in the following historical events. In 1547 Juan Ginés de Sepúlveda, who profited from slaves in Spanish colonies, argued that the indigenous people in the lands conquered by Spain deserved enslavement. Two of his major arguments were that God established the system in which men dominated women and masters dominated slaves, and that slavery benefited the enslaved. He actually argued, "What is more appropriate and beneficial for these barbarians than to become subject to the rule of those whose wisdom, virtue, and religion have converted them from barbarians into civilized men (insofar as they are capable of becoming so), from being torpid and licentious to becoming upright and moral, from being impious servants of the Devil to becoming believers in the true God?"[1] Sepúlveda seems to have believed that men, women, and children murdered by Spanish soldiers deserved the abuse they received because they were not civilized Christians.

Bartolomé de las Casas, a fellow encomienda (men granted ownership of land and the indigenous people living on it) and peer of Sepúlveda, was greatly disturbed by the brutality and slaughter he witnessed as a soldier and landowner. Unlike Sepúlveda, las Casas lived in the conquered Spanish islands. His writings reveal not only Sepulveda's lies regarding the behaviors of the natives in Hispaniola (a Caribbean island discovered by Columbus and conquered by Spain) but also the greed that motivated so-called Christians to ferociously murder and enslave the island residents.[2] Las Casas petitioned King Charles V with a proposal for developing Spanish colonies in a way that profited the indigenous people as well as the Spanish government and requested strict law be implemented prohibiting the mistreatment of the native population. Las Casas' proposal was called the "New Law" and was eventually ratified by King Charles V.

Seeing their future power and wealth threatened by this plan, encomienda opposed las Casas to the point that his life became endangered.[3] Spaniards who profited from slavery were so rebellious against the New Law that King Charles V found them unenforceable, and las Casas was forced to return to Spain.[4] (Does this not sound similar to the pattern used by today's politicians and Abusers of Power who identify their critics as unpatriotic and ungodly, calling them names and threatening their safety rather than having substantive conversations about what would be best for all concerned?)

Eventually, especially in British colonies, the use of indigenous people for labor was replaced by the importation of laborers in the form of indentured servants from various countries. White Europeans as well as Africans were put into contracted servitude (many without their permission) for a specified period of years. It is interesting to note that the first record of slaves in the Americas occurred in 1612 when a shipload of Irishmen were sold in the Amazon,[5] demonstrating that slavery was not just about racism against Blacks. Seven years later, the first ship of Black servants arrived in Jamestown, Virginia.[6] When these ships reached their destinations, contracts were made between the ship captains, who transported the "servants," and the landowners who needed workers—usually without input from the "servant." During the agreed-upon time (three to ten years), servants worked to pay off the fees for their transportation (kidnapping).[7] If servants converted to Christianity prior to the end of their terms, they were immediately released from their contracts because it was considered wrong for Christians to enslave other Christians.[8]

Oppression by Racists

In 1676, Nathaniel Bacon organized a large group of previously indentured servants to rebel against the government of the Virginia colony. The uprising became known as Bacon's Rebellion. An unintended consequence of this rebellion was a rapid switch from the use of indentured servants to the use of African slaves because the Abusers of Power feared the uniting of former Black and European servants they had observed during the uprising. By the late 1600s, African slaves replaced indentured servants in the colonies.[9]

To justify the cruelty rained down upon their captives, slave owners labeled their African slaves heathens, imbeciles, and lower-class species.[10] At the same time, white landowners suggested that slavery increased society's morality and safety.[11] These Abusers of Power often used passages from the Bible to gain social support. They quoted passages such as Ephesians 6:5 from the King James Version (KJV) of the New Testament portion of the Bible: "Servants, be obedient to them that are *your* masters according to the flesh, with fear and trembling, in singleness of your heart, as unto Christ." We suspect they often read Exodus 21:20–21 from the Old Testament KJV just before beating a slave. It says, "If a man smite his servant, or his maid, with a rod, and he die under his hand; he shall be surely punished. Notwithstanding, if he continue a day or two, he shall not be punished: for he is his money."

Abusers of Power excused their inhumane acts to ensure a continued increase of the wealth generated from the blood of their slaves. Whether it was outright deception or mental and emotional blindness, slave owners reported themselves to be merciful. James S. Green, Esq., proclaimed to the Colonial Society in the early 1800s, "There is no people that treat their slaves with so much kindness and so little cruelty."[12]

Even after Great Britain and several other countries abolished slavery in the early 1800s (without experiencing the predicted social or economic upheaval of white society),[13] Southern slave owners continued to perpetuate the notion that not only society, but people of African descent benefited from slavery. Representative John Calhoun inserted this Kafkaesque belief into his speech to Congress in 1837, in which he stated slavery was necessary in all cultures to support the rich and slaves in America were far better off than "free" people in Europe because their masters took care of them when they were old.[14]

Throughout America's history much of the upper echelon agreed with Mr. Calhoun's assertion, but there were some Abusers of Power who did not relish the idea of enslaving other human beings. However, they did not see an alternative that would allow them to maintain their financial and social positions. Both George Washington and Thomas Jefferson spoke out for the elimination of slavery.[15] Thomas Jefferson reasoned that slavery was a contest between justice and self-preservation. He explained this concept in a letter to John Holmes regarding the Missouri Compromise where he stated, "We have the wolf [slavery] by the ears. We can neither hold him, nor safely let him go."[16] President Jefferson's metaphor was prophetic, for the Civil War's triumph of abolishing slavery almost devoured our nation, but the racism generated by slavery continued to flourish.

We still face issues today as a result of this conflict even though logic would have predicted its death within one generation of 1865. According to the U.S. Census Bureau, only 8 percent of Americans owned slaves in 1861.[17] That small minority of rich plantation owners was able to convince the majority of Southern citizens to fight for a cause that only reduced the value of their own labor and pay, and diminished their quality of life. We contend that this display of extortionate influence is being repeated today by a small number of felonists manipulating the majority of our society and imposing the same detrimental effects.

Oppression by Sexists

Those who promoted the institutional oppression of women used the same tactics for the same reasons. With a few exceptions, Abusers of Power convinced society that it was wrong for women to obtain a divorce (even when being beaten), vote in public elections, make medical decisions about their own bodies, receive an equal education, own property, and the list goes on.[18] The propaganda used to support the abuse of women was usually linked to Bible verses that were taken out of context to "prove" women's inferiority to men.[19] Further enticements were offered by promoting fears that suffrage and equality would diminish the power and wealth of men.[20] Men were shamed into compliance by being told only henpecked men would allow their women to get so out of hand as to claim political equality.

The alcohol and cotton industries invested great sums of money in the anti-suffrage movement, asserting that voting women would bankrupt their industries.[21] The lies were many, but they centered on the ideas that men would be degraded and society would suffer if women achieved equality with men. Some of the predictions made by anti-suffrage proponents did come true: Cotton mills eventually had to pay better wages to women (and end their practice of subjecting children to abusive work environments), but they did not go bankrupt as a result of these changes.

While the pocketbook of a few corrupt politicians may have flattened after suffrage was granted to women, the government did not collapse when women voted, despite the predictions that it would. In fact, contrary to the propaganda presented as reason for preserving the status of women as second-class citizens, America continued to thrive as a nation and gave birth to the "Roaring Twenties."[22]

Oppression by Felonists

Thanks to the civil rights movement, profiting from prejudice has lost most of its legality and much of its profitability. However, the struggle for equality is not over. Legalized prejudice against segments of society continues to be encouraged by those who have no scruples about inflicting cruelty to increase their own interests—even when these practices harm our nation.

In his letter to such Abusers of Power from a Birmingham jail, Dr. Martin Luther King Jr. said, "Lamentably, it is an historical fact that the privileged groups seldom give up their privileges voluntarily."[23] And so it is that these Abusers of Power have skillfully reframed their focus toward people with criminal records, those suspected of committing crimes, and those who love accused/convicted individuals. Excusing themselves as righteous protectors of society, Abusers of Power have used legislation, corporate policies, and mainstream media to disenfranchise, marginalize, and segregate the majority of people who have ever been arrested and their supporters. As a result, these Abusers of Power have soared in status and affluence.

We believe felonism in America has its genesis within the Thirteenth Amendment. It seems men of power revealed that they just could not accept total equality among all citizens when they wrote, "Neither slavery nor involuntary servitude, *except as a punishment for crime whereof the party shall have been duly convicted*, shall exist within the United States, or any place subject to their jurisdiction."[24] (The emphasis is ours.) From the framework of that legislative language, many schemes have developed since 1865 to infringe upon the freedom of those without power or economic clout. The racist Jim Crow laws in the South were the support beams of discriminatory criminal codes written over the next one hundred plus years. These written and unwritten rules infiltrated all segments of the government to ensure the oppression of African Americans, other minorities, and powerless and economically challenged whites.

Over the years, America developed a love-hate relationship with criminals, from Billy the Kid to John Dillinger and Bonnie and Clyde. These criminals were seen as both villains and folk heroes, bucking a system that was perceived as unfair and lopsided. During the Great Depression, many farmers and factory workers blamed the banks for confiscating their livelihoods. They read about the wealthy and powerful segments of society doing all manner of vile and immoral acts without ever being challenged. At the same time, citizens witnessed small-time bandits being taken off to prisons, proving that hardworking, honest people had been abandoned by their government. Faced with those realities, people gave gangsters a status that was the antithesis of the negative stereotype applied today.[25]

It can be inferred that J. Edgar Hoover, the first director of the FBI, was aware of the pop culture's admiration for American gangsters and criminals. Whether intentionally or subconsciously, motivated by righteous indignation or a desire to advance his career, Mr. Hoover used the media and changed that image, reframing the American psyche to being more restrained and compliant toward authority figures. Television, the newly emerging media outlet of the day, jumped on board with Mr. Hoover's desire to change the minds and hearts of America regarding their perceptions of the American criminal. Ironically, Mr. Hoover himself employed burglary, sabotage, illegal wire taps, planted evidence, lies, deceptions, and a host of other dirty tricks while demonstrating no mercy toward those he arrested who used the same abusive acts. At the same time, Mr. Hoover consulted for the popular ABC television show, "The F.B.I."[26] and portrayed the Bureau as evenhanded, fair, honest, and successful. He was neither the first nor the last Abuser of Power to employ gross propaganda.

Predicting the motives of such a conflicted man is a difficult task. Did Mr. Hoover create drama around a potential problem so he could present himself as a savior and hero? Could he have truly believed that any means he employed to save America from Communism would be justified in the end, or was he motivated by a thirst for power? Witnessing Blacks and whites working together in criminal enterprises, legitimate art establishments, and social reform movements may have triggered the same fears in Mr. Hoover as those that influenced land owners after Bacon's Rebellion. This is implied in his statement, "The Reds have done a vast amount of evil damage carrying the doctrines of race revolt and the poison of Bolshevism to the Negroes."[27] If Mr. Hoover had believed the Blacks and people suspected of committing felonies were his equals, would he have used criminal acts against them? Isn't it possible that Mr. Hoover was more dedicated to the salvation of his powerful position than the safety of American citizens? Considering his willingness to violate the Constitutional rights of American citizens, we suspect something other than patriotism directed many of his behaviors.

When Dr. Martin Luther King Jr. insisted on organizing a "Poor People's Campaign" in which one million people would march on Washington, D.C., Mr. Hoover told President Johnson that such actions were aimed at undermining America.[28] Allegedly desiring to protect his view of American capitalism and defend us from Communism, Mr. Hoover targeted a multitude of Black organizations and individuals whose only "crime" was seeking justice and a better standard of living.[29] Launching a major FBI effort (called POCAM) under the Ghetto Informant Program (GIP), agents and informants distributed misinformation (lies) and rumors through individuals and the media to destroy plans for the march.[30] We cannot help but believe Mr. Hoover's racist/felonist bias was showing when he masterminded these programs.

What would have happened to the ruling class if all people of poverty united and began asserting their rights? Who would have the power if a successful Poor People's March demanded an end to war, poverty, and injustice? James Earl Ray, who was convicted as the assassin of Dr. Martin Luther King Jr. but who had maintained his innocence throughout the years, told Andy (co-author) shortly before his death that he believed the government killed Dr. King because they did not want the Poor People's March on Washington, D.C. to take place.

While the march went ahead as planned three weeks after Dr. King's assassination, we are certain it did not have the participation or create the impact it would have if Dr. King had been alive.[31] Mr. Ray's theory of a government-supported assassination has some credence; newly released FBI files prove the agency feared Dr. King's power as early as 1955.[32] If that was the reason Dr. King was executed, the strategy was effective, but his dream lived on.

As the depiction of heinous crimes became more common in American media, to some it seemed like the very fabric of society was unraveling. Outrageous crimes committed by mentally ill people—serial killers and those who kidnapped and murdered children—began making their way to the headlines and shifting society's ideas about the word "criminal." While there were fewer of those types of crimes (compared to theft, assault, and property crimes),[33] increased media attention made them seem epidemic. Atrocious acts by mentally damaged individuals, such as Jeffrey Dahmer and Ted Kaczynski, moved America's attention from the previously respected criminal to the vile criminal with a damaged mind. Yet, the love-hate relationship of the past continued on a new path: as moviegoers romanticized and glorified individuals, such as Al Pacino's character in *Scar Face*, they vilified people convicted for driving under the influence of alcohol.

Rather than casting all criminals as evil minions, we believe criminal activities are rooted in one of three origins: mental, economic, and environmental deficiency, with the majority falling on the economic side. Not only is poverty a motivation for crime, but the prosecution of crime—targeting ethnic gangs who live in poverty—has become as American as apple pie. Black communities have experienced a plethora of government-sanctioned discrimination, which has contributed to years of economic struggle and injustice. Such practices have sabotaged efforts to integrate the Black population into the melting pot of America's middle class. From share-cropper slavery and Jim Crow laws to racist legal systems that routinely give a disproportionate amount of harsh and unfair sentences to African Americans,[34] it is evident that felonism and racism are offshoots of classism.

That pattern has played out in more recent times with the implementation of mandatory-minimum sentences. Although these federal and state laws were officially motivated by a desire to ensure equal and objective sentencing, the laws were tainted with racism, classism, and felonism. Possession of 500 grams of powder cocaine had the same mandatory five-year sentence as possession of 28 grams of crack, even though they are the same drug. The difference is that crack is cheaper, so it is used more often by low-income individuals, thereby increasing the frequency and length of incarceration for Blacks and others living in poverty. Even after the Fair Sentencing Act (which changed the sentencing disparity ratio from 100:1 to 18:1—still unfair)[35] was passed in 2010, disparity still exists in the number of Black versus white citizens incarcerated for drug use. Although whites use cocaine and other illegal drugs more often than Blacks, and are a larger part of the population, police are more likely to stop and search a group of Black teens hanging out on the street corner than a group of white teens.[36] In that pattern, it is obvious that felonism is an extension of racism.

Accelerating Felonism

Looking back to the development of felonism, we see the 1960s were violent times. Dr. King's assassination was followed by the murder of Bobby Kennedy. Police murder squads targeted Black Panther Party members.[37] Violent riots and war protests broke out, as well as the Tet Offensive in Vietnam (which led to President Johnson's eventual refusal to run for a second term).[38] All combined to yield a growing loss of trust in the United States government. From those ashes, however, grew a brief period of positive reforms, both in criminal and social justice.

The United States Supreme Court came out with many rulings that strengthened criminal justice reform. For example, Gideon v. Wainwright (circa 1963) guaranteed the appointment of an attorney for all criminal defendants,[39] and Miranda v. Arizona (circa 1966) ruled that suspects have the right to refrain from answering investigators' questions without the presence of their attorneys.[40] In cases like Furman v. Georgia (circa 1971), the Supreme Court declared the death penalty violated both the Eighth and Fourteenth Amendments,[41] a ruling that temporarily abolished the death penalty in America.

Unfortunately, these reforms had not been fully implemented when America was exposed to the harsh reality of prison life in 1971, as New York's Attica state prison blew up in a massive riot. Rather than continuing efforts to negotiate a solution, officials stormed the walls, killing forty-three prisoners and ten hostages.[42] Had felonistic attitudes gotten out of the way and allowed a speedier implementation of reforms, fifty-three lives might have been spared in Attica.

Yet, as a result of aforementioned judicial changes, and other influences, the rights of America's prisoners were soon given more credence. This was especially true when Wolff v. McDonnell's decision was announced in 1974: For the first time, prison staffs were barred from interfering with mail from attorneys to prisoners. This ruling also ensured due process for prisoners when charges from prison staff were made against them, creating the position of quasi jailhouse lawyers (inmate advisers) who could act on behalf of accused prisoners.[43]

With this new ruling from the Supreme Court, prisoners had open access to the courts. Grievances of both criminal and civil matters could finally be addressed in court. This access, while painful for prison administrators, was a safety net against abuse for prisoners, and it temporarily fostered honesty and vigilance among prison officials.

Though the focus on prisoner rehabilitation fizzled out after 1974, a popular American song performed by Tony Orlando and Dawn echoed the prevailing social attitude of that time, which allowed for the redemption of men/women who had committed crimes. The song is about a returning citizen who has just left a three-year stint in prison and is riding a bus home. Before leaving prison, he wrote a letter to his romantic interest and requested that she tie a yellow ribbon around a designated tree if she is willing to accept him back into her life. The returning citizen reveals this request to his fellow passengers and explains his plan to remain on the bus if the tree is not properly decorated. The song ends with cheers from all the passengers as they witness 100 yellow ribbons tied on the "ol' oak tree."

In America's current climate, the lyrics of "Tie a Yellow Ribbon Round the Ol' Oak Tree" are not acceptable for several reasons. First of all, it is not emotionally and/or physically safe for returning citizens to publicly announce their recent release from prison. Such a revelation often results in ridicule and/or isolation if not outright abuse. Secondly, the majority of Americans no longer demonstrate a belief in redemption. The idea that after paying the penalty for their offense, people are to be accepted back into society as equals no longer exists. Today, most bus passengers in such a scenario would probably hope for a different result. They would not want to see such a low-class individual succeed in a romantic relationship. A third reason that this song would not be accepted today is that returning citizens know prejudice against them easily spreads to their loved ones. While people with felony convictions may willingly subject themselves to ridicule, they usually protect their families by keeping their own criminal histories on the down-low.

Using Felonism to Weaken Civil Rights and Gain Political Power

According to *The Encyclopedia of Crime and Punishment*, by David Levinson, the 1970s saw the end of criminal justice reforms and the faith in prisoner rehabilitation that had begun in the 1960s. This decline was coupled with a push toward the closing of many mental health institutions when media exposure revealed the horrors inside mental asylums. Thousands of mentally challenged people were dumped onto the streets, multiplying the homeless population and expanding the population of prisoners.[44] As if mental issues did not contain enough social stigma, many citizens were given prison numbers that camouflaged their mental diagnoses.

The trend of abandoning prison and legal reforms continued into the 2010s. In 2012, the U.S. Supreme Court relaxed the laws regarding Miranda Rights, stating these rights do not have to be read to suspects

prior to interrogations if prisoners are given a choice between returning to their cells and answering interrogators' questions.[45] We interpret
this ruling as felonistic because it is reasonable to assume that prisoners
may perceive an interrogation free of their Miranda Rights being read
as also being free of potential prosecution after having their words used
against them.

This trend toward increasing felonism led to the creation of the
child-criminal. In the 1990s every state in the union passed stricter laws
that categorized more children as adults, even though violent crimes
among juveniles were decreasing during that time.[46] Today there are over
2,500 juvenile prisoners serving life-without-parole sentences.[47] Eighty
percent of these prisoners witnessed violence in their homes prior to
their convictions. Suspicions of felonism were raised in our minds when
we learned that the majority of juveniles with life sentences live in five
states: California, Louisiana, Massachusetts, Michigan, and Pennsylvania.
Isn't it more likely that these life-without-parole sentences are politically
motivated rather than the idea that youth in these states have a greater
propensity for homicide?

The most telling statistic related to this population of prisoners is that
ten times more Black children per capita are condemned to life in prison
than white children.[48]

Like dominoes, our constitutional amendments are falling down, out
of reach for low-income citizens. While our nation continues to be great
and powerful, the liberty envisioned by our forefathers is fading at an
alarming rate. Abusers of Power have created a fearocracy so that citizens
will seek their help. When enough fear is generated, Abusers of Power
step in and present "solutions." The pattern goes something like this:
"Are illegal immigrants stealing your jobs?" they might ask (even though
there is evidence that this is not true). "Here, pay us big money, and we
will build detention centers to contain them while creating job growth."
"Thirty-one percent of traffic fatalities are being caused by drunk drivers?[49] We can fix that. Let's stop every car on the highway to see who's
been drinking. We might do a bit of reconnaissance while we're at it: ask
people to reveal personal information; ask to search cars even though we
have no probable cause . . ."

Without any type of military coup, we have been persuaded to trade
our rights to freedom of speech, freedom from illegal search and seizure,

due process, freedom from testifying against ourselves, freedom from cruel and unusual punishment, and more, for the illusion of security. As Benjamin Franklin said in 1755, "Those who would give up essential Liberty, to purchase a little temporary Safety, deserve neither Liberty nor Safety."[49] In the following pages, you will see many ways in which our civil rights have been sold out in the name of security and for the purpose of giving power to politicians.

We begin with three-strike laws. The repeated commission of a crime after a person leaves prison has always been a possibility. In the early 1990s, Abusers of Power convinced the public that people with three or more convictions must be treated with more punitive laws to protect the public. Abdicating responsibly for healing those convicted while they were incarcerated, legislatures across the nation got on board with enhancement bills, bills that increase the length of prisoners' sentences. With the stated intent of closing the "revolving door," many enhancement laws have crossed the line into the area of double jeopardy: The Fifth Amendment makes it illegal to charge someone twice for the same offense, but enhancement laws allow this violation as well as imposing multiple punishments for one offense.[51] The few politicians, judges, and law-enforcement officials who recognize this breach of the Constitution seem unwilling to speak out against the practice of judging people twice for the same crime by giving one action multiple names.

Under the guise of Constitutional compliance, Jim Crow and Black laws have been replaced by prejudicial practices against individuals suspected and / or convicted of committing a crime. If that statement seems too bold, please consider the evidence. Instead of lynching, we now have thousands of citizens being killed by police officers. Many of those suspects were unarmed, displaying signs of mental illness, and members of the lowest social economic class.[52] Our First Amendment right to peacefully assemble has been repeatedly violated by government officials. Before going into detail, we want to emphasize that felonism is generated and sustained by Abusers of Power who are very crafty at tricking or forcing main stream society into performing their repressive deeds. We have met law enforcement officials and wives of police officers who disagree with the policies they are required to enforce. There are many officers who consistently display deep compassion and mountains of self-control as they compassionately interact with abusive, mean-spirited individuals and do their best to uphold the Constitution. We are sure it broke their hearts as much as ours to witness the peaceful protestors in Ferguson, Missouri (and other cities) who spoke out against the death of an unarmed teen, and systemic government abuse of citizens charged with minor offenses being met by agent provocateurs who escalated tensions. First, a police dog urinated on a memorial to Michael Brown. Then a police car drove over the memorial.[53] Later that day and in the following weeks, law-enforcement officials presented themselves in masse, wearing full military garb. Some even rode on top of armored vehicles poised in sniper positions with laser-guided rifles.[54] After weeks of investigating, U.S. Attorney General Eric Holder's 2014 report clearly outlined the repeated violation of citizens' First-, Fourth-, and Fourteenth-Amendment rights by local government officials for the purpose of generating government revenue. [55] We regret that the person who sparked the protests in Ferguson, Missouri, Michael Brown, did not have the credentials of Rosa Parks, but we propose that if felonism had not permeated the local government in the 2010's, like racism did in the 1950's, there would have been no riots after Mr. Brown's death.

The Sixth Amendment covers the right to a fair and speedy trial by a jury of our peers, a public trial, and the appointment of an attorney. Today, less than three percent of criminal arrests end in a trial by jury according to Jed S. Rakoff's 2012 report, "Why Innocent People Plead Guilty." That leaves over 97 percent to be resolved with plea-bargain agreements where the prosecutor has all the power to determine how a crime will be charged and what punishment will be imposed.[56] Prosecutors may charge a person with DUI or reckless driving; manslaughter or first degree murder. Defendants who choose to go to a jury trial in both state and federal systems will suffer more charges and harsher punishment for insisting on their innocence and using their Sixth Amendment right. Mr. Rakoff also stated that jury trials for narcotic charges result in average sentences of 16 years; however, defendants who accepted plea agreements to similar charges served an average of five years and four months in prison.[57] Prosecutors also get to set the timeline for a plea, often demanding a plea be accepted before defendants and their attorneys know what evidence has been built up against them. To say this pattern of prosecutorial extortion has a chilling effect is a gross understatement. For innocent or overcharged victims, that ground is not chilled; that ground is frozen solid.

Felonists have also affected the Eighth Amendment which covers excessive fines and unreasonable bail, and prohibits cruel and unusual punishment. Citizens are charged excessive fines almost every day of the week. Some jails seem to have a practice of letting people pay their bonds to get out of jail while a particular warrant is waiting to be heard by a judge. Then they re-arrest the suspect the next day for a different warrant, which they knew was in effect at the time the individual bonded out on the first warrant. Mr. Eric Holder's report on Ferguson, Missouri clearly demonstrates a similar practice in the following statement, "... in 2007, one woman received two parking tickets that—together—totaled $152. To date, she has paid $550 in fines and fees to the city of Ferguson. She's been arrested twice for having unpaid tickets, and spent six days in jail. She still owes Ferguson $541. And her story is only one of *dozens* of similar accounts that our investigation uncovered."

Also in violation of the Eighth Amendment is the creation of debtors' prisons. Today, thirteen states and over 1,000 courts use private companies to collect fines for minor offenses, such as expired vehicle tags. Defendants who are unable to pay have higher fees tacked onto their fines and are eventually incarcerated for non-compliance with a judge's order.[58] Such a travesty would not have been tolerated by our founding fathers.

Citizens on parole must pay fines. If they don't have jobs to pay the fines, they may be sent back to prison. Because felonists make it difficult to obtain employment after incarceration, this is a tangible threat to the freedom of returning citizens. If a wealthy person is arrested and given a bond of $500,000, that's reasonable. But if an average citizen is arrested and their bail is set at $500,000, that's not reasonable at all. This practice is equivalent to denying bail to people with low incomes. On any given day, 730,000 people are locked up in local jails because they are too poor to pay their bails.[59]

Now we come to our Constitutional guarantee against cruel and unusual punishment. If it is cruel to murder someone, then it makes sense that we would have statutes in our laws to stop citizens from murder. We agree murder is cruel. We can all agree that murder is punishment. Yet we are one of the few non-Muslim nations that claim to be civilized while enforcing the death penalty. Is torture and induced psychosis cruel and unusual? It occurs every day in jails, and prisons all over America, especially when long-term solitary confinement is implemented.

The Tenth Amendment states that the federal government only has the power that is delegated to it from the States and from the people and the Constitution. But with all of the federal prisons scattered across the United States, one has to ask, "Where did they get the power to create so many federal statutes as well as the power to dictate to the states what laws and statutes that they should enact?" The answer is a little thing called "interstate commerce," which says the federal government has the right to these broad controls. All federal statutes are tied to it in one way or another. Using interstate commerce for the creation of a bureaucracy of law-enforcement agencies, the FBI, ATF, DEA, etc., are suspected felonists at best and conspirators against their own citizens at worst.

As mentioned earlier, the Thirteenth Amendment has a savings clause in it that allows servitude for people duly convicted of a crime. Until this clause is changed, minorities and poor people will always be in danger of powerful people coming together and finding ways to increase their likelihood of becoming servants to the industrial prison complex.

Finally, we come to the Fourteenth Amendment. Again the Constitution talks about due process and equal protection; however, legislative trends have placed obstacles in front of citizens trying to achieve an appeal have made the pursuit of an appeal nearly impossible. It is as if the law assumes that after a conviction, prisoners magically understand and know all the nuances of law. It can take years to understand abuses of justice committed by an inept attorney or to discover new facts that prove a conviction was in error, yet citizens are allowed only a small window to appeal their cases (one year for most cases). As we will see in Susan and Stacy's story, if you fail to get your appeal in on time, no matter the reason, you lose your right to all future appeals. Even if new evidence can prove you're innocent, you are out of luck and out of options for getting out of prison.

Felonists Who Profit the Most

Mass incarceration and the denial of new beginnings to ex-felons is especially profitable for one segment of America's upper class—politicians. Many state and federal legislators, executives, and judges have been elected based on their promises to make America safer by being "tough on crime." Remember the Willie Horton advertisements that helped President George H. Bush defeat Governor Dukakis in 1988?[60] What about Bill Clinton's "tough on crime" stance in 1993[61]? Aside from gaining votes, elected officials also receive campaign contributions and other monies from private corporations profiting from the prison industry. We will reveal more about that later in this chapter.

President Clinton did fulfill that campaign pledge in 1994 with the Violent Crime Control and Law Enforcement Act. While his intentions appeared righteous, this act is riddled with laws that have actually made society less safe. Forbidding access to Pell Grants to prisoners with few financial resources,[62] denying them public assistance to housing when they leave prison, requiring long mandatory minimums for select convictions,[63] and demanding states create registries for all people convicted of sex crimes has greatly increased recidivism.[64] Twenty years later, we are learning that the slight reduction in crime during President Clinton's administration may have had more to do with a decrease in the percentage of citizens in the "crime prone" age (fifteen to twenty-four years of age)[65] than an implementation of harsher penalties. Studies are also indicating that the slight reduction of crime attributed to this act has been greatly overshadowed by the negative effects of mass incarceration.[66]

In lockstep with politicians, mainstream media companies have learned to increase their profits by promoting this prejudice against ex-felons. Sensational news stories are presented nightly regarding the arrests of individuals with previous convictions, as if past verdicts prove they are guilty of the latest accusations. In the 1960s, television and radio news reporters held themselves to higher standards. Personalities such as Rush Limbaugh and Nancy Grace could not have become millionaires using their current rhetoric (i.e., all suspects are guilty until they prove themselves innocent). Fifty years ago, personal opinions and assumptions about the motives of suspects were not presented as if they were factual news. "If it bleeds, it leads" seems to be the media's mantra today, and it feeds the power and profits of felonists.

According to Dr. Deborah Serani, fear-based reporting is designed to increase the viewers' anxiety or fear about a newly discovered topic so that audiences will stay tuned in for the next broadcast. Viewers can see this pattern for themselves when watching almost any news program:

Often an event is presented as if it can have a horrible effect on viewers' lives. Then solutions and methods for protection are promised to be forthcoming either later in the same broadcast or in the near future. In her 2008 article in *Psychotherapy and Psychoanalysis*, Dr. Serani reveals that news conglomerates hire consultants to script programs in a way that ensures the rhythm, grammar, graphics, etc., will elicit the necessary fear to maintain the audience's loyalty.[67]

Often commentators present their opinions with such passion that the vitriol they spew during a trial can't be retracted after the jury determines the potential felon to be innocent. In these situations, no apologies are given for past inaccuracies. They offer no praise for the court system in finding a just verdict. These corporate purveyors of propaganda simply switch their target. Such shows have caused grave concern for defendants and their attorneys because they blatantly taint jury pools. We believe widespread felonism is responsible for this one-sided focus on free speech (which is not always truthful) being given preeminence over the individual's right to a fair trial.

Because it's so rare for a news show to feature adults with previous convictions doing something positive, returning citizens can receive national attention when their good deeds are identified by local stations. This occurred on June 17, 2014, when Bryant Collins noticed an unattended three-year-old child on the side of a busy Georgia highway. After pulling over and notifying the authorities, Mr. Collins stayed with the child until she was in a safe and stable situation. Such an act would not usually make national news, but Mr. Collins had spent ten years in prison.[68]

While this was a positive story, it was also rather sensational. Sharing everyday success stories of ex-felons who overcome great obstacles to emerge as contributing members of society could be highly beneficial to viewers, but it would not contain a sensational or fear-based message to keep viewers coming back for more. In fact, making a practice of reporting on successful returning citizens would probably motivate felonists to change channels.

Wading past the media-focused crusade against returning citizens, we find a small group of individuals and corporations accumulating billions of dollars by investing in private prisons, prison phone companies, prison food service companies, and *many* other prison-related businesses. With the rise in felonism has come an acceleration of privatized prisons, or is it the other way around, are private companies quickening felonism?

According to the *Washington Post*, the top two private prison companies have donated $10 million dollars to political candidates and spent $25 million on lobbyists since 1989.[69] The privatization of juvenile correctional facilities was so lucrative in the early 2000s that two juvenile court judges were caught receiving over $2 million in exchange for sentencing a high percentage of their cases to these private companies. Not only were two judges corrupted but thirty individuals, most of them publically elected, were eventually prosecuted for their participation in this "kids for cash" conspiracy.[70] Keep in mind that even after paying these political contributions and bribes, private prisons still reported hundreds of millions in profits.[71]

Private telephone companies have also cashed in on politically accepted trends created by felonists. The fact that prison phone calls have to be recorded and monitored (to make sure no one is plotting an escape or some other nefarious activity) has been used as an excuse for charging outrageous fees for phone privileges. This argument sounds reasonable, but it fails to explain why millions of dollars in commissions (some call them concession fees, but we call them kick-backs) are paid to state and local agencies while the phone companies still make large profits for themselves.[72] Securus, the phone company holding 20 percent of this market, made a whopping $114.6 million in profits after paying concession fees in 2014.[73]

Richard Smith, Securus' CEO says his company has paid $1.3 billion dollars in concession fees over the last ten years.[74] That averages out to $130 million per year! What he fails to acknowledge is that it was the family members and supporters of prisoners who paid those fees to Securus as the result of their excessive pricing schemes. We believe paying commissions to government entities is equal to imposing a special tax unique to those who support prisoners. Such impositions are illegal, but we know of no court cases challenging these established practices.

In recent years public and private prisons have begun employing private companies as "bankers" for transferring money between families, and other sources, to or from prisoners. Ryan Shapiro, founder of JPay, started the first prison "bank" in 2002. He says his motivation was to help people send money to their loved ones in a more efficient and less time-consuming manner. When interviewed by Ariel Schwartz at *Business Insider,* Mr. Shapiro refused to divulge information regarding profits earned from the fees charged,[75] but we know they are substantial. When money is sent to a prisoner, a fee of up to 50 percent of the amount sent is added to what the customer must pay.

Once JPay or their competitors are established with an institution (prison, jail, or parole board), traditional money orders and cash are no longer accepted as tender for paying fines and fees, adding money to prison phone accounts, or purchasing items from the few vendors who are allowed to sell food, clothing, electronics, and toiletries to prisoners. In some cases, money orders can be used to pay these prison banks and avoid these fees, but there is a consistent pattern of long delays when this method is employed.[76] This can be tragic for parolees in jeopardy of being incarcerated for non-payment of their fees.

JPay, and its one or two competitors, have added services such as prison-approved electronic devices that allow music downloads and approved emails and video chats between prisoners and people on the outside—for a price. Just like prison phone companies, these banks pay commissions to the jails, prisons, or states who contract with them. We know commissions for phone companies can be as high as 93.9 percent of the amount paid for the calls,[77] but Mr. Shapiro refuses to disclose his commission rates or profit information to the public. We do know his company pays commissions of about $4,000 per month to the state of Illinois.[78] If that amount is typical of the thirty-two states with JPay contracts, we estimate that prisoners and their family members are paying over $1.5 million annually. Mr. Shapiro says JPay fees are designed to be as low as possible, even though at least one competitor charges significantly lower rates. He claims JPay fees are not high enough to impact the families paying them and that commissions are required by the contracted states. Do you think he makes similar justifications for the huge parties he pays for at conventions for prison vendors and the expensive gifts he distributes to directors of corrections in various states?[79]

It appears that institutions greedy for the profits generated by JPay's services have sprung into action in at least one public prison. When interviewed by the Center for Public Integrity regarding the electronic devices sold by JPay, prisoners in Ohio reported that the state department of corrections took away the radios they had legally purchased when JPay music players and tablets became available.[80] These tablets cost prisoners and their families about $70, but additional fees are added each time a prisoner sends an email, participates in a video chat, or downloads music. JPay commissions are paid to states (or whichever institution holds the contract) based on the amount of money that flows through the system, so eliminating JPay's competition for prisoner entertainment devices ensures higher revenues. We suspect the situation will only get worse for prisoners and their families when Securus completes its acquisition of JPay.[81]

While some companies enjoy profiteering directly off prisoners (and there are many more than the ones mentioned above), others believe they increase their bottom lines by isolating themselves from any person who has ever had contact with the criminal "justice" system. In 2012 the Equal Employment Opportunity Commission (EEOC) found PepsiCo in violation of Title VII of the Civil Rights Act of 1964. PepsiCo had a policy for denying employment to applicants with minor offenses and even arrest histories that never led to convictions. Charges with no relevance to the job were used as justification for denying employment. Because their policy mostly excluded Black applicants, Pepsi's actions were seen as racial discrimination. As a result of this policy, PepsiCo was fined $3.13 million.[82]

Pepsi was fined for their prejudicial behaviors, but they are not alone in their practice of racism via felonism. The policies of many major American corporations ban the hiring of applicants with any type of criminal background, including arrests for which they were not convicted. America recently witnessed the irrational logic of felonists when Apple abruptly ordered all returning citizens to be fired from their construction site in Cupertino, California.[83] Under public pressure, and insistence from union leaders, Apple has since rescinded this felonistic move, but it has not shared the reasoning behind their initial action.[84]

Having been unemployed ourselves, we know applying for a job puts a strain on currently limited resources. After arranging for childcare, finding transportation, and spending time completing applications, it is extremely disheartening to discover that the company advertising a need for your skills will not allow you to explain the circumstances around your arrests. They don't want to hear about the positive changes you have made since your conviction.[85] For millions of Americans, a five- to ten-year-old conviction stemming from a misdirected youth or thoughtless moment has become a life sentence of judgment and discrimination.

After years of witnessing and experiencing this monstrous, institutionalized prejudice against people with, or those about to receive, felony convictions (and their loved ones), we decided this phenomenon had to be given a name. Just as racism was not addressed in a meaningful way until after it had been named in 1938,[86] we knew this prejudice would continue its stealth invasion of American policy and culture as long as it remained unidentified.

Brainstorming led us to the word "felonism" because it identifies the heinous pattern of prejudice while reminding us that felonism is closely related to racism. (Both have been institutionalized for the same reasons—power and money.) In 2011 we presented the naming of this monster to the public while speaking at a 140 Conference in NYC. Just as it took some years for the word "racism" to become part of mainstream America's vocabulary, "felonism" has been slow to integrate into the English language. It is our hope that this book will speed up the process.

Because the word is new, current research does not sufficiently detail the destruction this prejudice has inflicted upon our nation, but felonism is present and pervasive. Parallel to Frederick Douglass's observation that racism heaped debilitating effects upon the plantation owner as well as the slave (although he didn't use the word "racism"),[87] felonism has stunted progress throughout our society and created a "them against us" attitude within our education, political, economic, and legal systems that affects everyone.

President Roosevelt indicated that oppression of any group is a matter of national security when he said, "We must remember that any oppression, any injustice, any hatred, is a wedge designed to attack our civilization."[88] Although neither was talking about felonism, the words of Dr. King Jr. applied the same reasoning used by Mr. Douglas and President Roosevelt when he said, "All segregation statutes are unjust because segregation distorts the soul and damages the personality. It gives the segregator [racist and felonist] a false sense of superiority and the segregated a false sense of inferiority."[89] When prisons are transformed into healing centers, when social and financial incentives for arresting, prosecuting, and housing citizens convicted of crimes are eliminated, and errant behavior is viewed as a community issue that requires healing, then we will know we have overcome all oppression. Then we can amend Dr. King's words to, "I had a dream, and it came true."

It is easy to see that the proponents of slavery were those who benefited socially and financially from racism, while abolitionists had discovered other ways to amass wealth. Would it be possible to fool members of the Aryan Nation or the KKK into believing their race was superior without the promise of increased power and/or wealth? Would any oppression of another human being be sustainable if there were no perceived benefit for the perpetrator? We think not, and we believe the same applies to felonism.

We invite you to read the true stories in the following chapters. After reading these narratives, please ask yourself, "Am I a felonist?" If your answer is "yes," then the next questions would be, "Do I want to continue playing the role of a pawn for the Abusers of Power and participating in damaging our nation? Do I have the courage to conquer the unsubstantiated fears I have accepted as truth and work to build up my country one neighborhood at a time?"

A question that we often ask ourselves is, "What will happen to America if we don't address and eliminate felonism?" With your help, we will never find out.

Chapter 2

Andy & Linda's Story:
The Authors' Journey

Two frogs fell into a bowl of cream. One didn't panic, he relaxed and drowned. The other kicked and struggled so much that the cream turned to butter, and he walked out.
                                                    —Anonymous

At the age of forty-two, I finally found the love of my life. He was tall, handsome, loving, spiritual, intelligent, creative, and much more. Andy possessed all the qualities I had enumerated in my spiritual request for the perfect mate. Following two divorces and years of dating, I was on clouds. At times, it literally felt like I was hovering a few inches above the ground as I walked. Friends even said I looked younger because my happiness was so complete.

But (there has to be a "but") lurking behind that budding relationship stood an unidentified monster. It's hard to pinpoint the exact moment this slimy prejudicial phenomenon (that I have named "Monster") first appeared and tried to cast a cloak of shame around me for developing this beautiful relationship. Maybe it was when I witnessed the horror on my friends' faces as I first told them about a particular aspect of my relationship with Andy. Maybe it was when the director of my graduate program called to announce my imminent dismissal if the rumor she had heard was true.

The prison staff member in charge of practicum students had called several weeks after I had finished my social work duties at the state's prison hospital (I will call it SNF for Special Needs Facility). She reported that I had been escorted off prison grounds for having an inappropriate relationship with a prisoner. The rumor was not true. I was never escorted off prison grounds, nor was I in an inappropriate relationship with a prisoner. Contrary to the dominate beliefs and policies accepted by prison staff, who view prisoners as subhuman, befriending a prisoner was not inappropriate in my mind, although it was true that my future husband had been incarcerated for twenty years before we met and was still in prison.

That slimy, monstrous mindset usually led to comments from others like, "he's not good enough for you," "you deserve better than a sexless relationship," "he's manipulating you," "he might try to hurt you if he gets out," "he's only using you," or (the hardest argument for me to confront) "you are only in this relationship because it is safe for you—he can't hurt you while he's in prison." Just like most fear mongers, this monstrous mentality mixed a little truth with lies and tried its hardest to obliterate the most intimate (although platonic) relationship I had ever known.

Monster's rhetoric probably would have come out of my own mouth if someone I knew had been in the same situation, but this was happening to me, and it felt dissimilar from my past, dysfunctional relationships. That didn't mean I was going to ignore possible red flags. As a precaution, and probably defending myself against the unrecognized statements Monster was making in my own head, I asked my adult daughter and two friends to meet Andy and give me their honest feedback. After all, I had spent the last three years intensely working on freeing myself from past patterns of codependency. It was possible that I was fooling myself yet again, but all three "investigators" met Andy and returned with positive reports. My mental monster was now mute to me but not to everyone around me.

During my practicum (on-the-job training), Andy had a prison job as an inmate adviser. This job was one of the consequences of the 1974 Supreme Court ruling on Wolff v. McDonnell, which maintained that prisoners have a right to due process. The ruling required legal representation be afforded to inmates who are charged with offenses.[90] Prisoners desiring this important position are trained to defend their peers before three prison staff members (also called a disciplinary board or a prison tribunal), who rule on cases and apply punishment for transgressions that range in severity from prisoners masturbating in their cells to murder.

For several years, Andy had defended men and women who had received write-ups from **correctional officers (COs)**, helped people file appeals on their cases, and even argued cases before judges in the "**free-world**." If found guilty of a write-up, prisoners can spend time in the **hole** (solitary confinement), be fined money (and they only earn 17¢ an hour if they have a job), or have time added to their prison sentences. He was so good at his job that one CO told me Andy was a "regular Johnny Cochran." Shortly before I completed my practicum, Andy's security level and job changed. As a minimum-security trustee, he began working outside the razor-wire fence in the warden's office.

A few weeks after my departure from SNF, Andy asked Warden H if it would be okay for me to visit him. She verbally approved, so I sent in a visitation request. In response to the application, I received a form letter stating that Department of Corrections (DOC) policy required a one-year waiting period before ex-employees were allowed to visit. Although I had never been an employee, we did not protest the letter's inaccuracy, figuring Andy would be released on parole long before the year was over. Even the prison psychologist had predicted Andy would be one of those rare men who are granted parole the first time they meet the Board of Probation and Parole (BOPP). Andy's sentence did not involve murder or rape, he had not received a write-up in over ten years, and he was consistently helpful and liked by most prisoners and staff members throughout the compound. We had set up a "home plan" detailing where he would live afterward (not my house because we were not married), and he had the promise of a job that would be acceptable to the BOPP. To say we were excited about our future would have been a grand understatement.

We later learned that my request for visitation had far-reaching consequences. About six weeks after I had finished my practicum, Andy was scheduled to meet the BOPP. Somehow, the man who had supervised my practicum at the prison learned I had applied to visit Andy. I suspect he thought this made him look incompetent, but regardless of his thoughts, his actions were harsh. He complained to his supervisor, Mr. B, whom I had met a few times during my practicum. In fact, Mr. B had hinted at the idea of us dating. Upon hearing about my visitation request, the judge who had resided over Andy's trial and sentencing was contacted.

The judge remembered Andy (the old, mean Andy) and was not happy at the prospects of his release. Two weeks before the scheduled parole hearing, Andy received a Parole Cancellation Notice and was informed that he would again be serving a life-without-parole sentence. The waiver agreement he had been asked to sign years earlier allowing him to accumulate "good and honor time" disappeared. Andy's job in the warden's office was ended immediately because prisoners with life-without-parole sentences are not eligible for jobs outside the razor wire. His status as a trustee vanished within minutes, and his security ranking increased, even though Andy had committed no violation to justify the elimination of his hard-earned trustee status. It was a difficult pill to swallow, but we would be able to visit on the weekends in less than a year, and we knew Andy's sentence was illegal according to Tennessee law. It was time to hire a lawyer.

Andy had a friend, A. C. Baker, who had been a skilled inmate adviser while incarcerated but now worked for various attorneys in the **freeworld**. Because neither of us knew any attorneys, we contacted A. C. and asked for his recommendation. It was not long before I was sitting in the office of Mr. Tom Bloom, explaining that the sentence of life without parole did not exist in Tennessee when it was imposed upon Andy in 1979. Because my funds were limited, Andy had already written a writ of habeas corpus. All Tom needed to do was file the writ and argue the case for us. Tom was interested because he had seen many other prisoners abused by the "justice" and prison systems, but he was unwilling to take my money on a deal he thought had a high potential for failure (obviously not your typical attorney). He said he had encountered many prisoners who thought they had a surefire way to overturn their cases based on a particular law they had come across, but they were usually wrong. Tom agreed to visit Andy, but he predicted this free consultation would end our business relationship. Even though I had no legal experience outside of divorce court, I suspected better, and I was right.

Within days of visiting Andy, Tom called and asked me to come back to his office. He agreed to take the case, but it would not be as simple as filing Andy's writ. Impressed by Andy's demeanor and feeling compassion for our situation, Tom was willing to do as much as possible to obtain a favorable outcome for us in court. Before filing, he wanted to consult with a couple of legal experts in this area since his expertise centered on appealing death penalty cases. Tom knew money could be an issue for me since I was still a full-time graduate student, so he accepted a retainer fee (luckily I had some money saved up) and allowed me to make monthly payments for as long as this ordeal lasted. Little did I know, I would send Tom over sixty checks before this "adventure" was over.

A few months after getting the DOC letter requiring us to wait for visitation, I received a phone call from a female inmate. At that time, both male and female prisoners lived at SNF, in separate buildings, because it was the only prison with significant medical and mental health treatment facilities. During my practicum, I met several female prisoners, but I never expected any of them to call me. I was not even on any female prisoner's approved phone list. Andy was so well loved by these women, whom he had helped as inmate adviser and informal counselor, that one loving lady found a way to let me know Andy had been attacked by a fellow prisoner the previous night. She feared Andy might be dead.

I later learned that Jerry, an inmate who had shared with me his delusions of being a spy prior to his incarceration, had experienced a psychotic break and attacked Andy with a **shank** and a sock full of batteries. Jerry was originally sent to SNF for a mental evaluation but had somehow been assigned to the worker's unit instead of the mental health unit. Although prisoners had tried to tell the staff that Jerry needed a psychological evaluation and assistance, they were ignored (as usual) until it surfaced that Jerry believed the government had sent Andy to kill him. Unfortunately, it took Andy being loaded into an ambulance and sent to a **freeworld** hospital for prison staff to pay attention to Jerry's needs.

Usually I'm a positive person, but that phone call devastated me emotionally and physically. I immediately had to sit down because my mind seemed to be frozen in a tornado, and my energy level had dropped to zero. Since we were not married, I had no rights to obtain information about his condition or to stand by his bed if he was alive. The next few hours were so devastating that I have little memory of them. That night, though, a miracle happened: Andy was able to use a phone and briefly let me know he was okay. He had a severe concussion but few other serious injuries.

As soon as he was healthy enough for regular calls, we began talking about the process required to be legally wed. It was a topic we had discussed in the past, but we thought we would wait until he was home so

our family and friends could celebrate with us. Jerry's attack had given us
a good reason to reconsider. We had already spoken vows to each other
weeks earlier, and that was enough for me. I had been married twice
before, yet our telephone vows impacted me more than those at either of
the previous ceremonies.

Getting married inside a prison is not nearly as fancy or time consum-
ing as in the **freeworld**—or so we thought. Within days, Andy followed
prison policy and petitioned the warden for approval of our marriage. We
were shocked to learn that we would not be allowed to marry. Monster
had struck again via Warden H. My multiple letters and phone calls to
her were met with silence. At one point, Warden H hung up the phone
when I tried to reason with her. We called Tom and asked him to file a
federal suit so that our civil rights to marry could be restored. Tom, with
his continued desire to help us reach our goals, agreed to take the case on
consignment without increasing my monthly payments.

Now we were fighting the courts on two legal fronts, Andy's illegal
sentence of life without parole in state criminal court, and a federal civil
suit involving our right to marry and visit. The wheels of justice are slow,
so it took many months before we lost our first of three appeals in the
criminal case. It took almost a year for our federal case to be placed on
Judge Trauger's docket.

Andy and I continued to grow our relationship with daily phone calls
and an exchange of mail. We did not see ourselves as having fallen in love
but as having chosen to rise in love with every conversation. Our hearts
were entwined long before our one-year waiting period for visitation
ended, but the weekend finally arrived when we could visit. It was the
first time we had ever embraced and kissed each other because we had
complied with prison rules during my practicum (and we had not known
each other very well at that time). After the initial short kiss and embrace
allowed by DOC policy, we held hands and talked non-stop during both
eight-hour visits on Saturday and Sunday. Although we were friendly
with the people around us, most of the time we were oblivious to their
presence. It was as if the world stood still, and we were free to bask in
each other's spirits—regardless of the watchful eyes of the ever present
COs. Once again I felt like I was walking on air.

The following Wednesday, I received a letter from the prison. It
said my visits had been permanently terminated because I had been an

employee of our state's DOC, and new policies permanently banned visitation between ex-employees and prisoners. This letter was erroneous for two reasons: First of all, because I was not paid for my services, my practicum put me in the prison's volunteer status. In fact, I had to pay tuition to be there. Second, at the time of my practicum, ex-employees were allowed to return to visit after a one-year waiting period, and the fact that the rules had been changed did not apply to me. By law, I was under the rules that existed while I was there. It was another sign of Monster's power, but my initial reaction was not worry. Surely one call to the warden would clear things up. After all, she had told Andy it was okay for me to visit before I had sent in my application a year earlier.

Apparently, Warden H felt a stronger need to support her staff than obey prison policies because she denied my request to overturn the permanent elimination of my visitation privileges. Gossip spreads around prison yards faster than beauty shops, so it was not long before everyone knew about the termination of my visits. One afternoon, a group of six COs gathered in Andy's cell during a shakedown. Their efforts to discover contraband were meek, so it seemed their real intent was to illicit an emotional response and remind Andy of his place. While rifling through his cell, the COs took turns saying things like, "You need to forget that little filly. You're never going to see her again." Familiar with the legal system, Andy suspected they might be right, and the last thing he wanted to do was cause me harm. After many private tears, he determined his next call to me would be his last. It looked like Monster had won a complete victory.

When Andy called and suggested it would be better if we broke off our relationship now rather than risking years of court battles only to land in the same position we were in, I laughed so loud that my upstairs neighbor must have heard me. With every fiber of my being, I knew we had not been brought together just to be torn apart by illegalities. I knew we would be together as soon as a court that was not subject to political influence saw that Andy had an illegal sentence and ruled in our favor.

It took several more months for a federal judge to rule on our civil case. Federal Judge Trauger required both sides to go through Federal Mediation rather than going directly to a jury trial. Sitting in a little courtroom, we were outnumbered by DOC attorneys and officials. In their opening statements, the DOC attorney claimed our only motive was to manipulate the prison system. They also stated that this was one more of Andy's "frivolous" lawsuits. The magistrate in charge of our case, Magistrate Brown, responded by saying he had read many of Andy's briefs filed on behalf of prisoners and had yet to see one that was frivolous. He also added that Judge Trauger would not have assigned this case to mediation if it had no merit.

After Magistrate Brown explained the process, the two sides were separated into different rooms, and mediation began. Initially, Magistrate Brown talked with each group separately to get a sense of our positions. Upon his second trip back into our room, he repeated the DOC's newest claim that our motive was monetary. Tom explained that the $250,000 lawsuit for damages and legal fees was not the issue and was not the reason for the lawsuit. It was about doing the right thing and protecting civil rights. To our amazement, Tom immediately stated that he would be willing to forgo his fee and any punitive damages if we were allowed to marry and visit without future harassment, adding that if the DOC insisted on keeping us apart, he would make it his life mission to right this wrong.

Finding that money was no longer an issue, the DOC granted our request on the condition that Andy be moved to a prison outside of our current location. Even though it would be a burden on me, due to the expense of traveling on the weekends, we agreed to their compromise on the condition that the prison be within 200 miles. Within a week, Andy was moved to the Morgan County Correctional Complex, and we were married in the prison chapel on February 24, 2000, surrounded by the love and tears of my daughter and Andy's fellow prisoners/friends. Seeing these tough guys fighting back tears at our happiness was priceless.

The phone call I had been anticipating arrived a year later. Andy called me in the afternoon and said, "Sweetie, I'm coming home. The State Supreme Court just unanimously agreed that my sentence was illegal." At that point, we thought his release from prison would occur within days. For over a hundred years, the granting of a habeas corpus had *always* meant a prisoner was re-tried in a timely manner or immediately released. Unfortunately, Monster had not dropped us from its radar, and the lower court judge chose to ignore the Supreme Court's instructions. In defiance of the Tennessee Constitution, Andy was given a life-with-parole sentence. Once again, the law was ignored by those sworn to uphold it.

After a second hearing before the BOPP, Andy was granted parole. Five years after our wedding, he was home.

Down but not out, Monster continued efforts to economically enslave Andy and degrade my status. Potential employers would not talk with Andy about the circumstances that led him to check the box admitting to his past criminal conviction, much less hire him. After Andy was home, a couple of people I had counted as friends no longer returned my phone calls or letters. Even some family members appeared leery. As Monster exerted its influence, one of our neighbors even made efforts to have us fired from our jobs. I assume she was hoping we would lose our house and have to leave the neighborhood. As bad as all that was, reports of Monster's hate manifesting upon thousands, even millions, of other Americans caused us greater concern.

Spending the last year and a half writing this book while building a trucking company has been a challenge and a blessing, but it is only the beginning. If our work is successful, felonism will be removed from all government policies. Prisons will be converted into healing centers, and people who present an eminent threat of physical danger to themselves or others will live in a secure environment and treated humanely with hopes of their redemption. All people will be treated as equal, criminal behavior will significantly decline, and all Americans will enjoy higher levels of security and prosperity than at any time in our history.

Commentary on Andy and Linda's Story

Life is hard, and anyone who measures their value by the success of others will only make it more difficult. A billionaire can become totally upset by seeing a millionaire with a better jet. The highest paid fashion models can be outraged when someone else gets to walk down the catwalk in the dress they wanted. Along those same lines, it can be *really* difficult for prison staff members with felonistic attitudes to see prisoners having advantages they don't share. It bothered some of the staff members at DOC so much that they were willing to violate the law in an effort to sabotage our relationship.

Felonism has become an everyday part of our society. Laughing about people being raped for dropping the soap in a prison shower is not yet seen as politically incorrect. Viewing women (or men) as somewhat deviant for being in romantic relationships with prisoners is pretty normal in most social circles. Both of those attitudes are blatant examples of felonism.

Today most incarcerated individuals receive few visits or letters from home after their initial year(s) of imprisonment. If Linda had not been assigned to work at SNF, her thoughts regarding prisons and prisoners would probably be similar. This attitude is reminiscent of society's view in the 1940s of children born with major deformities. Parents were often advised to institutionalize children born blind, deaf, or with Down's syndrome. "Let the state take care of them," parents were told. "You just forget they exist and go on with your life." It is not unusual for family members of prisoners to receive the same advice.

For anyone on the "outside" who has never interacted with prisoners or prison staff, the world looks pretty calm. Rumors of prison riots show up on the news now and then, but to people who might be driving past an American prison, there are no indications of the unique, macabre culture teaming within the walls. The dynamics of relationships between the hierarchy of staff and the hierarchy of prisoners is full of twists and turns that seem to make no sense at times. Most administrators will tell you security is their number one priority in the creation of all policies and the resolution of all conflicts, but it isn't. It has been our experience that possessing unlimited control is the real motivation behind most decisions. This dynamic was clearly demonstrated when our requests for visitation and then marriage were denied. It is also apparent in the accounts given by three prison staff members later in this book.

Prior to our visitation request, DOC policies never mentioned practicum students but did allow former prison staff to visit prisoners one year after ending their employment. This was confirmed by the first letter we received requiring a waiting period. After our application for visitation privileges, state-wide rules changed to permanently ban past employees from visiting. When it was learned that Linda had not been an employee, the rules changed again to ban interns and practicum students from ever returning to visit. Following institutional policy, Andy requested a hearing regarding the termination of Linda's visitation. That was when he learned someone had removed Linda's application forms from his

visitation folder. Tampering with a prisoner's records was a clear violation of the federal law, but staff members used it as an excuse to dismiss
his case.

When they wrote new visitation policies after Linda ended her service
at SNF, administrators revealed their true motive, control—not safety—
by allowing current staff members, but not interns or practicum students, to be grandfathered in, probably because that would have allowed
Linda to visit Andy. We know that sounds egotistical and farfetched,
but we ask you to consider the following questions. If the commission-
ers, wardens, and other staff members involved had been concerned with
potential security breaches, why would they make the rules less stringent
for ex-employees who have a working knowledge of the internal security systems and procedures? That information could have been used to
sabotage the system and help prisoners escape. Training for interns and
students never included this knowledge, so why would new policies be
more restrictive toward them?

To put this in perspective, think about a state-wide company, with
hundreds of employees and volunteers, changing its policies for all staff
and volunteers just because a mid-level manager wanted to make sure one
romantic relationship was squashed. It might seem like a preposterous
idea. However, time and again Andy has seen harmful, illogical decisions
made to keep a prisoner from being victorious in a conflict. According to
documents filed by our attorney, one warden told people that no volunteer would ever be able to marry an inmate under her "watch." Because
the administration initiated this battle and lost, it was seen as a victory
for prisoners. That's why prison officials wanted Andy to leave the facility where he and Linda had met. All across America, rules are made
on a regular basis for the purpose of stifling the potential happiness of
prisoners and demonstrating staff dominance, while the long-term consequences are not considered.

Five years after the DOC in our state changed their policy to prevent
staff members from ever visiting prisoners, a lady named Jennifer Forsyth
was hired as a nurse at a DOC prison. She fell in love with George
Hyatte, who was serving a forty-one-year sentence. Jennifer was fired
when she was caught sneaking food to George. Even though they were
allowed to marry (possibly because we had prevailed in our federal case
five years earlier), the newlyweds were not allowed to visit.

Apparently out of desperation to be with her husband, Jennifer made a plan to break George out of prison. When George went to court, she shot and killed a prison guard as George exited a court house. The couple escaped, but authorities discovered and arrested the Hyattes in Ohio thirty-six hours later. They are now serving life-without-parole sentences.

We cannot help but believe Officer Wayne Morgan would be alive today if the Hyattes had been allowed to visit after a one-year waiting period. Permanently banning visitation to increase security was a tragic failure in that situation, though we do want to note that policy 507.01 has been modified to allow staff visitation of family members four years after voluntary termination of employment by the employee. Still, this policy, which is detrimental to families with young children (discussed in Chapter 14), would not have been helpful in the Hyatte case because Jennifer was terminated.

There are not enough pages to recount all the instances in which petty issues influenced by felonism have exploded into massive control issues that falsely depict prison staff as the "good guys." One example, though, is currently ongoing in Florida. Recently, prison officials allegedly diminished a prisoner's right to personal hygiene. Bryan, as we'll call him, is confined to a wheelchair. The prison has a special hose that is attached to the regular showerhead so that Bryan (and other prisoners with similar issues) can dispense water where it is needed when they shower. Like mothers from a more modest time would tell their children, he needs to "wash down as far as possible, and then wash 'possible.'"

A few months ago, a pattern developed in which the hose would disappear. Bryan was instructed to get a coffee cup out of the garbage and use that to collect water and rinse himself off. Knowing his civil rights, Bryan filed a grievance. Some may interpret this act to be frivolous. If you have any experience with bedsores, you know this is actually a serious situation. In response to Bryan's grievance, an officer broke the shower hose just before it was time for Bryan's shower. Apparently, the officer was so confident in his immunity from prosecution for this vengeful act that he performed it in the presence of two prisoners. After all, who would believe a prisoner? In Florida, exercising such abuse, even to the extreme (i.e., so that it causes the death of prisoners), has publically gone unpunished for years.[91]

What are the financial consequences of these daily control struggles?

First of all, they create great expense for tax payers. In our case, tax payers had to foot the bill for the legal fees of six prison administrators as well as several years of Andy's incarceration. In Jennifer Forsyth and George Hyatte's story, a huge, multi-state manhunt had to be financed by tax payers. Bryan's case may be much less expensive if his pleas for assistance stay out of court, but the Florida tax payers still bear the expense of increased medical treatment when wheelchair-bound prisoners develop infections that can be prevented with a little soap and water.

Aside from monetary expenses, safety in the prison environment is diminished when prison officials insist on demeaning helpless prisoners just to prove their dominance. The old saying, "Necessity is the mother of invention" applies here. Prisoners who feel the need to save face after a senseless conflict, such as the one Bryan endured, can devote all their waking hours to inventing methods of revenge. It is fortunate for Florida tax payers that Bryan is seeking resolution through legal means, but many prisoners respond to their abusers by destroying property and/or attacking personnel. The accumulation of seemingly minor control struggles can eventually explode into prison riots. In these instances, the potential for suffering and loss for everyone involved is enormous.

These consequences can be avoided when prison officials and society in general stop allowing felonism to influence their thoughts and actions. A total overhaul of policies is not necessary. Protections are in place, and policies motivated by a desire to ensure civil interactions already exist. According to Supreme Court Justice Anthony Kennedy, "Prisoners retain the essence of human dignity inherent in all persons,"[92] and there are a multitude of state and federal laws that confirm his statement. What we do need is the public recognition that all human beings are valuable, even those who have made terrible mistakes. Changing our attitudes is not easy, but it is the one thing over which we have total control.

We do not count ourselves as poor, innocent victims deserving some sort of government or social handout. It was Linda's choice to develop a relationship with a man in spite of his incarceration. It was Andy's choice to live a life of crime that resulted in twenty-seven years of incarceration. The part that is disconcerting is that many agencies and individuals automatically assume couples in our situation should socially and economically be assigned to the "back of the bus" as a result of something that happened over thirty years ago.

By writing this book, we hope to put human faces to those who are living in atrocious environments and who are often seen as numbers rather than people. Our country does not have to be a felonistic society if we do not want it to be. What we need right now is an honest, open, national discussion about felonism, solutions to ameliorate the damage it has imposed, and specific methods for eradicating it from our policies.

Creating the changes necessary to eliminate felonism will not be easy or comfortable, but it will be joyous and beneficial to everyone in the long-run. We want to see children, especially children living in poverty, begin their adult lives with no stigmas attached to them as the result of their parents' past; to see people who make their living through law enforcement (whether they be attorneys, judges, police officers, or prison staff) have the ability to sleep at night knowing they played a part in keeping the peace without abusing another human being; and to provide a place where all people who believe harming others is their only avenue to happiness can receive healing, education, and a multitude of options for their future.

Throughout Andy's criminal career, each of his offenses against his victims were also offenses against himself. If there were some way to reverse the harm he caused, he would do it, but living in prison did not create justice for his offenses. Granted, removing him from society may have been the only way to change his injurious lifestyle at the time; it greatly stunted his ability to give back to the community when he came to his senses. While incarcerated, he studied the motivations and behaviors that led him to prison, and he investigated hundreds of his peers who admitted to atrocious acts of inhumanity. Except for prisoners with mental disabilities, all his fellow inmates told him they felt remorse for the harm they had caused and desired some way to live loving lives. Humans, even those in prison, are happiest when they contribute to the betterment of themselves and others. Felonism seriously inhibits that from happening.

Today, ten years after being granted the ability to live in the same house, our lives are happy—despite the many opportunities that are closed to us due to felonism. Our love continues to grow. We are generous with the blessings we have, and we strive daily to contribute in a positive manner to the lives of others—regardless of the negative attitudes we encounter.

Chapter 3

Ashley's Story:
A History of Problems

Religion without humanity is very poor human stuff.

—Sojourner Truth

When I was six months old, my family was split up because my mom went to prison. We lived in the projects (government housing) at the time, and there was this church group who kept coming around inviting everyone to church. Eventually Mom had studied the Bible with Sandra, and Sandra had helped her in other ways. When Mom was arrested, Sandra and her husband, Lytle, let me and my sister live with them. Part of my family didn't like that because they didn't think it was right for white people to raise Black children. My uncle came and got my sister when I was about three and she was six. He took her to Louisville so she could live with my granny, but it turned out bad for her. I didn't understand all of it, but I think it had something to do with money. Sometimes my auntie would bring my sister to our house for a few days, and I would get to ride with Lytle when he took her back to Louisville, Kentucky. When my siblings were with my granny and other family members, they heard a lot of stories about how white people used to own Black people. They were taught to hate all white people, but I didn't think that was right. I just didn't have any room in my heart to hate people.

Around third or fourth grade, I was picked on a lot for being in foster care. Kids would say mean things like, "Nobody wants you. That's why you're in foster care." There were also some teachers who thought it was wrong for white folks to raise me, and they said Sandra and Lytle weren't doing a good job. That just was not true, but even if it were, why would they say such things to a child?

Most of my life I didn't get to see my mom, but when I turned about seven or eight, I started to visit her, first with my people, and then Sandra and Lytle would take me. The first time I visited Mom, I felt really nervous. I knew the guards would keep me safe, and that I would be leaving afterward, but I was still nervous. Overall, I was ashamed that Mom was in prison, but I still wanted to be with her. As a kid I would think that maybe one-day Mom would come pick me up from school like other moms picked up their kids, but she never did. It really put a hole in my heart.

When I was about twelve years old, I heard the real story about why Mom was inside. I first heard that she had killed the post man so she could steal people's government checks, but actually she killed a guy named Jack. When I was twenty, Mom made parole and came to visit me, but she kept getting into trouble and went back in. We didn't see each other much while she was out. I would have liked to see her more, but it never did happen. Mom just got out last year, but she's already been back in for taking money at a convenience store. It seems that she has trouble with boundaries and authority figures. If I had walked in her shoes, I would probably have the same issues. From what little I know about Mom's past, I can tell she survived some pretty horrible situations as a kid, and that didn't change after she got married. Mom had to be tough to survive, but that toughness has kept her away from her kids.

I have had trouble with my husband being violent toward me too. I've called the police, and kind of feel like I've been manipulated by them. The police asked if I wanted to press charges while acting like they would do all the work. Later, I found out that I had to go down and press charges, and I had to pay to get him out once he had settled down. When he gets to acting good, I want to drop the charges, but they won't let me. Basically, they help me in one way but cause me more problems in another. The judge sent him to rehab for drug treatment, but he got out and went right back to it. I feel like I wasted some money, but I have to live and learn.

As a kid I first saw domestic violence in elementary school. I had a friend whose dad was in prison. She didn't want her dad to come home because he was so mean to her mom. One day she asked if she could come over to our house because her parents weren't home. Sandra had to go out to drive the Inner City Ministry bus that evening, and she and Lytle thought it wouldn't look right for my friend and me to be at our house with Lytle, so we took her home. Seeing that no adults were home, my friend returned to our house with us despite what the neighbors might think. Lytle put my friend's safety above his reputation because that's the kind of caring man he is.

After a while, her step-dad came over to get my friend. He had found out where we lived by listening to the phone message we left. It was about 8:30 PM, and he was being crude. Her step-dad kept saying he was going to beat my friend when they got home because she knew she was supposed to stay home after school. Lytle called the police, and it all turned out for good. We found out the step-dad had been kicked out of the house, and he was using my friend to try to get back into good graces with his wife. That girl was a good friend, and we were able to talk freely about our parents being in prison. The only difference was that she didn't want her dad to come home, and I did want to see my mom living on the outside.

I'm thankful that Lytle and Sandra raised me. I love my biological family, but if Sandra and Lytle had not stepped in, I would probably be where my mamma was. The constant teasing and bullying that peers heaped upon me in school was overcome by the benefits of being part of a loving, stable family. It makes no sense to me that kids and teachers thought it was wrong for a loving white couple to accept me into their family. The fact that many white people of the past have benefited financially from slavery and racism, and many still do, does not mean all white people are that way. Some people thought Sandra and Lytle were brainwashing me against my own kinfolk, but that wasn't true to me. Why would they regularly let me visit my granny (who practices racism) and Mom if they were trying to turn me against my own people?

About twelve years ago, I did have reason to become racist, but I didn't give in. One terrible night I received a call that my first husband, the father of my first child, had been shot and killed. Since he had never taken nor sold drugs, and he would never commit a robbery or any other type

of crime, I could not understand what had happened. When I reached
the place where he had been murdered, I understood. My wonderful
husband's only fault was being in the line of fire as gang members established themselves on the street where he had been driving. The saddest
part was that I heard two policemen in conversation as one of them
stated my husband's death was unimportant. "Just another dead nigger,"
he said. That white officer was living on the other side of the coin that
my grandma occupies. How sad for both of them.

I'm proud of the fact that I have never been arrested by the police. I
think I'm the only one of my siblings and other family members, parents,
aunts, uncles, and cousins, who can say that. All the rest have some sort
of record. In fact, my brother is in jail now for taking money from people.
Sandra and Lytle are not better than my biological family, but their attitude is better, and that is what they have bequeathed to me. It was hard
to grow up without my biological parents, but I am hoping we can get
together a lot more now that Mom is out of prison.

In the long-run, race, legal status, biological connections, and economic status only separate us from each other if we let them. People are
people. The men who wrote and signed the American Constitution said
we were all created equal. Most of them didn't really believe in or practice equality, but it is a founding principle of our country. We are better
off when our attitudes toward each other are guided by the belief that
we are all equal. Maybe when a rich person decides to treat my family
members bad because they have been to prison, or treat me bad because
I am a poor Black woman, they believe they can only practice equality
by giving up their riches. If that is their attitude, it is easy to understand
why they make up excuses to treat us as second-class citizens, but that
belief is wrong. I don't want rich people to become poor like me. I just
want all of us to have an equal chance at having opportunities to make
a decent living, earn enough money to pay for a good place to live, own
a reliable vehicle, buy insurance, eat healthy food, and get medical care.

If all Americans shared the attitude of equality that Sandra and Lytle
taught me by their example, maybe individuals would not feel the need to
retaliate against each other for past wrongs. I hear people say, "You can't
fix stupid," and prejudice really is stupid in my opinion, but I can hope.

Commentary on Ashley's Story

Ashley is one of those rare people who are snatched from the "cradle to the prison pipeline" early enough to keep her out of juvenile and adult jails before her twenty-first birthday. Being pulled in separate directions by her Black biological family, white adoptive family, and social environment caused a multitude of trials for Ashley. Now her children are in the same precarious position because they are Black, live in poverty, and have a father with felony drug convictions. Keeping her children out of prison will be a continuing struggle for Ashley and her husband unless our society changes. Currently, 1 in 3 Black males and 1 in 17 Black females go to prison at some time during their lives. If Ashley's children were white, their chances of incarceration would be 1 in 17 and 1 in 111 respectively.[93]

It is easy to ignore the combined impacts of racism, classism, and felonism on this family. Many explain away these prejudices by stereotyping Black people as just more violent than whites. To those people, we ask, "How would you behave if the police refused to investigate the murder of your loved one because they were viewed as 'just another dead honkey'" (or whatever slur belongs to the racial class you were born into)? What fibers would make up your moral compass if your childhood was filled with memories of police harassment in your neighborhood and of teachers ignoring your efforts to ask questions and giving you lower grades for work that was better than your peers', or if store clerks and other adults' showed expressions of dread, mistrust, or disgust as you entered their presence?

For every action, there is a reaction. Could it be that oppressive *actions* by those in power are the cause of *reactions* that include drug use, rebellion, and violence from America's children of poverty? How would you react to the accumulation of offenses that you did not create and were powerless to change? Might it be that the lack of cooperation between people in poor neighborhoods and local police departments is a cause–effect relationship?

If you interact with people living in poverty, it is not uncommon to hear the saying, "Snitches wind up in ditches with stitches." That is probably a major part of why the killer(s) of Ashely's husband was never identified. Why would people identified as "niggers" by the police cooperate in an investigation that appeared motivated by a desire for a paycheck and possible promotion more than a hope for peace?

Police officers use many tools to break through this culture of cooperative silence when a crime has been committed. They are allowed to lie during interrogations and charge uncooperative witnesses with obstruction of justice.[94] At the same time, police officers establish a protective muteness among themselves as a means of maintaining and enhancing their power. Most people know this as the "blue wall of silence."[95]

We believe felonism is responsible for this outrageous hypocrisy that flourishes in America. As long as suspects and people with felonies are categorized as second-class citizens, their actions will be judged as less righteous (maybe even criminal) than the exact same behaviors performed by government officials acting under the cover of law. The control struggle between law-enforcement officers and members of a community places a tremendous amount of stress on all participants. We genuinely empathize with officials who see themselves as equal to members of the community and only want to help but are distrusted and abused due to prejudice against the uniform and badge they wear.

Unlike most foster parents, Sandra and Lytle did not abandon their fifteen foster children at the conclusion of their eighteenth birthday parties. Not only was Ashley allowed to stay in their home after the state relinquished responsibility for her upbringing, but she continues to be part of Sandra and Lytle's daily lives along with several other foster siblings. Nationwide, the story is much different. In her doctoral thesis at the University of Tennessee in Knoxville, Samantha Leanne Stout reports that over 25,000 teenagers are forced to leave foster care in America each year when they turn eighteen.[96] Usually, these teens are abandoned by their foster families. As the most susceptible population for homelessness in our nation, about 25 percent will be homeless soon after their eighteenth birthday, 20 percent will be in trouble with the law within two years, and almost 60 percent will be unemployed when they are twenty-four.[97]

It is no surprise that a disproportionate number of these children are of minority races and from poverty-stricken families because those are the groups most often arrested and convicted of crimes.[98] With the increased rate of incarceration since 2007, we have seen a sharp increase in the number of children in foster care. With bleak prospects for employment, housing, and having their basic needs met, many of these young adults will turn to criminal activities, such as prostitution and selling drugs, to attain basic necessities.[99]

When we approached Ashley to contribute her story, we were struck by her perception of normalcy regarding her situation. We are grateful that she has not defined herself by her mother's actions or allowed the pain induced by a prejudicial police officer to rule her life. Ashley is also unique in her refusal to accept any type of racism or see herself as the victim of the family that abandoned her when she was just an infant. Her tender, loving spirit is proof that we can overcome our pasts. It is our hope that all children of incarcerated parents are assigned to loving foster parents similar to Sandra and Lytle.

Chapter 4

Austin's Story: Justified Felony Murder?

Life's tragedy is that we got old too soon and wise too late.

—Benjamin Franklin

Life has a lot of twists and turns. Mine started before I was even born. My parents were not rich, but they managed to support seven children and hide their dance of domestic violence from public attention. My mom, I'll call her Sara, was a strong woman, but when my four-year-old brother died just before she delivered my twin brother and me, she was wise enough to know that allowing another family to raise my brother and me was the most loving thing she could do for us at the time. We were adopted into a family of five that lived fairly close to my parents' home. Our paths probably crossed many times, but I didn't find that out until I was forty-eight years old.

Although I don't remember being told, Jeb and I always knew we were adopted. Maybe it was because we witnessed the adoption of an infant sister when we were about four years old, or maybe we were just told when we were younger. Mom and Dad's three biological children were about six, eight, and ten years older than us, and my parents also took care of foster children when I was a bit older. Dad worked at several different jobs while we lived up North. He must have made good money because we lived on a big farm, we raised our own food, and Mom stayed at home.

My memory of those days is sparse, but I do know we had daily chores and attended a charismatic church on a regular basis. I didn't mind the speaking-in-tongues and faith-healing frenzies because we were allowed to play outside during much of the service. Even though I was a bit of a cut up at the private school we attended, my grades were passing and life was pretty good.

That all changed when I was nine. One dark night, my eighteen-year-old brother had a BIG argument with Dad. It ended with my brother walking off the farm toward town and being killed by a drunk driver. Things were never the same after that. Without any explanation that I remember, Mom and Dad moved us all to a Southern state, and for the first time we lived in a city. Gone were the goats, hogs, cows, chickens, gardens, and others things we used to raise, but the chores continued. We were put into another Christian school where Jeb and I had to repeat our last grade because of the differences in the school requirements, but that didn't really bother me.

I guess Dad turned to religion to help him deal with Paul's death. In less than a year, we moved to a Midwestern state so Dad could attend seminary for a conservative Southern-style denomination. After being ordained, Dad was given a church in a neighboring state, but we only stayed there about a year before moving back to the same Southern city we had lived in after leaving the North. About that time, Jeb and I started high school, and my youthful aversion to girls vanished. Kathy and I started dating in ninth grade, and unlike many teenage guys, who switch girlfriends every time they open a new bottle of pimple cream, I stayed with Kathy all through high school. That didn't seem to be a problem for either of our parents until Kathy's family moved into town my junior year. That's when Dad found out Kathy's father smoked cigarettes and didn't take his family to church on a weekly basis. That was all he needed to know to forbid me from ever seeing Kathy again.

Being a typical teenager, I wasn't going to end a two-and-a-half-year relationship just because my dad told me to. Kathy and I kept seeing each other on the sly. Since we both went to the same Christian school, I don't know why I thought they wouldn't find out. One day I was informed that my parents and the preacher/principal in charge of our high school had decided to send me away. The next thing I knew; I was living at a Christian boys' ranch where I bunked with eight other guys in a sort of foster-home setting. Not letting a little distance separate me from my sweetie, I would sneak letters into the mail when we went to town on the weekends, and Kathy would write me using different names. Sundays were my favorite days. The church attended by the ranch residents was several miles away, so we'd spend the entire day at church. After lunch I could just about always slip into the church office and call Kathy without anyone else knowing.

Unfortunately, two of the other ranch residents ruined it for the rest of us. After learning about an old cemetery near ranch property, they decided to dig up a grave. I couldn't believe it when they told us to look down into the hole they had dug and saw human remains. Disgusted, I fled the area, but it didn't take long for ranch leaders to hear about the tooth that had been removed from the remains. When the house parents couldn't identify the perpetrators, they gave a sound beating to all the guys in my cottage and sent us home.

By this time, I was a senior in high school and just a few months from turning eighteen. When I admitted that I would not stop seeing Kathy if I returned to Dad's roof, I was sent to a place called Good Shepherd's Children's Home. On the day of my eighteenth birthday, Kathy's parents picked me up and allowed me to move in with them. I'm not sure why, maybe because we were no longer united by our defiance, but we broke up pretty quickly. At first I rented a room in a stranger's house, but it was not long before I moved in with a guy at work, Jeff, who needed help with the rent. Since we were both eighteen and feeling elated about our newfound freedom, our apartment soon became known as party central. Eventually there were five guys at this apartment. We made a steady habit of drinking, smoking, and just enjoying life when we weren't at work.

On October 8, 1984, I woke up and found the apartment filled with our friends, as usual. Even Jeb was there. He had moved in a few days earlier after some sort of disagreement with Dad. Jeb had even been defiant enough to skip church that day, so I figured it was a serious argument. The guys continued the conversation that had started before I got there. They were planning to rob a guy Jeff knew because the old man always carried a wad of cash. The victim was one of those country fellows who was raised during the Depression and still didn't trust banks. Someone came up with the bright idea that I would hit the man in the head with a baseball bat, and they would take his money. As soon as I heard that plan,

I told them to leave me out of their scheming, and I left the apartment. My friends from work had just arrived to pick me up for a Sunday outing that didn't include church.

That day is a blur to me because we dabbled in all kinds of drugs that were pretty new to me. I know we did some Quaalude, alcohol, pot, and who knows what else. Late that night, the guys took me home. We arrived just as Jeff and three of our friends were about to drive off. Not ready to hang out in an empty apartment, I got into Jeff's car, and we took off. Immediately, I grabbed up the lid of a Styrofoam cooler in the floorboard for my pillow and drifted off into a drug-filled haze.

The next thing I know, the guys are calling my name and telling me to get out of the car. We were out in the country, and the hood of the car was raised up. Stupidly, I lumbered toward the house the other guys had already entered and reached the threshold just in time to see Jeff shoot an older man. Since he remained standing, I thought Jeff had missed, but I wasn't sure about what I'd just witnessed. I immediately ran back to the car and was followed by two other guys. After hearing another shot, one other fellow got in the car just before Jeff arrived. I had no idea where we were, and I didn't care. I just wanted to be away from there.

When we got back to the apartment, Jeb was there. Jeff passed around part of the money he stole (even giving Jeb a couple hundred), but that didn't impress me. Stealing had never been a part of my lifestyle, much less murder. When and where did Jeff get a gun? All that would come out later during our trial. Due to my lack of participation, I really didn't think I had done anything wrong, but I knew from what had happened at the ranch that all of us would be seen as equally guilty. Rather than implicating myself by reporting to the police, I agreed to the oath of silence Jeff demanded (instead of shooting us in the head), just like the other guys in the room.

One week later, all five of us were arrested. Despite our agreement to never talk about that night, one of the guys in the car that night had told his roommate every detail. The roommate had been arrested for a separate crime and bargained with the police, information about a double murder that had stumped them for a week in exchange for a big reduction in the consequences he would pay for his crime (rape, I think). The police had solved a much publicized murder mystery within hours.

We were arrested separately, so I thought all five of us would stick with our original agreement. I refused to say anything to the police. When investigators presented me with three pieces of paper that they said were signed confessions, including one from my brother, I didn't believe them. Unfortunately, Jeb did believe that I had signed a confession implicating him, and it motivated him to say anything the prosecutor wanted to hear. Jeb took the deal and got a ten-year sentence, most of which he spent on probation rather than in jail. It was almost thirty years later that I learned the details: The district attorney (DA) was planning on charging all of us with capital murder, but he didn't have any evidence against me. Jeb was told that if he testified that I knew about the plan and the gun, he would spend little time in jail. You can probably guess the rest.

Fast forward twenty-eight years, and I am finally granted parole. I'd earned my GED, gotten a job as a cook, and pretty much kept my nose clean throughout my incarceration. Mom and Dad kept in contact and visited me regularly through all those years, but I didn't have contact with Jeb. As a condition of my parole, I was required to live in a halfway house where I could attend Twelve Step programs (even though I hadn't failed a drug test in years). I had learned my lesson about using drugs to numb my mind back in 1984 and didn't need any refresher courses. I'd never been addicted, so having a beer after work didn't put me in danger of a binge, but my opinion did not match the halfway house staff's. They believed that having one beer a week was confirmation of an addiction. Eventually, that difference of opinion led to a problem.

Several of us guys at the house had the same parole officer (PO), and we were required to report to him once a month. To save time, the PO (I'll call him Matt) came to the halfway house where he could talk with each parolee as well as confirm what we reported about our "clean living" with the house staff. At our very first meeting, Matt let me know that he didn't like felons with murder charges, much less double murder. He assured me that I would be violated (i.e., returned to prison) if he had anything to do with it, and of course he did.

Getting a job wasn't easy with a felony conviction even though there was a staff person at the house whose main assignment was to assist with employment. After he helped me get a social security card and birth certificate, I spent a month applying to just about every business on the bus route within ten miles of the halfway house. Finally, I had gotten an interview at McDonald's and was close to being hired when I met the fellow, John, who conducted AA meetings in the house. Knowing that McDonald's would not be a good fit for me, the staff member asked John if he had any openings at his place. John asked if I knew how to install sheet rock, and within minutes, I had my first **freeworld** job.

Possessing alcohol in the house was forbidden, but most parole conditions allow drinking as long as we don't get drunk. One night a resident handed me a glass of whiskey thinking he was doing me a favor. Since I had told him I didn't want the drink, I gave the glass to the night duty staff man when he asked about my drink. Wouldn't you know it, Staff Man was one of those guys who couldn't stop at one drink. When the day staff arrived the next morning, he was a bit tipsy and there was alcohol on his breath. They asked Staff Man how he got alcohol in the house, and he said I gave it to him. True enough I had given him the first glass, but I don't know where he'd gotten the rest because I was asleep. Surprisingly, Matt didn't violate me, and Staff Man was transferred to a different facility since he was from a rich family. The resident who brought the alcohol into the house had no consequences, and I was assigned to live at the mission for two weeks. That didn't seem fair to me, but it was better than returning to prison.

When my time at the mission was up, I returned to the house. Now that I had been there about two months, the head counselor, Ed, finally decided it was time for me to have a program plan that would allow me to get a certificate of completion. Ed outlined what meetings I would have to attend and all the other hoops I would have to jump for the next thirty days. Earning a certificate of completion was required as a condition of my parole for me to move out of the house, and I was really looking forward to being on my own. I worked the program and went to all the meetings, but my honesty got me in trouble.

During the AA and NA meetings, I was expected to talk about my regret at all the times I had squandered my life getting wasted and pursuing the next high. From listening to other guys, I could have made something up, but this was supposed to be a program where people were brutally honest. Counselor Man didn't appreciate my honesty. I think he believed my felony guaranteed that I was an addict and a liar. One week before I was scheduled to earn my certificate, Counselor Man convinced

Ed that I wasn't working my program and was a bad influence on the rest of the house. Neither man had the courage to talk with me. They called Matt and told him I was being kicked out of the house. Before leaving the halfway house, I confronted Ed and asked what part of his thirty-day plan I had omitted. Supporting his staff over his plan with me, Ed claimed ignorance of the plan we'd written together and suggested that I'd forged the plan he had signed.

Matt still didn't violate me; instead he let me share an apartment with another parolee who had left the same halfway house but was still on his caseload. A month after moving into this guy's apartment, I found him dead in the bathroom. He had overdosed on heroin. The apartment was in my roommate's name, so I had to move out. Relocation also meant I no longer had a ride to work because my new apartment was too far off my co-worker's route. After I lost my job and my apartment, Matt sent me to a Salvation Army program called Bootstraps through which I was able to secure a place to live. Unable to find steady employment, I started going down to the day-labor company closest to the apartment. It took two weeks of sitting in their lobby, and me finally complaining about being ignored, to get my first job. After that, the work was pretty stable.

On Valentine's Day, I just happened to have brunch with a friend and drank two beers. I knew the Bootstraps program would have me blow into a breathalyzer when I got back that night, but I was confident the beer would be out of my system by then. That was a tragic miscalculation on my part. The program director told me I would have to go to the mission for a week, but he didn't call Matt. My next appointment to see Matt was the day I was to return to Bootstraps, so I hoped I could slide by. It seemed to me that since I had not gotten drunk or broken any laws, and I had been working, it would be okay to omit my week at the mission when Matt and I talked. I was wrong about that too. Matt fulfilled his promise to violate me.

During my first week back inside, I had to attend a class called "How to Survive in Prison." If they had been giving out grades, I would have made an A++. It was not much better than the class on re-entry I had been required to attend before leaving prison a year earlier. In that class, the male teacher didn't seem to care if we learned anything or not. We all sat around talking about everything other than the life-skills curriculum he was supposed to cover. Basically, he got paid, and we got credit for just jacking our jaws. After a week of that, the unit manager took over (an unprecedented move on her part), and she covered every page. I liked the class and picked up a few good tips on how to resolve conflicts in a positive way. Eventually I went through a very good class designed for people with technical violations.

About nine months after returning to prison, I was granted parole again, but this time to an area of the state that was much closer to my parents' house, and there was no requirement that I live in a halfway house. Since my parents had visited me for years, and always told me they would support me if I ever got out, I was floored when, within days of my release, Dad said I couldn't live at their house. He wouldn't even let me know their address. Eventually I accepted his explanation: Mom was in the early stages of Alzheimer. Dad thought it would be devastating to Mom if I got out and was violated a second time. I think he was also afraid of how I would react to Jeb. After going to prison, I hadn't spared any words in expressing my anger toward Jeb for lying about my involvement. It finally occurred to me that Jeb had not been given a choice. Jeb and I had just turned eighteen when we were arrested. Not only did he have police investigators lying to him about what I was saying; he had an intimidating district attorney blackmailing him to get a conviction against me. I'm glad Jeb was able to start a family and build up a business instead of wasting away in prison. I don't wish that on anyone, especially not my twin brother.

With my parents' house no longer an option, I had to submit another parole plan. My second parole experience was totally different from the first. In exchange for free housing, I agreed to live in an approved halfway house and attend classes designed to help parolees adjust to their new surroundings. Another parolee and I were put on a bus early in the morning for a four-hour trip west. Upon arrival, we were supposed to be picked up by someone at a halfway house. I'll call them Huggs because their motto is "Humility, Understand, God, Grace, and Spiritual Strength." The prison had given us $30 cash, and we each had a small bag of our belongings. I spent my money to buy a cheap little cell phone and started making calls. A buddy of mine who had been out for a while lived in the area, but I didn't know his number. I tried calling my new PO, Mike, and the halfway house's office, but there was no answer at either place. Finally, I used what little battery I had left to ask for help via Facebook. Thank

God the account I had started at the first halfway house wasn't taken down while I was inside. After twelve hours at the bus station, a fellow returning citizen picked me up and took me to my friend Larry's house.

It was great to be out of the bus station, but Larry's house was out in the country. He and his wife, Ann, were driving all over America as truck drivers and didn't know when they would be back. They had food in the freezer, but I ended up spending the next two days at their house all alone with no transportation and no phone. After my last experience, I certainly didn't want to go somewhere other than the halfway house without Mike's approval, but I had no choice.

On Monday, Larry and Ann had another friend, Frank, drive about forty miles to assist me with transportation and food. That same day Ann was able to remotely put money on my phone, so now I had transportation and communication, but Mike and the halfway house's phones continued going to their answering machines, and no one was calling me back. It was Dr. Martin Luther King Jr.'s birthday, and their offices were closed. Frank agreed to stay at Larry's house that night and take me to the halfway house the next day.

I thought my troubles would all be over, but they were just starting. My top priority was having a face-to-face meeting with Mike as required by my parole conditions. Participating in these classes was my second priority. When I arrived at the halfway house, I went straight to the CEO, Ms. S, and explained my experiences of the past few days. She apologized and claimed that she had gone to the bus station the previous Friday, but I was not there. Knowing I had not seen her at the bus station even though I'd positioned myself at the front door for twelve hours, worry began rushing into my mind.

Before the day was over, Ms. S. took me to an almost empty house in a high crime area of the city. There was one resident besides myself, no food, and almost no linens for bathing or covering our beds. Record low temperatures had hit the country, yet Ms. S. insisted that we keep the thermostat at sixty degrees at all times. I only had the two sets of clothes I'd been given by the DOC and a jacket Frank had given me two days earlier. There was not much furniture, so the place looked abandoned.

After Ms. S left, a man claiming to be a previous resident of the program came in and said the television was his. Then another man, this one claiming to own the house we were in, came in and said we were being evicted within the week. According to this gentleman, Ms. S had not paid rent on this place in three months. She was supposed to have been in court that day to state her case. Since Ms. S had not shown up, the judge had ruled against her and begun the paperwork to evict us.

The next day, the other tenant and I reported these visitors to Ms. S when she picked us up for breakfast, processing, and the re-entry class. She was not the least bit happy about her television being taken, but she understood our position. We could not get into a physical confrontation having just left prison, and we didn't know if he was telling the truth or not. Regarding the eviction, Ms. S was sure it was just a misunderstanding that would soon be worked out. She dropped us off at our re-entry class, but not before I asked to call Mike. The forty-eight-hour mandatory meeting with my PO had expired. Considering my past experience, following this rule was very important to me. Ms. S assured me it would be taken care of soon, a false statement she would repeat to me daily for the next nine days.

When Ms. S returned us to the house that night, we were given two boxes of food containing two gallons of milk, a loaf of bread, two packs of lunch meat, two boxes of cereal, eggs, oats, a few cans of vegetables, and two packages of meat. Even though we had given Ms. S authorization to use our food stamps earlier that day, we were instructed to make this food, which was less than the food stamps should have gotten us, last a week. Two months later, when I was still unemployed, I learned that Ms. S had been using my food stamps card the entire six weeks after I had left her program.

As a condition of his parole, my roommate had to attend a Twelve Step program within the first seven days of release. The halfway house's van never showed up to take him there, so I agreed to walk with him the two miles, through a strange neighborhood containing several crack houses in single-digit temperatures. Neither of us had ever lived in this town, but with the help of the map on my phone and directions from strangers, we managed to get to the meeting before freezing. It was our understanding that the DOC paid the halfway house about $2,000 per month, per person, as long as we participated in the assigned program. We were totally baffled as to why we were not being given contact with parole officers, clothing, sufficient food, and the other items advertised to be part of the package. Within a week, we had to get food from a charity organization. When I finally was able to meet with my PO, I learned that his office was just a few blocks from the classes I attended during my first week out. If the program leaders had given me a heads up, I would have walked to Mike's office and relieved myself of a mountain of stress.

On the ninth day of our stay, I received a call from Ms. S asking for my new address because we had to be out of the house within twenty-four hours. This was the first time she had mentioned eviction, and she didn't offer for me to move to a different house within her program. In a panic I called Larry and Ann to ask for assistance. I could just see myself being violated for not meeting Mike the first, and now second, week I was out. Now I was being forced to change my address without getting approval, a clear violation of all parole conditions. While driving in another state, Ann was able to contact someone in the re-entry program conducted by the DOC. Apparently they were aware of my situation but said they didn't have a way to call me. That was strange since the halfway house office had called my cell phone several times and was supposed to be in close contact with the DOC.

As a result of Ann's intervention, a DOC staff member called and told me I didn't have to stay in a halfway house as a condition of parole, but she had been investigating several houses just in case I wanted to stay in the program. Even though I wasn't learning much from the six-hour class we attended (they taught a curriculum for thirty minutes per day and told us to just hang out the rest of the time), I agreed to try another facility. Since I still didn't have my driver's license or a job, it wasn't much of a choice.

A few minutes later a woman from a different halfway house called and told me they would pick me up if I wanted to attend her program. The program sounded wonderful, so I agreed. She forgot to mention the part about me having to turn over my phone and not being able to communicate with any of my family or friends for the first six weeks I was there. That rule was introduced after I arrived. I felt totally duped, betrayed, and frustrated, so I left.

To shorten an already long story, I have been living at Larry and Ann's house for almost a year. Although I don't see my parents very often, I have reconciled with my brother and work as a part of his construction crew. The best news of all is that I have finally met Sara, my birth mom, and all my siblings. Since getting away from halfway houses, I have had no troubles from people telling me one thing and doing the opposite (with the exception of a PO). I'm still learning how to navigate this outside world, but I'm pretty sure my days behind razor wire are over. It is my hope that, sometime in the future, I'll be able to help someone else get their **freeworld** legs and make a smooth transition as a returning citizen.

Commentary on Austin's Story

Austin's initial police interrogation brings up a story by Frederick Douglass that demonstrates how slaves would feign stupidity to protect themselves from their masters' wrath. During Douglass's slave years under Master Thomas, food allotments for slaves were of smaller portions and lesser quality than for the dogs and pigs. When he discovered that slaves on the neighboring farm had plenty of food, and that the horse recently purchased from that farm would return home if released, Mr. Douglass developed a plan. When the master wasn't looking, Mr. Douglass would free the horse and tell the master about its "escape." After receiving the master's scathing lecture about how thoughtless he was, Mr. Douglass would falsely agree to his stupidity and fake sorrow while accepting his punishment—a four-mile jog to retrieve the horse. Upon Mr. Douglass's arrival, Aunt Mary, the head kitchen slave at the neighbor's farm, always provided him with enough bread for one or two days' sustenance. Eventually this plan backfired on Mr. Douglass because Master Thomas sold the horse and sent his slave to a different farm to be "broken" by a man more savage than himself.[100]

The same sort of scenario became true for Austin, as it does for many people who try to protect themselves by feigning ignorance to the police. The long-term effect of Austin's silence led the prosecutor to employ perjury from Jeb to get the conviction he wanted against Austin. If the prosecutor had not gotten someone to falsely testify that Austin knew about the plan and the gun, it would have been impossible to convict Austin of felony murder.

The trending mentality of "lock 'em up and throw away the key" has created a culture in which it is acceptable for police investigators and prosecutors to use lies, deception, and intimidation to interrogate and prosecute suspects. As we noted in Ashley's commentary, these practices become a double-edged sword. Like Austin, many suspects will refuse to talk, even if they are innocent, because they believe anything they say will eventually be manipulated to condemn them. In their zeal to catch the "bad guy" and achieve success at their job, prosecutors often focus on the person arrested to the exclusion of other possibilities. Knowing they are rated by the number of annual prosecutions, investigators are motivated to convict as many people as possible with each case.[101] Austin's case is evidence of this.

Even though Austin's friends corroborated his story about being gone for hours prior to the murders, prosecutors insisted on charging Austin with the same offense as those who planned the crime. When they found they had no evidence to convict Austin, they blackmailed his brother (exchanging freedom rather than money) so Jeb would lie on the stand. Even Austin agrees that not reporting the crime merited some degree of punitive action, but convicting him of felony murder was more than overkill (pun intended).

Felony murder is a term that applies when a person dies as a consequence of someone committing a felony offense. Philip Workman's case is a prime example. At twenty-eight, with a history of cocaine addiction, Mr. Workman robbed a Wendy's restaurant in Memphis, Tennessee, in 1981. When the police arrived, a gun battle ensued, and a police officer, Ronald Oliver, was killed by the bullet of a fellow officer. This fact was not shared with the defense or the jury during Mr. Workman's trial. After losing a multitude of appeals, at great expense to the state of Tennessee, Mr. Workman was executed by lethal injection on May 9, 2007.[102] As with Austin's case, a felony murder charge can also be applied to any accomplices of a felony in which a murder occurs as a result of that crime.

A case more similar to Austin's, but more tragic, occurred in 2003 when Ryan Holle lent his car to his roommate. In this Florida case, the gun used to kill a teenager was obtained at the house where Mr. Holle's friend and three other men went to steal a safe from a marijuana dealer. Though Mr. Holle had lent his car to his friend many times in the past, without incident, this time he was shaken from his alcohol-induced sleep and arrested. In his hungover state, Mr. Holle made statements indicating that, though he didn't know guns would be involved, he may have known his roommate planned to rob a dealer. Now he is serving life without parole for felony murder. The prosecutor had offered Mr. Holle a deal, plead guilty and only serve ten years, but Mr. Holle did not believe he was culpable for his roommate's offense[103] and refused the plea.

The prosecutor argued before a jury that if Mr. Holle had not lent his car, the robbery and murder would not have happened; therefore, he should receive the same sentence as the men who planned and implemented the robbery and murder.[104] David Rimmer did not really believe the argument he presented to the jury, that Mr. Holle shared equal blame. He even stated that his motive for offering Mr. Holle a better plea bargain than what he offered the other men was that he saw Mr. Holle as less responsible; however, the jury never heard that part of Mr. Rimmer's reasoning.

We must examine the flip side of the coin: Let's say Mark Zuckerberg, or some other inventor, asked to borrow your car to drive to the patent office, stating that he was going to write down his latest brainstorm for his next invention. You agree with Mr. Zuckerberg's intention and cheer him on (which Mr. Holle did not do). Once the idea is implemented, should you receive half the profits? Of course not! People against this line of reasoning could claim that Mr. Zuckerberg would have used some other form of transportation if you had not lent him your car, so you don't deserve any credit for his actions. Why wouldn't the same logic apply in Mr. Holle's case? His roommate could have borrowed a car from someone else, and the murder would have been fulfilled just the same. Mr. Rimmer's argument is that the roommate's only transportation option was Mr. Holle's vehicle, and that was just not true. On a prosecutor's resume, however, multiple felony-murder convictions for one case is more impressive to future employers or conservative voters than convicting someone as a minor player in a murder case.

Most countries, and four U.S. states, have eliminated felony murder from their laws. While we sincerely acknowledge that murder is a horrific crime, it is not justification for mass revenge: Imposing life-without-parole sentences upon people whose actions were on the fringes of a crime does not honor the murder victim. It disgraces our "justice" system and deepens the divide between our government and our citizens. In both Austin and Mr. Holle's cases, it is easy to see that revenge, and possibly job status, blocked intelligent prosecutors from engaging logic and true justice.

We believe encouragement to increase the number of incarcerated at the expense of wrongfully convicting a few people who are innocent, or at least less culpable, is fostered by rich and powerful corporations, such as Corrections Corporation of America (CCA) and GEO Group, two private prison companies that provide correctional and re-entry services. The existence of private prisons was mentioned in Chapter 1, but here we provide more information about specific corporations. According to an October 1, 2013, article, "Last year, CCA sent letters to forty-eight governors, offering to take their prison systems off state hands at a less expensive rate in exchange for a guarantee that their states would keep their facilities up to 90 percent full—regardless of crime rates."[105] This offer was made in spite of the fact that the nation's crime rate has been decreasing throughout the last fourteen years.[106]

While we know of no state with a public policy of intentionally incarcerating innocent people to save money for the state, the positive relationship between mass incarceration and the increasing wealth of private prisons implies the possible existence of such an unwritten policy. This theory is supported by the fact that the U.S. Department of Justice reported crime rates consistently fell from 1990 throughout 2010[107] even though CCA reported in 2005 an ever increasing rate of incarceration. This same CCA report admitted that a reduction in crime rates could reduce its profits.[108]

As long as private prisons profit from warehousing prisoners, they will have a strong motivation to lobby for laws that increase their clientele. Items identified as threats to CCA's stability in its 2005 report include: sentencing patterns ("currently threatened by leniency in conviction and sentencing practices"); reputation of state and private facilities; decriminalization of certain activities, such as drug use and immigration; early release for good behavior; sentencing alternatives; public's lack of acceptance of the privatization of prisons; and the FCC's possible elimination of commissions being paid to prisons by phone companies, such as Global Tel Link.[109]

Because CCA officials profit from increased bodies in beds within their prisons, we believe they have motivated many states with which they have contracts, especially Arizona, to increase the incarceration of immigrants. Several organizations have reported relationships between CCA officials and lobbyists who worked with government staff to create and pass the anti-immigrant law, Senate Bill 1070. Evidence to support this statement is seen in Senator Russell Pearce's attendance and actions at a meeting held by ALEC (American Legislative Exchange Council).

This organization is a 501(c)(3), which means it is not supposed to participate in the development of legislation, but that's what ALEC does.[110] Intent on passing conservative legislation on state and national levels ALEC establishes private, collaborative meetings between politicians and officials in private industries. Legislators do not report the meals, events, and other perks received at ALEC meetings because they pay membership fees of $50 per year and identify ALEC as the giver of gifts. Lobbyists avoid the necessity of identifying which lawmakers they wine and dine by paying ALEC hundreds of thousands of dollars in annual membership fees.[111] This process generates about 1,000 new bills per year. With the help of lobbyists and public relations firms, about 200 model bills are passed annually.[112]

Senator Pearce freely admits that CCA officials/lobbyists spent three days in meetings with Arizona congressmen to obtain assistance in writing Senate Bill 1070. Some call it the "Breathing While Brown" law because it seems to target Latino immigrants for arrest, prosecution, and long periods of incarceration. Of the thirty-six congressmen who cosponsored this bill, thirty were either at the meeting or were members of ALEC and received donations from CCA.[113] Shortly after Senator Pearce introduced this legislation to the Arizona Senate, CCA hired a public relations firm, Highground Consulting, to ensure its passage. While debates regarding the passage of this bill were raging inside congressional halls, the public was fed a flurry of propaganda that said illegal immigrants were increasing unemployment and driving down hourly wages for American citizens.[114] Following the pattern of past Abusers of Power, these commercials gave mainstream Americans an excuse for oppressing an identified segment of society. These CCA supported messages directly contradicted messages by conservative publications, such as AEIdeas, which presented evidence that seven million immigrants in America have no negative effect on the employment rates of Americans but actually increased the value of real wages.[115]

Once the bill was passed, it was up to Governor Brewer to sign it into law. It turns out that her communications director, Paul Senseman, had been a lobbyist for CCA prior to joining her staff and that his wife still worked for CCA.[116] Mr. Senseman went back to work as a lobbyist for Policy Development Group (who contract with CCA) after his two-year stint with the governor. Another one of her top aides and campaign manager, Chuck Coughlin, had formed his own lobbying firm in 1998 and is still lobbying for CCA and other private prisons.

As if that corporate-political web was not tight enough, CCA had one more key player in its pocket. From 2005 until the end of 2007, Mark Brnovich was a registered lobbyist for CCA while serving a host of private and government positions. He was a director of the Center for Constitutional Government at the Goldwater Institute, a judge pro tempore for Maricopa County, and an assistant U.S. attorney for the District of Arizona.[117] It seems a bit suspicious that a judge who is in charge of housing men and women in prison facilities would concurrently work as the senior director of business development for CCA.[118] With Senator Pearce, Paul Senseman, Chuck Coughlin, Mark Brnovich, and many others spinning between public and private "service," how can tax payers escape their web? It is important to note that by 2011, private prisons housed almost 50 percent of all ICE (Immigration and Customs Enforcements) detainees, and CCA had the largest share of those contracts.[119]

Wouldn't it be more ethical to return to past policies in which the government was totally in charge of all prison operations? That system was not perfect, but we can subject public prisons to media and public scrutiny, thus holding individuals accountable if they misuse their positions. Because they are private corporations, most private prisons refuse to share information that is subjected to "sunshine laws." How can they be held accountable for the tremendous flow of taxpayer revenues they receive annually when they are not subjected to the Freedom of Information Act?[120] It is bad enough that punitive prisons exist. It is much worse that we allow a handful of executives, shareholders, and spin-off companies to accumulate *billions* of dollars in annual profits from such misery and then protect them from public inspection. Our citizenry has been pulled into the subterfuge, but it's not too late to escape. We hope you will read Chapter 17 to learn about things you can do to help.

Outside of private and public prisons, many returning citizens find life much more difficult than it has to be. Because most of them cannot vote, these sixty to seventy million citizens have little legal recourse to improve their plight. In response to this, some people say, "Don't do the crime if you can't do the time," but in our current culture, that cliché should be changed to, "Don't do the crime if you can't stand being seen as the scum of the earth for the rest of your life."

There is no way to pinpoint when America became a systemically felonistic society, but the 1974 Supreme Court ruling that legalized the disenfranchisement of all ex-felons was definitely a signpost. In his dissenting opinion with Judge Brenner, Justice Thurgood Marshall quoted the California Secretary of State:

It is doubtful . . . whether the state can demonstrate either a compelling or rational policy interest in denying former felons the right to vote. The individuals involved in the present case are persons who have fully paid their debt to society. They are as much affected by the actions of government as any other citizens, and have as much of a right to participate in governmental decision-making. Furthermore, the denial of the right to vote to such persons is a hindrance to the efforts of society to rehabilitate former felons and convert them into law-abiding and productive citizens.[121]

Because Austin made a bad decision to get in the car with his roommates while he was under the influence of drugs, because Austin lived by his code of not being a snitch, because he learned to mistrust authority figures as a teen, because a prosecutor was willing to employ perjury, and because his eighteen-year-old brother was bullied into lying on the stand, Austin will never be able to vote, own a gun, work in a multitude of jobs, or be fully rehabilitated in the eyes of our felonistic society. He will also have to pay a monthly fee so that a parole officer can monitor his actions for rest of his life and possibly re-incarcerate him for something as simple as a traffic ticket or making the acquaintance of a vindictive woman (see Renegade's Story, Chapter 12).

Who profits from Austin's disenfranchisement? Who profits from police being able to lie and destroy evidence in order to gain a conviction? Who profits from prosecutors using immoral tactics? Who profits from private prison officials and public legislators working together to draft new laws? Well, we can state with confidence, it's not the American people!

Chapter 5

Bob's Story:
Disadvantages of Being
"Inmate Friendly"

Do something. If it works, do more of it. If it doesn't, do something else.

—President Franklin D. Roosevelt

H ere's the way our correctional system is supposed to work: a guy (women are included, but I'll stick with referring to men because they were my main clientele) commits a crime. After being arrested, he's told about all the evidence against him, so he confesses and accepts probation—which means he still lives at home and works at his job while meeting regularly with a probation officer and paying his fees. Fees are monies collected from the probationer or parolee to help offset the cost of supervising them. Some fees are also paid as restitution to victims. Of course, probation is not offered for serious offenses like murder, but it is a consequence for many crimes.

If he does what he is supposed to do while on probation, he is released from probation and does not spend any time incarcerated. If he fails to report to his probation officer, uses drugs, or gets arrested for something else, then a hearing is held to determine if he should remain on the street or go to prison. If he goes to prison, he should serve a percentage of that sentence before he is eligible for parole. Say the offender was sentenced

66

to three years at 30 percent, the 30 percent means he has to serve one year, before he becomes eligible for parole consideration.

When he gets out of prison on parole, he reports to a parole officer, pays his fees, and ideally stays out of trouble. He may live in a halfway house at first to make sure he gets daily supervision and has success at finding a job and adapting to life outside of prison. While on probation or parole, he is supposed to have access to assistance from his PO with things like housing and employment. He's also supposed to have access to his PO as a "go-to guy" if he encounters problems that could pull him back into criminal activity. Once the length of his original sentence has been fulfilled, he has "**flattened**" his sentence and he is now "**off paper.**"

These terms make sense if you think of a metaphor where a big folder is being filled with one sheet of paper for each day of a sentence, starting with the day of a conviction. Let's say a man, Joe, gets a three year sentence. That would be 1,080 sheets of paper. If Joe was in jail for a year while waiting for his trial (not an unusual occurrence), 365 days are immediately removed from his folder. If Joe goes to a "time building" institution, two sheets may be removed from his folder each day if he does not get any "write-ups" from a CO.

Write-ups are like tickets with different levels of severity. Things like fighting to keep from being raped or having his belongings stolen are serious offenses and can actually add sheets of paper to Joe's folder— especially if Joe was protecting himself from a CO. A host of minor write-ups can have Joe put into solitary confinement but do not add paper to his folder. These offenses include things like having too many books or articles of clothing in his cell, having thirty-one aspirin in a bottle marked for thirty tablets, or arguing with a CO—especially if Joe is right. You get the picture. I have heard that the legislature passed a law that would add 365 sheets of paper to Joe's folder if he's caught with a cell phone, but I haven't seen it applied too much—and there are a lot of cell phones in prisons. It's difficult to get all the papers out of Joe's folders, but when he's "flattened" or "off paper" he's released back into society without any type of supervision. If Joe has a five-year sentence and is granted parole after three years, his parole will be over in two years. Should Joe have a life-with-parole sentence, he will be supervised for the rest of his life.

While a person is on probation or parole, he doesn't get good time taken off his sentence. He serves the rest of it day for day. His good time is basically being free and living outside the prison. It is the unwritten "hope" of the system that once a person has flattened, he is so afraid of returning to prison that he never commits another crime, or does anything that would allow him to be accused of committing a crime, for the rest of his life. That's how it is *supposed* to work.

Because I was a parole officer (and sometimes a probation officer) for fifteen years, I can state with confidence that the above is *not* how it works. Not being a lawyer, I don't have too much firsthand knowledge regarding the initial phase. I know how plea bargaining versus a jury trial is supposed to work, but I've not been behind the scenes to witness what really happens.

I have been the probation and parole officer of the same individual at times, but I never understood the process that caused a client to be in both categories of supervision simultaneously. In these cases, I would supervise a person as their parole officer. When they flattened that charge, I continued as their probation officer. The funny thing is, I never had a probationer flatten his original sentence. They always seemed to do something to get themselves violated or revoked.

I want to tell you that probation is no picnic for most people. You would think a person given a three-year sentence for something like theft would have to report to a probation officer for three years or spend a total of three years in prison. Most people don't know this, but that's not generally how it works. I have seen probationers with three-year sentences that took ten years to flatten. In one instance, every time the guy would get on probation, he would eventually do something minor, like have marijuana in his pee. After being arrested and thrown in jail for a few months, the judge would re-release him from jail and start his original three-year probation over again, ignoring the weeks and months of successful probation my client had achieved earlier. I don't know why that is legal, but apparently it is.

Unlike a lot of parole officers and COs today, I was a pretty seasoned fellow when I was hired by the Tennessee Department of Corrections (TDOC) back in 1996. I had retired from twenty-three years in the military and worked three years in the private sector at a steam plant. My military experience and training had certainly qualified me to work in a prison setting, so I took the job with the expectation that I would retire after twenty years. My wife and I looked forward to being financially carefree in the last twenty to forty years of our lives with three pensions to support us. That's still our plan, but we took a small detour. You'll see what I mean soon.

The TDOC can be a good place to work. The benefits are good. The pay is relatively low, but it's a living if you put in some overtime and work at it steadily. I quit high school to marry my high school sweetheart and join the military. It wasn't a mistake to marry my sweetheart. She's still the light of my life to this day, and I did get my GED and take several college courses relating to positions I held in the Army. I didn't, however, tie it all up and get my degree, so working for the TDOC was a pretty safe, reliable career, but I was not going to reach top management positions. The worst thing about a job at the TDOC is the need to watch out for people who will stab you in the back and even break a few laws to get rid of you if your views are different from theirs. You would think I'm referring to prisoners, but I'm not.

On my first day out of the Academy, I was assigned as a CO to a prison called MTRC. That facility has a new name now, but back then it was where newly convicted men waited to be assessed and assigned to a different prison. They were supposed to be sent to a prison that had the programs they needed to correct the issues that got them in trouble to begin with, but that's pretty much a game of smoke and mirrors. Anyway, as soon as I arrived, I was told I would be trained as an institutional parole officer (IPO) because that is where I was needed. I did get to finish out that night shift as a CO.

As I had expected, one of the prisoners, I'll call him Butler, challenged me just because I was the new guy. Rather than giving him a write-up, I arranged for Butler to be locked in his cell for the night. All I could do was smile while I listened to Butler's screams about what he was going to do to me the next time he saw me on the compound. The joke was on Butler because if he ever came up for parole, which he did years later, I would be the guy arranging his presentation with the Board of Probation and Parole (BOPP). Lucky for Butler, I'm not a vengeful person, and I was a PO by the time he needed an IPO to prepare for his parole hearing.

At the time of my training, the BOPP used a point system to assist board members in determining parole. Points were given for such things as completing programs, having a stable relationship with people out-side of prison, not getting any write-ups in the last year (or longer), and being a dependable worker at a prison job. The seriousness of the crime for which a person was convicted also had a big impact on a prisoner's points. In reality, if your offense in any way harmed a wealthy or politi-cally connected person, the offense was much more serious than if a poor person was affected by your crime. No matter how good a prisoner's point system looked, no matter how many years it had been since a write-up, and no matter how much support a person had to start a new successful life outside of prison, if a well-connected person wanted them to stay inside, their offense was always "too serious" for them to be released "at this time."

Along with preparing a prisoner's point sheet, it was my job to orga-nize all the paperwork (letters for and against parole, certificates showing programs prisoners had completed, copies of the prisoner's police reports and judgments from their original offense, etc.), get copies to all the board members, schedule a hearing date, make sure everyone who needed to know about the hearing was informed (including their victims), and make sure a piece of paper documented that everything I was supposed to do had been done.

On days when the BOPP met at the prison where I was assigned, my job also included making sure prisoners were at the right place at the right time. Since certain COs are the only ones allowed to walk around the prison during "count time" (prisoners are physically counted six or more times each day to verify that no one has escaped), making sure a prisoner was at a meeting on time was trickier than it seemed. Having too many prisoners waiting their turn to meet the BOPP could be just a bad as not having them ready when the BOPP was ready. Along with that issue, it was also my job to get the protestors and supporters in the right places at the right times and make sure everyone knew the rules.

During the BOPP hearings, prisoners were not allowed to talk to anyone other than BOPP members. They could not respond to anything anyone said to or about them during their hearing unless told to do so by a board member. The same rules applied to those present in support and in protest of parole. To be granted parole in Tennessee, prisoners have to get four positive votes from any of the seven board members. Because board members rule on over 10,000 cases per year, they do not attend many of the hearings, and they often vote on the cases remotely. Instead, most prisoners meet with board member representatives called hearing officers.

These cases used to be sent around by mail to the different board members in the various parts of the state where they lived and maintained their offices. (I understand that these days they are sent by computer for faster consideration and efficiency.) At each hearing, notes are taken. These notes are later shared with board members. In the first part of the hearing, prisoners are required to explain why they committed their offense, and why they believe they will live a crime-free life if they are granted parole. Audio recordings are also made of the hearing; in case a board member wants to get a sense of the hearing's emotional content. However, the recording devices do not accommodate the acoustics of the brick walls and concrete floors: When the recording actually picks up voices, it is often difficult to understand what was said.

The board members preside over the high profile cases and more serious crimes. This is called a "board level" hearing. Such a hearing requires four concurring board member votes with the chairman of the Board of Probation and Parole serving as the tie breaker in the event of a tie. In high profile cases, such as James Earl Ray's, at least four board members attend the hearing and announce an immediate decision. In 1994, James was denied parole but told he could ask again in five years. That's called "being put off." There was a time when the BOPP would put people off for ten or twenty years. In a way, it was good because it didn't give false hope to men whose cases were too politically volatile or who had committed serious enough crimes. In some cases, it was a foregone conclusion that an offender was not going to get parole. Sex offenders are a good example of this. Eventually a lawsuit led to a rule that prisoners could not be put off for more than six years because that is the length of one term for each board member. Unfortunately for some prisoners, many board members are hired for several consecutive terms. In fact, the last chairman of the BOPP held his position for almost forty years. If two or more board members have a social, political, or personal bias against a given prisoner or type of offense, they can make parole impossible for that prisoner.

It was rare for a hearing to end with a definitive decision regarding a prisoner's parole status. Added to my job a few days after each hearing was the task of checking whether board members had logged in their decisions. It could take a month to get four "yes" or four "no" votes, but it usually took about two weeks. Along with giving prisoners the final decision of the BOPP, I had to enter information regarding home and work plans into the computer system for men who were granted parole. Parole officers were supposed to make personal visits to these sites—at least the homes—to make sure the home owners agreed to the terms of the parolees' conditions, and that the locations were legitimate. We didn't want men moving into crack houses even if they did own the property. They didn't want that either because a condition of parole is that a PO can search the property where they live without cause and without a warrant. After a home plan is approved, I would let everyone know, arrange transportation, and let the prisoner know when he would be going home. Due to glitches in the system, and people messing up, there were many times when men were not sure they were getting out of prison until the day they actually left, but I did my best to provide as much warning as possible.

Once a fellow was out of the gate, I would speed back to my office to close his case and start on a few others. Being an IPO was a pretty interesting job. Some of my peers were high-quality people, and I really enjoyed sharing good news with guys who had turned themselves around, so to speak. I liked the challenges and appreciated the fact that there was *always* something to accomplish while I was at work. At times I didn't agree with the BOPP's decisions, but overall I thought the process was fair and objective for most prisoners.

Although this particular part of the correctional system (the BOPP) wasn't broken, they fixed it anyway when a new governor was elected. The point system was modified so that programs became the core focus for determining if a prisoner would obtain parole. For prisoners, the problem with the new approach was that there were not very many programs. Of the few that did exist, most didn't have a set curriculum, and some were taught by volunteers or staff members who didn't believe in rehabilitation. The one program that was structured, employed trained counselors, and had a great reputation for reducing recidivism was the one designed for men with sex offenses. Like I said, I'm sure it wasn't written anywhere, but there was *no* way these guys were going to be released on parole no matter how well they did in the program.

The program-centered process turned out to be a nightmare for IPOs.

They still had to keep up with the point system, but since several steps had been added to each case, it was almost impossible to keep up with the demand. Even though many of the programs for prisoners had not even been developed, IPOs were expected to make compliance look good for the BOPP.

Just two months after IPOs were trained in the new methods, their records were audited and some IPOs were issued warnings for noncompliance. A few of the older IPOs complained to their supervisors, even to the head of the department, that the new system just wasn't working. Without sharing private information, let me just say that the higher ups did not appreciate their truthfulness.

After five years of being an IPO, I wanted a change of pace. Thinking the job would have a slightly slower pace, I transferred to the downtown parole office and became a "field" parole officer (PO). As far as workload was concerned, being a PO required about the same amount of work. A PO's goal is to keep society safe by helping parolees adjust to life outside of prison. I wanted to see all ex-felons have good jobs, have stable families, and abide by all laws. To move toward that goal, POs are supposed to have a face-to-face meeting with each man within three days of the time he is released. As parolees demonstrate compliance with parole conditions, we increase the time between office visits. When I was confident in a man's ability and determination to be a contributing member of society, I sent recommendations to the BOPP for him to be moved to a lower supervision level. There was an unsupervised level, but in my ten years as a field officer, I was able to place only one individual in this status.

The main tools POs use include 1) checking for drug use with urine tests, 2) checking with local and state police sites to make sure parolees have not been arrested since their last meeting, and 3) making sure they are paying their monthly fees (if applicable). The urine tests were pretty easy to perform, but checking on recent arrests could be a challenge. Often, I would squeeze in some computer time only to find out that the police sites were not communicating with the TDOC computers. By the time police sites were functioning, I would have clients in my office or need to leave the office for a home visit or some other task. A few parolees made my life easy, but others were constantly adding more work to my load. I tried to give everyone the benefit of the doubt and provide as much help as possible with men who needed jobs or housing. Knowing it's hard to transition from a prison to a "free" culture, I really tried to give guys lots of support and leeway, but if I had reason to believe someone was participating in illegal activities, I had no problem gathering the necessary evidence and revoking their parole.

During my fourteen years as a PO, I got one mandatory promotion and was never promoted after that. In the way of raises, I received only the 1.5 to 3.5 percent annual cost-of-living increases that everyone else received. My workload, however, became much heavier. Instead of having caseloads of 75, which was considered a high number by Tennessee standards, we were consistently assigned 160 to 170 parolees. I was also assigned to be the district safety instructor for the board. That meant I was sent for up to a week to distant cities to learn how to train others on these courses. Then I had to prepare and present classes once per quarter to the two probation/parole offices in our district. These assignments would take me away from my primary duties, but no one was provided to take over my cases or help with them while I was conducting those duties. Obviously, I put in lots of unpaid overtime.

Board policy prohibits overtime pay; you had to take comp time instead, but I received very little time off. On top of that, I was placed on the Administrative Case Review Committee (ACRC). When parolees were found to have a technical violation (not paying fees, missing appointments, being charged with minor crimes, etc.), it was the ACRC's responsibility to plan for the individual's success as well as plan ways to reduce the chance that they would commit another crime. We could require parolees to attend Twelve Step programs or receive counseling or classes in things such as anger management. We could impose curfews, increase supervision level for a time, or do a host of safe guards before sending men back to prison. While some of the men on my caseload met the ACRC, many did not. Either way, it meant more of my time was taken away from men who were my responsibility.

With the added positions, I never had enough time to catch up on my main responsibilities. I am the first to admit that I took short cuts to ensure the compliance of as many of the men on my caseload as I could. Let me say here that everyone had trouble keeping up with the workload, and the stress was horrible for all of us. We all had huge caseloads; everyone in the office consistently ran behind schedule. It was not too big of a problem with management until the day I seemed to have committed the ultimate crime—I acted in a way that made me appear "prisoner friendly."

One of the many disadvantages of men living in prison is the limited education they get on being able to distinguish safe women from dangerous ones. Rob was one of those guys. When he saw "red flags" around a woman, he interpreted them as signs of a coming parade rather than imminent doom. When Rob finally realized that Ann was trouble, though, he had the sense to leave her. The policy of the parole board was that anyone in a domestic assault situation would be revoked and sent back to prison with almost no questions asked. In a lot of cases, the parolee is at fault and does deserve to be revoked. Domestic assault cases are the bane of a parole officer's existence. They are hard to prove and some women take advantage of this.

Ann was a veteran of playing the system. She knew all she had to do was report that Rob had assaulted her, and he would go back to prison. So she contacted Rob and told him that if he didn't come back to her, she would report him. By this time, Rob was living with another woman and that infuriated Ann further. She called him all kinds of dirty names and made multiple threats about what she was going to do. Rob came to me with a recorded message that Ann had left on his phone: Her plan was to bruise her face and report him for domestic violence if Rob didn't deliver. (There's one thing I can say for Ann; she was a woman of her word; she had already done that to another individual in another city.)

Soon, Rob was hauled in front of a judge, and Ann was there. Women often don't show up in court when making accusations like this, but Ann did. When the judge heard Ann's phone messages threatening Rob and learned that this was not the first time she had cried "domestic violence" to get what she wanted, he threw Ann out of his court room and dismissed the case. Still, as an automatic part of the parole process, I had to request a parole revocation warrant, and Rob was locked back up pending a parole revocation hearing.

At the initial hearing, I recommended that Rob be reinstated to parole and all charges be dropped. The hearing officer concurred with my recommendation. But when the case came around for voting by the board, it set off a firestorm. They could have (and should have) just disagreed with my findings and revoked Rob's parole. Instead, politics reared its ugly little head and the case was drug out through two more hearings, with another hearing officer writing a lengthy statement to the board stating that he thought my findings were correct, and that he couldn't see any guilt on Rob's part.

The attention I had drawn to myself by defending Rob sparked an investigation. One particular board member seemed to have taken special offense at my actions because she and a TDOC attorney went through my files with magnifying glasses to glean a mountain of charges against me. Until the judge overruled her, she even tried to have me punished for not reporting the misdemeanor arrest of a man who had flattened his sentence two days before his arrest. Ultimately, I was suspended without pay for thirty days, and I lost my appeal of that decision. Because my caseload was still active, I was ordered to divide my suspension into sections so I wouldn't get an entire month behind schedule. It was difficult, but I decided to swallow my pride and return to work when my suspension was complete.

About the time I was getting back into the groove, my supervisor approached my cubical and told me the same lady at the board was complaining about some minor problems with my files. She even took issue with tasks that were not completed while I was suspended from my duties! That was enough for me. I retired that very minute. Sure, I would have preferred staying another five years to double my pension, but some things are worth more than money.

Looking back, I am proud of my accomplishments. I never had a write-up and never got a warning in the fifteen years I served. All my evaluations were excellent, except for in the case involving the board member; however, disciplinary protocol was not followed then. I did the right thing, and if I had to do it over again, even knowing the outcome, I would do it the same way. I wouldn't think twice about it.

Everyone who was involved with that case and demanded my head is gone now except one. Accused of misdeeds themselves (including the chairman of the board), they were forced to either resign or retire. I worked with a few men whose bad behavior made all parolees look bad, but there were a great many more men who came out of prison, moved past their mistakes, and are now contributing members of society. I am proud to have helped with that in some small way.

For anyone who might be looking for some final words of advice, here they are: don't go to prison, and especially don't get assigned to parole in

Tennessee. While some fine people work in the system, plenty of others just don't know what they're doing. Promotions (when they are given) are based on seniority rather than merit, and there is no system for training people to develop leadership skills as they move up the management ladder. If you think you might get caught doing something illegal, or being with someone who does something illegal, go to another state. You don't want to do time in this one!

Commentary on Bob's Story

Working for a government bureaucracy will always have advantages and disadvantages. Job security and structure are seen as positives. People usually know where they stand in the hierarchy and what they have to do to reach the next level. Knowing guidelines exist for every situation that can arise in a day can be a comfort for many employees.

The fact that it is easy to get lost in the shuffle is considered a disadvantage to some, and an advantage to others. Having a large stack of policies and procedures for every scenario can feel comfortable as long as unexpected situations do not arise. The reason unique situations are a problem is that it can take extraordinarily long periods of time to work through the chain of command to find resolution. Because bureaucracies are rigidly structured, any break or block in the chain of command can be impossible to resolve. Bob was constantly bombarded by a caseload that was double its normal size, and he had no recourse for resolving that issue. When someone above him in the chain of command decided she did not like Bob, there was no way for him to go above her head without expending a great deal of energy that would probably have been wasted in the long-run.

We recently spoke with a woman in Washington, D.C., whose story unwittingly revealed the appearance of a felonistic attitude within her parole board. We will call the narrator Ms. BW for "beautiful woman." Ms. BW was proud of her progress until "that day." For the first time in her life, Ms. BW was not using drugs. She was attending meetings, interacting with positive people, and fulfilling her employment and family responsibilities. Ms. BW was even enjoying her job until the day her parole officer showed up. The fact that the PO came in unannounced was not the problem. Ms. BW was initially happy to be "caught" in the act of turning her life around. The problem was the PO's attire. The fact that the lady had felt the need to wear a bullet-proof vest, side arm, and Taser mystified Ms. BW.

Readers may be thinking, "What's wrong with that? POs are similar to police officers." The problem is the message to Ms. BW and her co-workers. Ms. BW had never shown aggression toward her PO and was not aware of any other returning citizen acting out toward this woman. It was as if the PO had come in ready to engage in battle with an attacker where none existed. It would be like your doctor entering the examination room wearing a full-body hazmat suit when you came in for an annual physical. Wouldn't that make you a bit uncomfortable? The PO has been assigned to assist people who have proven their compliance with the law. Other than prejudice against her clients, what could possibly motivate her to dress as if her life were in danger? We hope parole officers will consider the confrontational message they send by wearing military garb to a parolee's jobsite.

Another argument that presents evidence of felonism within the BOPP is the way they undervalue POs. The American Probation and Parole association recommends caseloads of 30 for probation officers dealing with parolees who are at high risk of recidivism, 60 for parolees at medium risk, and 120 for parolees at low risk.[122] In 2008, the ratio of parole officers to parolees in Tennessee was about 1 to 110, but no distinction was made between low-, medium-, and high-risk parolees. At the high end, Tennessee's ratio allows each PO to spend about an hour on each parolee's case per month,[123] but Bob's case load gave him less than fifty minutes per parolee during months he was not called out of town.

Maintaining a pattern of adding other out-of-town responsibilities while continuing to expect Bob (and other parole officers) to complete a caseload appropriate for mostly low risk clients appears to us to be employee abuse as well as client abuse. Bob has a passion to help individuals and society. His caseload included a multitude of high-risk clients sprinkled in with less disadvantaged clients, so a caseload of 70 or 80 would have been sufficient. Assigning him over 160 clients on a regular basis—along with other duties—significantly reduced his effectiveness in assisting returning citizens with locating good jobs, housing, or appropriate treatment programs.

Some could argue that these abuses occurred in an effort to fire Bob or have him voluntarily quit. They could say it had nothing to do with Bob's clients. We could accept that argument if it were not for the fact that the people covering Bob with a mountain of work had to have known the effect it would have on his clients. The men Bob served had spent years in prison. They had stayed out of trouble and demonstrated their readiness to return to society. How could anyone angry with Bob put over 100 people in danger of losing their freedom without being hard-hearted toward these men as well as Bob?

Our own experiences with the BOPP were no better: Andy (co-author) has been routinely treated with suspicion no matter how compliant he has been with inappropriate demands that were outside of his parole contract. One PO told Andy he was missing four payments and would have to get them caught up or risk incarceration. The next day, Andy brought the original receipts of his payments for her to see, and copies for her to keep in his file. Even with the evidence in her hands, the woman could not admit that his claims of being on time with every payment were truthful or correct. Her response was, "I'll look into it and get back with you." Months later, after not hearing back from the first PO (it is rare that they return phone calls or acknowledge messages), a second PO made similar claims but could not pinpoint which payments were missing. Rather than risking the possibility of angering his PO by arguing with her, Andy just paid the extra $180, even though she could not identify the reason it was owed or how she came up with that amount.

The overall negative attitude many POs display toward parolees provides more evidence of felonism being a systemic problem. We have witnessed many interactions in which POs spoke in demeaning tones and belittling words to parolees who were trying to demonstrate compliance. Andy (co-author) witnessed one PO pull out his gun and aim at a parolee as the parolee left the building to keep his anger from overcoming his actions. Obviously, the parolee had not violated his parole because he was not arrested. To us this dynamic seems to parallel the master–slave relationship of the old South. If this sounds too drastic to be true, we invite you to sit outside a parole office and observe for yourself.

The situation may not be so bad if an isolated bureaucracy practiced felonism, but the BOPP is not alone. Many agencies whose stated purpose is to serve returning citizens are tainted with felonism. The really frustrating part is that bureaucracies are difficult to change. While the heads of bureaucracies are often politically appointed, the lower-level workers remain with the agency for twenty to forty years, and those are the people who set and maintain the agency's culture.

When these workers forsake felonism and strive for equality, then real progress will be made in accomplishing equality throughout America.

Chapter 6

Dean's Story:
Sex Offense or Jealousy?

Be impeccable with your word. Speak with integrity. Say only what you mean.
Avoid using the word to speak against yourself or to gossip about others.
Use the power of your word in the direction of truth and love.

—Don Miguel Ruiz

Growing up in a town of about 15,000 has its ups and downs. My parents were middle class and raised all three of their children to be God-fearing adults. During the early part of my life, you might say I had a Beaver Cleaver existence. While I was not a star athlete, I had my own corner of fame because I was blessed with a "pretty" face, a good singing voice, the ability to play the guitar, and a knack for writing songs. Getting a date was never a problem, and I dated a lot.

Immediately after high school, I got a job at a tool factory where I supplemented my gym workouts with strenuous lifting and shifting of machinery in the factory. Life was good. I had plenty of money. I played music for small local crowds, and I was living as an independent man. Around the age of twenty-three, I got married to a beautiful gal. We enjoyed working and partying as much as any young couple in our area. Weekends were for drinking and smoking a toke or two, and I took care of my obligations as a family man—until I didn't.

About the time I turned twenty-five, I had an accident at work. My left arm was injured so badly that all the muscles and tendons were torn in multiple places. I'd never been hurt like that before, so I tried to shake it off and didn't report the damage the day it occurred. When I finally did get an appointment with the company doctor, he was positive my injury was not work related, and soon I was fired because the injury kept me from performing my job. The worst part of the damage from that accident was not my shoulder but my view of myself. My self-esteem was in shreds: I could not make a living, exercise, maintain my buff physique, or play my guitar. As my esteem plummeted, my drinking and drugging rose, and my wallet deflated.

It came to me that since I couldn't work, I would need to steal something in order to rejuvenate my billfold. None of my friends were thieves, but I figured I was smart enough to put a few coins in my pocket without input from anyone else. Violence was not my thing, so I made one clear rule for myself, I would not hurt anyone. Determined to "make" a little money, I was driving around a country road when I spotted a nice house on a hill with a pile of newspapers gathered around the base of the driveway. It was a sure sign that the residents were on vacation.

After parking in the driveway, I knocked on the front door. If someone answered, I planned to ask for directions. Surprisingly, the door swung open with my first rap on the wood. It was a *nice* house. Announcing myself with tentative "hellos," I walked through the home and found that it was indeed empty. These people had plenty of entertainment devices and computers, so I reasoned that their insurance would replace anything I took. In my mind, I was not hurting them in the least.

Like I said earlier, I was new at this profession, so turning my stolen goods into money was a bit trickier than I expected. I did have the presence of mind to stay away from pawn shops. As it happened, I ran into a friend and asked if he was interested in purchasing any of the items in my vehicle. He didn't own a VCR, so I made my first sale. Soon, my friend's lead foot attracted the attention of the local police. In the course of giving him a speeding ticket, the police officer inquired about the VCR in the back seat. I guess the officer reasoned that this expensive item didn't belong in a clunker. It didn't take long for my friend to reveal my name. That's when I found out I had stolen from the local judge.

Looking back, things worked out pretty well for me. The judge was furious and let me know I had stolen more than his family's property. I had stolen their sense of security, and that really bothered me. I received a four-year sentence, but I only had to spend the first year in that judge's county jail. He let me out early for good behavior, saying I was a model prisoner, and I was.

Since I had no confidence in my ability to steal for a living, and I'd realized it didn't fit my peaceful personality, I fired myself from that job. Unfortunately, I did not fire myself from my practice of booze and drugs. In fact, my habit got so bad that I would blackout. Although it looked to others like I was functioning normally, I would have no idea how I'd gotten to a strange location or what happened to the little money I had in my pocket. Although my first wife stuck with me while I was in jail, it didn't take her long to decide to get away from my downward spiral.

I married on the rebound, but that didn't last very long. Like I said earlier, finding dates was not a problem for me, so it wasn't long before I located wife number three. Amy was not the most beautiful woman I had ever dated because her abusive ex-husband, I'll call him Earl, had hit her and messed up her bottom teeth. Before meeting me, Amy had gotten away from Earl by taking up with an older man who carried a gun with him at all times. The thing that really drove Earl away, though, was the court order that Earl had to pay child support for their two daughters. Being the dead-beat dad that he was, Earl left the state.

Amy's childhood had contained one tragedy after another. Although she was a wonderful lady, her family was filled with troubled people. By the time we married, I had a welding job that was good enough to pay most of the bills. Amy took up the slack with her florist job. We were happy and had a good relationship with all our in-laws, until Amy's Grandpa made his move. Acting as if he were doing Amy a favor, Grandpa bought a broken-down trailer, moved it to one of his properties out in the country, and told Amy she could have it as a gift. Grandpa had given a similar gift to Amy's sister, but we came to learn that this one had strings attached. We had signed a lease for the trailer we were renting in town, so moving was a burden and didn't release us from the monthly payments we had agreed to pay, not to mention, the trailer on Grandpa's land looked as if it were a Jeff Foxworthy reject.

The deal we had with Grandpa was that he would supply the materials while I applied my carpentry skills to rebuild the structure. Basically, we had to camp out until I could make the first room livable. This project required me to quit my welding job in town because my shoulder was still healing, and I was not physically able to do both jobs. Living out in the middle of nowhere with no money in my pocket became a second low point in my life. To add to my misery, Grandpa informed us that he expected us to start paying rent, so our financial situation quickly became disastrous. I had never lived off my wife's income before, and I didn't like doing it now. I felt totally trapped.

It was about this time that Earl returned to town. His family had told him about our marriage, and he mistakenly thought our nuptials eliminated his responsibility to pay child support. While Amy and I were building our love nest, Earl was visiting with his daughters and poisoning their minds against me. It was obvious they weren't warming up to me very fast.

One morning it occurred to me that if they saw how much I loved their mom, maybe they could see me as a good guy. Amy entered the kitchen while the girls were having breakfast, and I grabbed her up in a big embrace. When the girls saw my hands on their mom's butt, they both began giggling. I noted their approval. Later that week, I playfully squeezed their butts, and they giggled again. It seemed to represent a bonding between us. At the ages of nine and ten, they were not think-ing about sex, and neither was I. For a few days, this was a bit of a game between the four of us, but Amy asked me to stop. She didn't think I was doing anything wrong, but she said Earl would love to use something like that against us. Of course, I stopped immediately. The girls were warming up to me, and there were plenty of other ways for us to enjoy being a family.

About two years later, a local daycare worker was charged with molesting children at his center. This occurred close to the time that new laws were being passed in my state, to increase punishments for people who committed any type of sex crime, especially against children. Then a coach at the local school my step-daughters attended was publicly accused of molesting girls on his team by touching them on the butt. Around that time, Amy let her daughters have a sleepover at the home of Earl's sister. When the subject came up, the girls' aunt asked what they thought of the report about the coach at their school. Both girls said they didn't think it was a very big deal. They stated that Dean had touched them on the butt. They didn't see what the fuss was about.

That same night Amy received a call from Child Protective Services stating that I needed to go to the police station. In a panic, I spent the night at my sister's house. Although I didn't hate the police, my experience eight years earlier had left me with quite a few bitter memories. The following day I entered the police department and was escorted into an interrogation room. Thinking I had nothing to hide, I answered all the officer's questions truthfully. When he asked if I had ever touched the "buttock" of my step-daughters, I said yes and explained the situation. Immediately, I was placed under arrest and told I would be serving up to twenty-five years in prison for sexually molesting minors.

Dismayed and devastated, I was placed into custody and didn't see the outside world for almost three years. I never did find out what happened to my car after I parked it at the police station that day. Unbeknownst to me, Amy was being instructed to refrain from contacting or helping me in any way. The police stated that if she violated these instructions, she would be arrested, charged as my accomplice, and lose custody of her children.

Eventually I pled guilty to a Class E felony, just one step above a misdemeanor. Because my "offense" had occurred two years before these new laws went into effect, I was given a sentence of four years instead of twenty-five years. Included was the stipulation that, after being released, I report to the local police department once per year for ten years. After that, I could file to have the charge expunged.

Not long after my incarceration, I had some serious medical problems. My spleen burst as I was lifting weights. At the time, I was at a prison called a "reception center." It was a brutal place with lots of fighting among prisoners—mostly because rival gang members were being housed right next to each other. Exercising was a good way to deal with the stress as well as to protect myself, because guys with big muscles are less likely to be attacked. While examining my spleen, the doctors discovered I had congestive heart failure.

After having surgery for both conditions, I was moved to a prison that had hospital facilities. Shortly after arriving, I was asked if I would like to participate in their Sex Offender Treatment Program (SOTP). I had learned that it was wise to accept any programs that are offered, so I said yes. One of the tools used by SOTP is called a plethysmograph. It's a biofeedback machine that measures changes in certain body parts; in this case, they measure the circumference of the penis. While hooked up to the plethysmograph, you're told to watch images of people of various ages, of different genders, and in varying stages of clothing as they flash on a screen. When the machine indicates a rise in penile blood flow, it is assumed that the picture shown at the time represents the type of person that is a sexual turn on for the client. When it was my turn, the doctors concluded that I was not sexually attracted to children. I knew that before starting the program, but I did learn a few things about myself from the SOTP.

Due to good behavior, I **flattened** my sentence in thirty-four and a half months. It was great to be home! When people asked why they had not seen me around in the last few years, I wanted to be honest, so I told them what happened. I made the mistake of telling a few people that I shouldn't have. One person I shared with turned out to be the "town crier" and also felt the need to get attention by awfulizing situations to everyone who would listen. It wasn't long before people who had once been my friends changed the way they looked at me, if they looked at all. Each time I saw someone avoiding me, I asked them why they had changed. Eventually I found out what Ms. Awful-izer was saying and got people straight on the truth. I looked the people who had believed her exaggerations, embellishments, and lies right in the eyes and told them I was the same person they had always known. I told them we could talk about their opinion of me, and about my past, anytime they wanted to. The last thing I said was that I was not going away. I would not run from their judgment, fear, or anger. They would be the victims of all that crap, not me. It took a while, but things were back to normal within a year. In the meantime, I had learned a valuable lesson: Give people the chance to jump on you like a pack of dogs, and they will. The solution is "Don't jump in the fighting pit." A second lesson I learned was to only share my full story with people who are emotionally safe and strong enough to handle it.

Probably the worst part about keeping myself out of the dog pit is that I have to remain on constant vigil when I'm in my hometown, which is about twenty miles from where I live today. This is a lesson I learned the hard way. I had been out of prison for about two years when I was doing a job in my hometown. I went to a fast-food place for lunch. When I stretched my hand out to receive my change from the drive-thru operator,

I realized the lady giving me change was one of my ex-step-daughters. Delighted to see how much she had grown up, I touched her fingers as she dropped coins into my palm and gently said, "Hey there." Without realizing that seeing me could be traumatic for her, I followed my routine and parked nearby to eat my food. In less than two minutes, I was surrounded by police and arrested for assault. My vehicle was towed to the police impound, and I spent the night in jail.

The next morning at my arraignment, I was adamant that I was innocent and wanted a fast trial. There would be no plea bargaining this time. After a court date was set, I borrowed $300 to post bond and hired an attorney. While walking out of the courtroom I noticed Earl standing behind a pillar next to a balcony. From the way he was peeking around the pillar and the expression on his face, it looked to me like he intended to throw me off the balcony. Earl yelled at me to stay away from his family, so I calmly told him that I had no intentions of interacting with his family and would appreciate the same courtesy.

When I arrived at the impound lot to retrieve my car (another $250), there was Earl. Considering his past violence toward Amy, I'm sure he would have attacked me if my brother had not been with me. A few weeks later, I stood beside the attorney I had hired for $1,100 to learn that the case would be dropped. Realizing they had no case against me, neither Earl nor his daughter bothered to show up for court. Their accusation (that I had yanked my former step-daughter's hand and tried to pull her toward me) disappeared. I had escaped the dog pack, but not without great expense to my bank account and my emotions.

About seven years after serving my sentence, the state legislators changed the rules. Historically, it had been illegal to make a new law apply to people who had violated it in the past. For example, when the DUI blood alcohol level was lowered to 0.08, prosecutors could not go back and arrest people who had previously scored 0.1 on a breathalyzer. In their misguided zeal to eliminate sex abuse, the legislature decided that everyone convicted of a sex crime would now be on the Internet Sex Offender Registry. When a few people noticed my name on there, I had to repeat the process of letting them know I would continue to look them in the eye and treat them with respect. One very negative consequence of this was that my brother lost friends and customers at his business when people mistook him for me.

Another problem my infamy created is that it's tainted people's vision and hearing. Living in a relatively small community tends to have a bit of a fish-bowl effect. For a while I would go to the same fast-food chain restaurant during my lunch break. Since I am usually rushed for time, and in my work clothes, I always get my food at the drive-thru, park, and eat in the parking lot. I noticed that people seemed to gather at the window as I received my order. It finally occurred to me that someone inside was announcing my presence, so everyone came to gawk at the "pervert" on the other side of the glass. It didn't really bother me until people at the window started "mishearing" what I said in polite conversation.

While accepting my lunch order one day I said, "Excuse the mess. I live in my van." I don't really live in my van, but it can look that way sometimes. The woman taking my order reported to her husband that I had invited her to get in my van. He approached me the next day and threatened to call the police. Whether people mishear me based on their prejudice or fears, or whether they want an excuse to alienate me, I may never know. After a few incidents like that, I changed my tastes in hamburgers.

Another time, a couple of friends fixed me up with a double date. Betty was a pretty girl, and before we even met she told my friend that my past incarceration didn't bother her. I think she was one of those ladies who liked "bad boys," but that didn't prevent her from having a subconscious fear of me.

We had a good time on our double date, so we all ended up at Betty's house. After a while Betty went into the kitchen to make drinks, and my friend followed her to assist. Betty whispered, "What does Dean think of me?" He told Betty that I had said she was "Killer!" In shock, Betty yelled out, "Kill me? What did I do?!" He calmed her and cleared up the misunderstanding. We went on to have a three-year relationship and are still friends today, but only because she was willing to listen long enough to overcome her fears.

The most heartbreaking incident happened a couple of years ago. Sue and I had known each other for over twenty-five years and had always been friends. In our younger years we were married to other people, so we hadn't acted on our attractions to one another. Being single when we met up years later, we started dating. I tried to tell Sue about my past, but she said she didn't want to hear the details. Sue and I had wonderful conversations without discussing the past. She loved watching me play music, and I loved spending time with her. We always made each other laugh, and I thought we were moving toward a long-term relationship. I had dated a lot of women, but it felt like Sue was "The One."

Even though Sue didn't want to hear the story of my past, she had heard some of it from a relative. After a period of dating, I wanted to tell her everything. I explained the whole story in great detail, and I thought we were fine. One day I received a call to come to the police station. When I arrived, I noticed Sue's car in the parking lot, so I was a bit concerned. Immediately I was escorted into a conference room and told by two officers that if I ever called or tried to see Sue again, I would be arrested for stalking. Later I learned that Sue had gone to the police to check out my version of my history. One of her friends was a sergeant, so she asked him to check me out. Sergeant Felonist earned this name by telling Sue that I had raped my step-daughters and that nothing in my story was correct. Sue was terrified. Had Sue thought it through, she would have realized that I would still be incarcerated if I had raped two children, but Sergeant Felonist had manipulated her into an irrational state.

I was heartbroken, so I called Sue's father. We had been friends a long time, and I explained the entire situation to him. Sue wouldn't listen to him. Months later Sue was visiting her uncle (also a friend of mine), and we ended up talking on the phone. Finally, we smoothed things out, but I was still hurt. She has called a few times since, expressing interest in our getting together, but I'm just not willing. This public outcry against sex offenders has put me in a vulnerable position, and I am not going to do anything that risks my returning to prison.

It has taken a while for me to realize how vulnerable I am, but once I see a situation in which I could be susceptible to wagging tongues, I vamoose. One time, I started going to church. I really enjoyed the fellowship, the message, and the positive community. After hearing me sing and getting to know me a bit, the fellowship invited me to work with the choir and teach Bible classes. I loved the validation and being treated as an equal, but one day it hit me that I was too vulnerable in that setting. With children all around, anyone could accuse me of anything. Sergeant Felonist had provided all the evidence I needed to realize the police had no qualms about lying to make me look like a monster. I'd have no way to defend myself. Rather than exposing myself to another Ms. Awful-izer, I just quit going to church, thus taking myself out of the dog pit.

I do the same thing with many situations. Using computers is one of them. From what I know about social media, it would just take one person with a vendetta to send me some sort of incriminating tweet or email, and there I'd be. So I don't use social media or anything related to the Internet. I would love to advertise my business or my music, but it's just too risky.

Since leaving prison I have not consumed any type of mind-altering substances, not even a beer. I don't want anyone saying they saw me intoxicated to fuel any possible negative view of me, so I stay out of that dog pit.

Legally, there are no restrictions on my actions. I cannot be arrested for, nor am I restricted from attending school functions or being around children. I know children are safe near me, but it is the wild fear of others that I worry about. Once, I was hired to do some repairs on a daycare facility. Because I had bid the job at night, I didn't think anything of it until I arrived at the job site and realized there were children in every room. On another occasion I was working on a home where adolescent children lived. The parents had to run to the store and asked if I would mind them leaving the children at home. I made sure to do outside repairs until the parents returned, but I was still nervous once I realized what a vulnerable place I was in.

After what happened with my step-daughter at the drive-thru, I don't hang out much in my hometown. I still take jobs there, but I never go shopping without a witness by my side. It saddens me that so many people choose to live in fear and believe lies regarding my past, but there is nothing I can do about it. Most people do not have the courage to engage in an honest conversation with me once their minds have been polluted by dishonest gossip.

On several occasions I have seen an interesting-looking woman and re-visited her place of business or the coffee shop where we first made flirtatious eye contact. That has been my style since my earliest days of dating in high school. What has changed is that now, when I cross their paths the second or third time, sometimes, the lady or a male friend, will insist that I'm stalking her. I am resigned to the fact that I cannot stop people from talking about me behind my back. I know that these people don't know me. No matter how beautiful a woman is, if she's a gossip,

I'm not interested. There is one blessing that I hold onto throughout all this: I know who my friends are, and every one of them is a great treasure to me. Though my wallet is still flat, I am an emotionally wealthy man engulfed by a society of emotionally impoverished, fear-filled adults. I pray for their healing.

Commentary on Dean's Story

Writing about sex offenses is a delicate task. Any type of explanation or sympathy for the person committing the offense can be interpreted as an offense to the victim or a cold-hearted denial of the trauma created by such offenses. Lest anyone believe we are inexperienced with or insensitive to this topic, it might help readers to know that we have endured our own experiences with this issue. While minors, both of us were inappropriately sexualized by adults. We have family members and friends who have been sexually assaulted. However, we also have friends who will experience severe consequences the rest of their lives for moments of indiscretion during their youths or while in altered states of mind.

Given the frequency and traumatic effects of these crimes (an estimated one in six women and one in thirty-three men have experienced some sort of sexual assault),[124] we do not wish to minimize victims' experiences. At the same time, we believe the current trend of lumping all sex offenses into the same category and burdening all offenders—even those who are very unlikely to reoffend—with the same lifelong restrictions on housing, career, and civil rights is damaging to victims, offenders, and bystanders alike. It's also of grave concern when legislators and judges obliterate the Constitution and Bill of Rights for any reason.

When Dean was told about the topic of this book, he responded that he hadn't really experienced felonism but had seen it happen to others. Dean had not perceived the gossip behind his back, his need to stay away from church, or the slandering of his name by a police officer as felonism. Along with mainstream America, Dean did not realize that the abolition of America's long-standing tradition of preventing new laws from being applied retroactively was a felonistic act.

Lawmakers are deluding themselves when they allow the ex post facto application (applying law passed after the crime was committed) of new sex offender laws. This is a clear violation of article 1, section 9, clause 3 (which prohibits ex post facto laws) of the Constitution.[125] Courts have presented the idea that retroactively applying sex offender registry and civil commitment laws to people like Dean and George (see Chapter 7) does not violate the Constitution. Judges claim these laws are civil protections and not punitive; therefore, they are not ex post facto punishments.[126] Dean, George, and just about everyone on the sex offender registry will tell you that the placement of their picture, name, and contact information on these lists has caused them harm. Courts in South Carolina and Judge Mary Donovan of the Second District Ohio Court of Appeals agree with them.[127]

As we applaud the reversal of past trends, e.g., where women were blamed for being raped, sex acts that are not agreed to by both (all) participants are always wrong. Blaming the victim for the actions of the person who executed a sexual violation is never appropriate. While loudly proclaiming both of those facts as principles to live by, we call for a repeal of today's current inclination, generated by felonists, to depict people convicted of sex offenses as unworthy of humane treatment and incapable of redemption. Readers who disagree with this stance are invited to keep an open mind as we investigate current trends that reduce society's safety, especially our children's.

Just the title of the registry dehumanizes men and women. Registrants are no longer *people* with felony convictions. They are "sex offenders." To many, this title yields the belief that all people with this conviction will reoffend, and thus deserve a designation that says they are worthy of segregation, constant insults, public humiliation, torture, individual and gang rape, and even murder. Even in the few states that now distinguish three or four degrees of severity committed by people with sex offenses, just being on the registry casts a huge stigma upon all its registrants. A nineteen-year-old teen who has consensual sex with his seventeen-year-old sweetheart is cast into the same category as a seventy-year-old man who rapes his grandchildren. A fifteen-year-old girl who sends her younger boyfriend a picture of her naked breasts can receive the same classification as the woman who forces children into performing sexual acts for her movie business, as both could end up on their state's sex-offender registry.[128]

When a person's picture appears on the Internet registry, viewers rarely know the circumstances. Because prosecutors and police tend to load charges (e.g., charge a person with "armed robbery" and "using a gun in the commission of a felony" for the same offense) to enhance their advantage in winning plea bargains,[129] on the registry, the person's offense may appear more severe than it was. The unintended consequence of this practice is an enhancement of the general public's fear of registrants.

A recent example of this carte blanche isolation and rejection of people with sex offenses—and those willing to befriend them—was seen on the TLC show "Here Comes Honey Boo Boo." When allegations and photographs surfaced of June Shannon, mother of Honey Boo Boo, having a relationship with a man who had just gotten out of prison after serving his time for a sex offense, the entire show was canceled.[130] The outrage and judgment toward Mark McDaniel is understandable since he had been convicted of molesting Honey Boo Boo's older sister ten years earlier.[131] We understand the horror felt by onlookers who believed Ms. Shannon had abandoned her relationship with her older daughter in favor of rekindling a romantic relationship. Still, if critics had walked in Ms. Shannon's shoes, they may have reacted differently, or they may have followed the same path.

We can empathize with Honey Boo Boo and her sister while expressing our belief that a witch-hunt occurred once these relationships were revealed. After abruptly canceling the show, a public investigation of all the men in Ms. Shannon's life was exposed on television and the Internet. Even men who had never been on this "reality show" were investigated and publically scrutinized as the result of having been in a relationship with Ms. Shannon.[132] Aside from being felonistic, this move was also hypocritical since so many shows, such as "Breaking Bad" and "Dexter," glorify people who commit crimes.

The network did not mind exploiting this family's culture, a culture created by the poverty from which they came, as long as the more unpleasant parts of this culture remained in the shadows. Performing background checks on people working around the children on this or any show is logical, but publishing their findings related to people who were not on the show seems felonistic. Unnecessary damage was incurred by innocent people by this prejudicial act. Because the show was canceled, about thirty cast and crew members became unemployed, not to

mention the emotional and monetary damage the cancellation and exposure caused Ms. Shannon and her daughters. While we applaud all steps
taken to insure the safety of Honey Boo Boo and her siblings, we believe
such steps could have been taken without producing collateral damage.

TLC is not alone in their unfair practice of distancing themselves
from people with felony convictions. Most game shows promote felonism by performing background checks on potential contestants. Shows
such as "Survivor," "Extreme Weight Loss," "The Bachelor," and "Wheel
of Fortune" require potential participants to pass criminal background
checks.[133] Would it be so bad for a person who made a big mistake in their
past to better him- or herself by winning a large sum of money in their
present life? How would the administrators of these shows feel if the 70
million Americans currently being boycotted by these shows imposed
their own sanctions, stopped watching shows that ban their employment and refused to purchase products from their sponsors? As they say,
"Turnabout is fair play," but we doubt the decision makers of these programs would appreciate seeing the stance they use being applied to them.

Many people have developed an irrational fear of everyone on the Sex
Offender Registry and do not realize that men and women with sexual
offenses have some of the lowest rates of recidivism. A study conducted
by the U.S. Department of Justice collected data in thirty states to determine the rate of recidivism during the first five years of release. Data from
2005 to 2010 revealed the average rate of recidivism for both technical
violations as well as new criminal offenses was 67.8 percent among those
charged with crimes unrelated to sex, yet for people with sexual assault
convictions, the rate was 1.7 percent.[134] Research in this area varies according to the length of the study and the definition used for recidivism, but
a multitude of studies consistently reveal a significantly lower rate of
recidivism for people who commit sexual offenses when compared to
those convicted of other offenses. Yet the impression given by the media
and the existence of the registry contradict the facts.

We suspect most people searching the Sex Offender Registry are motivated by a false belief that knowledge will empower them to protect their
families. They may think they can watch for these individuals and warn
their children about these nearby "monsters." However, the Bureau of
Justice Statistics has found that 93 percent of minors who were victims of
sexual abuse knew their offender prior to the offense.[135] Adding to this are

two studies conducted by the U.S. Department of Justice, which conclude, "... this study is the first of its kind to demonstrate that SORN (Sex Offender Registry and Notification) as a policy has little effect on two related and socially important recidivism outcomes using the trajectory methodology: 1) reducing/deterring sexual recidivism and 2) reducing/deterring recidivism in general."[136] In other words, registries do not affect the likelihood of a returning citizen committing another crime.

According to the Center for Sex Offender Management (CSOM), there is no blueprint for identifying an individual with tendencies to sexually offend another person. Research has shown that people of every age group, every intellectual level, either sex, and every socioeconomic level have committed sexual offenses.[137] Yet the few common characteristics for recidivism that have been identified include an unstable lifestyle, employment problems, and an attitude or belief that justifies their criminal or antisocial behaviors.[138] Would you not agree that if these qualities are common to reoffending, we should take care to prevent the exacerbation of these factors? Instead, our government registry requirements increase the potential for these characteristics. By limiting employment and social opportunities, the likelihood for new victims is increased. By ignoring the topic of rehabilitation success achieved by men and women on the registry, a lack of healing and high potential for recidivism is implicit. What message do we send registrants who are trying to overcome deviant sexual tendencies when we apply restriction and public notifications that subject them to public humiliation?

As we have stated, socially and economically isolating people who have difficulty with positive relationships enhances the problem. If you were repeatedly accused of infidelity (or some other offense) after years of demonstrating loyalty, wouldn't you eventually be tempted to accommodate your accuser? Similar thinking can easily be duplicated, especially in people who are trying to live a better life but are continually met with opposition as their "reward."

While we are not saying recidivism is society's fault (we believe all people of sound mind who commit such acts are responsible), we do ask readers to consider the consequences of their actions toward others. Isolating individuals with tendencies toward committing sex offenses (especially by banning them from churches[139] or other community building organizations) has the net result of making our neighborhoods less safe.

Considering the potential consequences identified above, the registry provides false hope of safety to parents who check it as a substitute for spending time training their children on ways to keep safe and monitoring their interactions on a regular basis. Let's keep the *intent* of these laws, to protect all members of society, while treating men and women who have offended in a manner that will support their rehabilitation—thus actually protecting society. If we treat a person like our enemy (or like a sexual pervert) long enough, that is what we can expect them to become.

Chapter 7

George's Story:
A Wounded Life Overcome

The ultimate measure of a man is not where he stands in moments of comfort and convenience, but where he stands at times of challenge and controversy.

—Dr. Martin Luther King, Jr.

Trust has always been difficult for me. As you read the following story, you will understand why. Although he shows up later in my story, my biological dad was absent from every part of my memorable childhood until the end of my fourteenth year. After my conception, Dad1 abandoned Mom and me to enlist in, first, the Navy, then the Army, and then Hell's Angel's. Mom had hooked up with Dad2 long before I knew Dad1 had skipped out on us. I will never know which man would have been better as a father, but I know Dad2 was an abusive drunk from hell even if he didn't join a motorcycle gang.

Dad2 had his good points, but they were greatly overshadowed by the bad. Each having sons from a previous relationship, he and Mom gave me a little sister, Helen, when I was about three years old. Two more half-sisters arrived as I grew older. Dad2 also gave me a good work ethic, and he taught me to adapt to whatever situation I was in. I learned that lesson mostly because Dad2 moved us all over the country without regard to the needs of his family. Out of the blue, he would come home and announce we were moving. Between my fifth and fifteenth years, we lived in New York; Washington; Oregon; Washington, D.C.; Pennsylvania; Texas; Georgia, and Arkansas. In some of those states, we lived in two or three different towns before moving on to the next state. I never got the sense that he was in trouble with the law. It always seemed to me that he was just bored with his latest job and ready for a change. Back then, kids were pretty much kept in the dark regarding the reasons behind parents' actions, so I can only assume that Dad2 was part nomad.

He also taught me to fear for my life. Dad2 was a mean man who didn't mind beating on women and small children. More than once, Mom, my step-brothers, and I became his personal punching bags. We seemed to be his "favorite" offspring, because we bore the brunt of his most violent attacks. Dad2 also taught me to treat people like sex objects. While all those are pretty awful lessons, Dad2 constantly schooled me in the fine art of emotional self-degradation—the hardest of his lessons to unlearn. I have overcome many prejudices, many trials, and many deceptions over the last forty-plus years, but the toughest things for me to do, even today, are see myself as a worthy person and allow myself to trust others.

Added to my distorted thinking were two physical traumas in my early years. When I was four years old, I was playing on the teeter totter with a friend. Not knowing about the laws of gravity, my friend hopped off his seat while I was up in the air. As my seat crashed down to earth, my head slammed into the metal handlebars and put me in a coma. Mom says I was in the hospital for four days, but that was nothing compared to what happened a year later.

We were living in New York at the time, and I had just started kindergarten. While waiting for the bus, a drunk driver hit me with her car and nearly ended my life. The initial impact propelled me into the air in front of her car. So drunk that she was not aware of my flight, the woman ran me over. It was terrifying when I awoke from my second coma a few months later to see my body wrapped up like a mummy and tubes suspended from all parts of my body. I had to be strapped to a wheelchair during most of my elementary school years as Mom carried me from one specialist to another, hoping for a miracle. That experience definitely caused me to see myself as different from most.

The details related to my accident are not a part of my memory. I have heard that the driver was an aunt or somehow a relative of mine, but I don't believe we ever met after the accident. I do remember that $500,000 was put into a savings account of some sort. Throughout my childhood, I looked forward to the day I turned twenty-one and would be allowed to cash in that principal and all the accrued interest. More on that later.

After two years of watching other kids play, I was pretty depressed, and Mom was about to give up on me. It was then that my Aunt Rose and Uncle Bill introduced us to my "savior." The specialist's name escapes me, but I remember the day I was able to walk on my own two feet after five years of being confined to a wheelchair. We moved three or four more times within the same number of years. I didn't miss leaving my wheels behind.

You would think this event would be the beginning of huge improvements in my life, but my life got worse. I hadn't even hit puberty yet, but Dad decided it was time to embark upon my sex education. Under threat of a severe beating, Dad would instruct me on the finer points of intercourse—with my mother. Even though he told me it was okay, I knew what I was doing was wrong, but there was no one to turn to. A cloud of terror prevented us (even Mom) from joining against Dad2, and we were always too isolated from the community to reach out for help. Dad2 had already sexually abused my step-brothers, half-sisters, and me. Mom and I had no support system after moving all over the country, and all of us shrank into obedience under Dad2's dominating rage and abuse. Dad2 had always told me I was born of bad blood and would never amount to anything in life. Knowing what I had done to my mother and what he had done to me, I believed him.

About the time I turned fourteen, we arrived at a small town in Arkansas. Soon I discovered that I could collect the soda bottles stacked up at the back of the local convenience store, enter the store from the front door, and "return" the bottles for cash. I'm not sure how they figured it out, but it was not long before a policeman arrested me at school, and I was sent to the Pine Bluff Training School. The six months I spent there weren't too rough, but I did set my mind to staying out of trouble when I got home. Mom got some sort of job at the courthouse while I was gone. When I was released, she warned me that she'd overheard uniformed officers talking about my homecoming. She said I was being closely watched by all the officers in town, so I had better be careful. I didn't understand what she was talking about until later.

Moving around a lot means changing schools frequently, and that means always having to prove yourself as the new kid—especially after returning from a juvenile "training" facility. I was surprised during lunch one day when this beautiful girl in my class asked me to have lunch with her behind the gym. At first I said no because I knew Judy was dating Bobby, and we were on the football team together. After she told me they had broken up, I agreed to the lunch date. Judy's sexual education must have been similar to mine (that people are to be treated as sex objects), or maybe she had been instructed to treat boys like pawns. Either way, before lunch was over, Judy held my hand and put it on her breast as she invited me to come over to her house that night. Judy didn't act mad when I told her my evening was filled with football practice and homework, but I think she was. Not long after getting back to the main part of the school, Judy's boyfriend grabbed me from behind and started pounding me. Judy had lied to me about their break-up and to Bobby she reversed the roles about who made sexual advances toward whom.

Being a pretty big fellow myself, I figured I could hold my own in a fight with Bobby, but Bobby's cousin was a popular senior. Along with being a huge fellow, Bobby's cousin had a reputation for his athletic skills. In the back of my mind, I just knew his cousin would be assisting Bobby in beating me into a pulp. When I felt someone else grab my collar from behind, I reared back and swung around with every intention of keeping that cousin out of our business. My fist landed right in the middle of the band teacher's face, broke his glasses, and knocked him out.

This was back in the olden days when boys were allowed, even encouraged, to duke it out (off school property) if they had a difference of opinion, and principals still used paddles. Bobby and I were both taken to the principal's office and informed that our punishment would be twenty-five licks with the "board of education" on our naked butts. Bobby got his licks first. When my turn came, the paddle broke on the twentieth stroke. Since there was only one "board of education," my licks could not be completed, and I was suspended from school for two weeks. (Due to our joint punishment, Bobby and I became great friends that very day, though I have no idea whatever happened to Judy.)

I worked at odd jobs after school and while suspended. Because Dad2 was a drinker, Mom needed help keeping the bills paid, so I always gave her most of my wages. One day my uncle told me he would sell me a sweet, '57 Chevy, two-door hard top for $50. Arkansas law at that time allowed fifteen-year-olds to have driver's licenses, and I really wanted that car. Mom had already spent my wages, so I asked Dad2 for a loan. He knew I would pay him back because we lived at the same place, and he was still big enough to beat it out of me, but Dad2 said no. He told me to be a man, quit school, and get a real job.

Halfway through my school suspension, events caused me take an emotional roller coaster ride. My little sister, Helen, came to me sobbing. One of the bullies in her class had stabbed her vagina with a pencil. Lucky for the bully, the police arrived before I could finish pounding him into the ground. Since it was a small town, everyone instantly knew all the details. I could just see myself having another date with the "board of education," or worse since I was not supposed to be on campus while suspended.

Expecting an immediate summons to the principal's office, I got the shock of my fifteen-year-old life. Instead of an escort from the principal's office, a very tall (6' 7"), dark-haired man, whom I'd never seen before, walked into the gym and asked if I was George. Then he introduced himself as my father. Before saying anything else, Dad1 told me he was proud of me for stepping up to my little step-sister's bully and defending her honor. As quickly as Dad1 appeared, he disappeared, but after hearing his words, I didn't care. Whatever consequences I had to face for having another fight at school—while suspended—didn't matter. I read Dad1's reassurance as my being "man" enough to quit, so I did. I took a job at the same place Dad2 worked. We spent our days catching and processing turkeys. It was not fun, but I got that $50 and the car.

I thought quitting school and "being a man" would be a good move, but my life took another downward spiral. Like many country boys will do, I went fishing by myself in a flat-bottomed row boat. While on the lake, I realized my intestines would explode in my jeans if I didn't hightail it onto shore and relieve myself. Quickly, I rowed my boat to the nearby woods and cast a couple of hooks into the water so a passerby would know the boat had not been abandoned. Squatting down in the bushes, I took care of my bathroom needs and made sure the leaves I wiped with were not poison ivy. Just as I was pulling up my pants, a lady appeared out of nowhere. I don't know of any fifteen-year-old boy who wouldn't have been as embarrassed as I was when this strange lady said, "Hello."

Without saying goodbye, I hightailed it back to my boat and resumed my fishing.

I was blindsided that evening when the sheriff came to our house and arrested me. Remembering me from our first interaction with the soda-can scam, the sheriff believed the lady in the woods when she filed a report saying I'd tried to rape her. There was no way that had happened, but it was a grown woman's word against that of a kid—a kid who had recently gotten out of a juvenile facility. *Now* I understood Mom's warning. Eventually I was told that if I pled guilty to indecent exposure, the rape charge would be dropped. I took the deal.

Getting counseling was part of the program, but the counselors were not very good in my mind. From the counselors' point of view, they probably thought they were helping, but I had this one lady who kept insisting that I confess to trying to rape my accuser. Basically, she tried to bully me into a confession. In one session our conversation became heated, so I stood up and took a step toward her to make my point and end the conversation. The counselor called security and put her arms up to deflect my phantom punches. Then she told me my actions proved that I had tried to rape the lady I met in the woods. So much for getting to know your client. I later learned that her strategy is pretty typical of prison counselors.

Breaking from their old nomadic pattern, my parents still lived in Arkansas when I got out of juvenile detention. Not wanting to work with Dad2 again, I took a job at a chicken processing plant and got married at the ripe age of seventeen. We rented a little apartment right next to the county jail, and I thought life was finally going to turn around for me. The situation definitely became better for Wife1 because I did all the cooking, cleaning, bill paying, and working to pay the bills.

One day the tides almost reversed for me. Dad1 made a second appearance in town, and this time he came bearing gifts. Although he left before I even knew he was in town, Dad1 went to Helen's house. Giving her $60,000, he told Helen to equally distribute it between Mom, my step-sister, Helen, and me. By this time, Helen was married and living with her husband, Mark. I didn't like Mark because he had raped Helen before their marriage, and I definitely thought fourteen was too young to get married. Since Helen seemed to love Mark, and they were about to have a child together, I tolerated him. Anyway, Mark came to me at work and showed me part of a scorched $1,000 bill. He said it was the last one. Helen had gotten it into her head that Dad1 had stolen that $60,000, or obtained it in some other illegal manner. Mark arrived home just as Helen was putting that last bill into the burn barrel. I'm not sure what caused me the most anger, the fact that Dad1 came to town and left without seeing me, or the fact that Helen burned up the money he had left. Since I never saw him again, I will never know where the money came from or why he gave it to Helen.

Hearing about this event only magnified Wife1's demand for more money. I thought our income was decent at the time, but she insisted that she needed more. Learning the night shift pay was much better, I transferred to the midnight cleaning crew at the same chicken plant. One of our jobs was to sanitize the hooks on the conveyor belts that moved the chickens throughout the plant. As we worked one night, a screwdriver got stuck in one of the belts and everything stopped. We were sent home early, so I happily anticipated a good night's sleep with my wife. Instead, I found Wife1 in my bed with four strangers.

Devastated, I had to leave town, but I did two things before leaving. First, I took Wife1 to a doctor and made sure she was not pregnant. I didn't want to abandon a child the way my father had. My second task was to visit my mother and ask her to check on the $500,000 that had been accumulating in New York and awaiting my twenty-first birthday. Mom said she would take care of it, so I went off to boot camp with the Army National Guard. It may sound crazy, but I really enjoyed boot camp. The work was no harder than what I had been used to, and the abusive rants of the drill sergeant didn't hold a candle to what Dad2 could dish out.

The party stopped four months later when I got home. Wife1 was pregnant. I immediately filed for divorce, and her dad made her have an abortion. This was in the early 1970s. Having children out of wedlock was just not accepted in small Southern towns at that time. I tried to escape my hometown by joining the regular Army, but my last conviction made me ineligible. Being the emotionally damaged fellow that I was at the time, it only took me three months to hook up again. I married Helen's youngest sister-in-law, Wife2.

Once again there was a need for money, more money than I could make on any shift while working security at the furniture factory where

I was now employed. Dad2's message that I was a "bad person born of bad seed" had been bouncing around in my brain for nineteen years, and I gave in. A couple of friends and I started robbing houses and storing our booty in Ricky's dad's garage. We knew better than to sell everything at once, so I would visit the garage every few days to add or remove our stolen items. At seeing a stranger in the area, one of Ricky's neighbors got suspicious and called the police. Ricky was arrested first and provided the police with abundant details about my behaviors and those of our accomplice.

Because the stolen goods were recovered, and no one had been hurt, we were each sentenced to a year in prison. Ricky was given six months of probation as his reward for being the first to cooperate with the police. At that time, prisoners worked hard on farms or highways during their incarcerations, so if they stayed out of trouble, they were often released after serving only 30 percent of their sentences. After being incarcerated for over a year with no disciplinary problems, I finally got the attention of the **whole squad rider**, the gun-toting correctional officer who guarded us in the field. I explained that it was past time for me to be released. Unlike most COs, this whole squad rider checked out my story when we got back to the prison, and I was released a couple of days later.

Wife2 was waiting for me when I got out of prison. That may have had something to do with the fact that I had just turned twenty-one and would finally be able to collect the bankroll that had been accumulating since I was five. I opened a bank account in a brand new bank that had appeared in our town. The bankers and I were excited about the $725,000 deposit I would be transferring to my new account from New York. (Not disturbing trust funds with compounded interest really pays off.) Just like the windfall from my father, I learned that this treasure had been stolen from me.

It turned out my mother had not followed my instructions to contact the New York bank when I was seventeen and about to go into the Reserves. Since the New York bank had not heard from my guardian, and had no way of knowing where I lived, they had turned the entire sum over to the state of New York as abandoned property. For several months I clung to the hope that an attorney could prevail in court, and I would collect at least 60 percent of my money, but I never found a lawyer who was willing to do the job without taking at least 70 percent for themselves.

Some of them even wanted 85 percent of my money. I knew such fees were illegal, so I held my ground and received none of my money. If you asked me today, I would settle for $108,750 (15 percent), but I just couldn't do it back then.

With that defeat, Wife2 and I decided to move to Arizona. Our first child was born there, but the birth almost took Wife2's life. JJ was a wonderful little boy and has since grown into a fine man with children of his own. Before our second child, Alisha, was born three years later, we moved back to Arkansas. Wife2 wanted to be near her people before delivering because she had experienced such grave complications when JJ was born. In the long-run, that was a terrible move because I caught her in bed with another man. I'll call him Horrid.

Horrid and Wife2 married as soon as our vows were severed in divorce court. While I fought for custody of JJ and Alisha, I met and married Wife3. I was her sixth husband, and with her came one child by each of my predecessors. No one can say either of us was afraid of commitment. As a blended family, we were very happy. All of our children accepted each other and enjoyed the times we were together. When I was not working or playing with the kids, I restored classic cars and motorcycles. It was a good way to teach the boys and possibly put a little extra (legal) money in our pockets.

One dark cloud had hung over my head since the beginning of this relationship. If I failed in getting custody of JJ and Alisha, I had told Wife3, I'd have to leave town. I wouldn't be strong enough to stay in the same community as my children without seeing them. When JJ was seven, I learned that Horrid had burned him on the chest with a lit cigar. It was not long before Horrid had a few bruises and a matching scar on his chest. Thankfully, I didn't get arrested for that, but Horrid and Wife2 had one more trick up their sleeves.

After a great deal of finagling, Wife3 and I managed to arrange a week-long camping trip with all seven of our children. We had a fantastic time picking berries, fishing, swimming, hiking, cooking on a campfire—the works. It was a wonderful bonding experience for all of us. At the end of the week, I took JJ and Alisha back to their grandma's house (our court-ordered neutral zone) with promises of seeing them soon. Monday morning there was a sheriff at my door to arrest me. My initial thought was that Wife2 was upset about the kids getting poison ivy. I later learned that Wife2 and her mother had held Alisha down on the floor and pierced her hymen so they could charge me with rape. To this day, I feel anguish for Alisha because she went through this monstrous ordeal, knowing her step-father and grandfather would not save her. At the time, I filed a warrant out on Horrid, believing he had raped Alisha. Horrid failed the same polygraph test that I passed, but the prosecutor refused to charge him. I suspect they turned a blind eye to Horrid's probable guilt because he was a good old boy from the community, and my past felony had blinded them.

As I was taken into custody, I instructed Wife3 to use the two classic cars and classic Harley I had restored as collateral for the bondsman. Even though I won in court, I lost my Harley because Wife3 misunderstood and gave the title to the bondsman. Before my innocence was established, it was determined that my precious children would be placed in foster care for their own protection. After being found innocent of the rape charge, I had to climb one more mountain: Between grandparents, foster parents, Wife2, and me, there were now five claims for the custody of my children. In the end, the judge awarded custody of JJ and Alisha to Wife2.

Just as I'd told Wife3 years earlier, I *had* to leave town. Unfortunately, she refused to go with me. Looking back, I can't really blame her since the fathers of her children and other family members lived nearby. At the time, I was devastated by the loss of seven children and a wife that I loved all in one blow, but staying in that town would have given Wife2 a second chance to frame me for child abuse. She was not successful the first time, but I didn't want to give her another opportunity. The only way to keep me safe from her wrath was to leave town. I hoped my absence would also protect JJ and Alisha. For the next two years, I wandered around the country, medicating my sorrow with alcohol and drugs. I was so messed up that I don't even know where I went during that time.

At the end of those two years, I stumbled into Wife4. We were both a mess throughout our marriage. Being good alcoholics, Wife4 and I had the habit of frequenting the neighborhood bar before going home at night. One evening, I got home first and was hanging out when Wife4 burst through the door in tears. She said she had just been raped while at the bar. Immediately, I went in search of the rapist, but he had been smart enough to leave before I arrived. In my inebriated state, I figured punching anyone at the bar would be almost as good as getting the rapist, so I hit the next guy that crossed my path. It only cost me one night in jail for public drunkenness. It felt like I had gotten a break from the law, but now I see that I was missing a big warning sign.

Not long after the alleged rape of Wife4, I was sound asleep after pulling a night shift. It felt great when my wife snuggled into bed beside me until I realized it was her seventeen-year-old daughter. After jumping out of bed and recovering from the shock, I had a sincere conversation with her and made it clear that we would not have any sort of a sexual relationship. When Wife4 arrived, I told her about what had happened. I thought we were all on the same page until it happened again. The second time she crawled into my bed, I left everything except the clothes on my body and walked out of town.

One and a half years later, I was living in Memphis, Tennessee, and found myself married to Wife5. She had children of her own, but I never met them, just as Wife5 never met mine. Following the pattern of many couples, we had a honeymoon period that disintegrated into constant fights and accusations of infidelity. It was probably our frequent use of alcohol and drugs that corrupted our marriage, but we didn't recognize it at the time. After five years of matrimony, I put Wife5 on a bus to Arizona where we had arranged for her to start a new life with her friends.

On the way home from the bus station, I stopped by a bar on Beale Street and ran into a guy who called himself Willy. Due to my past convictions, frequent moves, and addiction issues, it had been difficult for me to find work in Memphis, but I had a landscaping job with the Housing Authority. The job included an apartment in public housing, which most people call "the projects." Willy said he had arrived in town that very day and needed a place to stay. We had so much in common (alcohol and drugs) that I told Willy he could crash at my place for a while.

Before Willy's arrival, I had spent quite a bit of time helping a family who had moved into the neighborhood with nothing but the clothes on their backs. Desiring to help them, while putting a little extra change in my pocket, I agreed to assist in furnishing their house. After visiting a multitude of yard sales and flea markets, I finally managed to get the beds, couches, bedding, and other things they needed to settle in. Since the parents were drug addicts just like me, their lack of money paralleled mine, but I had a steady job. After four months of waiting to be reimbursed for things I had purchased with my own funds as well as the time and energy I had invested, I struck an agreement with the wife. Having no woman in my life, I agreed to swap their debt for sex. The wife told me her husband agreed with this arrangement, so at the appointed time, I left Willy at my apartment and went to collect my "payment."

Willy must have sensed that something was out of the ordinary because he followed me to the neighbor's house. He later told me he tracked me to protect me, but he was so messed up on drugs that maybe he doesn't even know for sure. Our barter seemed to be going just fine until my neighbor saw her husband at the bedroom door, and Willy was right behind him. The moment the lady yelled "rape" was the moment I knew another woman had lied to me. Ignorant of our agreement, the husband lunged for me, Willy lunged for the husband, and all hell broke loose. Hearing the children screaming in the next room caused me to go into the living room and herd them into the kitchen. Unfortunately, I missed the thirteen-year-old girl who Willy had managed to seclude and rape while I was in the kitchen.

It was when we arrived at the police station that I learned the truth about Willy. The day we met, he had just been released from prison as a sex offender. Although Willy told me he was visiting Memphis for the first time, he had actually lived in that area before his incarceration, had a bad reputation, and was recognized by people in the next apartment building. As the prosecutor read the list of charges against us, I couldn't believe how things had gotten turned around. Along with aggravated rape, I was charged with aggravated kidnapping for moving the kids into their own kitchen. No one believed my story, but the judge certainly believed the prosecutor's theory that Willy and I had spent four months conspiring to take revenge against this family for not paying me. Because of our past records, they also theorized that we had planned to commit other violent acts in this neighborhood. Refusing to accept the plea deal of life without the possibility of parole, I was eventually sentenced to eighteen years in prison.

About a year into my sentence, I asked to attend the treatment program designed for people with sex offenses. I reasoned that I may find a way to turn my life around, and it couldn't be any worse than the prison. I had forgotten about the first prison counselor who had tried to bully me into a false confession, but her tactics came flooding back into my brain shortly after I joined the new program. The counselor I was assigned to had full access to my files and took time to read all the prosecutor's theories about what had occurred. He believed every theory to be factual and any contradiction on my part to be a lie.

At first, I liked the program because it addressed anger and self-esteem issues in a way that was helpful. At one point we were told to keep a diary regarding our thoughts and feelings, especially focusing in on our esteem. Well, Dad2's abusive statements were still rumbling around in my head. Finding myself in prison only magnified them, so my diary was pretty bleak. While I had no intention of killing myself, I did write about wishing for death as an escape from my current agony.

Just before Christmas, my counselor came into my cell and started reading my diary while I was at lunch. Rather than talking to me about what I had written, he assumed I was about to commit suicide and had me locked in a padded room for suicide watch. Since all the counselors went on a two-week winter break the next day, that is where I spent my Christmas—wearing paper clothes with absolutely nothing to do twenty-four hours a day. Do you think that "treatment" helped improve my thinking? Hell no! I spent much of that time thinking about how stupid I had been for trusting a prison counselor.

Even though the program had pretty much screwed me over, I wanted to stay because it was better than most other parts of the prison. We had a lot more privacy, and most of the prisoners were pretty good people. There were some sick puppies in there, but the only time I had to be around them was in group. After a year or so, I had worked my way up to the next level of the program and was moved to a different prison.

It was here that the counselors turned into real hooligans (I'm being polite by using that word). They too had read reports from the police, prosecutor, and judge, and they too believed every word of their theories to be accurate. Reasoning that they had to *make* me take responsibility for my actions, they repeatedly pressured me to replay the activities of the night of my offense in a way that matched what strangers had theorized rather than relying on my own memory. In order to stay in the program, I had to say I had planned to rape my neighbor for four months—the entire time I had waited for them to pay me for my services. They also wanted me to say Willy and I had conspired to commit rape and that he had been my lookout while waiting for "his turn."

Eventually, I left the program because the emotional abuse was harder than the physical hardships I could face in the general population. When my prison term was up, I was assigned to an officer of the Tennessee Bureau of Investigation (TBI) and given a list of stipulations that I, even today, have to follow religiously to maintain my freedom. Some of the stipulations include staying at least 1,000 feet away from any park or school. If I sell my car, leave the state for any reason, or move from one apartment to another, I have to notify the TBI case manager.

Along with my face and place of residence being advertised on the Internet, I have to physically check in with my case manager every three months. One time I reported a day late due to car troubles. When my officer joined me in the crowded lobby, full of people who were there for a multitude of reasons, she loudly berated me for my tardiness and let me know that the next time it happened, I would be in jail for eleven months and twenty-nine days. I don't know who she thought would benefit from her humiliating public jabber, but it certainly wasn't me.

On the issue of the sex registry, I would like to say that most of the people on there are not a threat to anyone. It makes total sense that people would want to know if an acting pedophile lives next door. I want to know that myself. But the overall result of the Sex Offender Registry is to instill fear where no fear is needed, and that fear often damages relationships. At the time of this writing, I have been out of prison about twelve years, and I am positive that I will never do anything that will cause me to return. I am now in a loving relationship with a wonderful lady named Lynn. Thankfully the stipulations of my release do not ban me from being in the presence of children because she has two beautiful girls who now call me Dad. But Lynn has experienced difficulties because of my presence on the Sex Offender Registry.

A couple of years ago, Lynn was surprised to see that someone she thought was a friend had posted my picture on Lynn's Facebook page and publicly shamed her for allowing me to be around her children. Both of us have lost friends who will not openly talk with me/us about their fears after seeing my picture on The List.

Another thing that really hurts at times is the physical restrictions. We have a friend who is dying at home from cancer. I very much want to spend time just holding his hand and letting him know he is loved as he struggles on the verge of death, but his house is across the street from a park. I would love to write him a poem or letter of comfort, yet each time I pick up a pen, it triggers memories of that isolated Christmas when the prison counselor misunderstood my journal, and my hand refuses to cooperate with my mind.

Fifty years of believing no one was worthy of my trust has been a tremendous struggle. I would not wish such a life on anyone, especially now that I know how good it feels to trust Lynn and one or two other people. Oddly, my lack of trust has now been turned around so that people see me as unworthy of trust when they see my picture on that website, but I'm still the same old George—mostly.

It is my hope that as people read my story, they will begin to understand that seeing a person's picture on the Sex Offender Registry is just a small segment of the person they are viewing. If you want to help in reducing the probability of more sex offenses by people on The List, go meet your neighbors before passing judgment and before looking at The List. Take someone with you, just in case, but go. Be kind to kids who seem to have a habit of getting into trouble, because they are probably coping with some really big problems at home. Most of all, be kind to yourself. If someone, even your parent, says negative things about you, like Dad₂ did to me, *don't believe them.* You are as wonderful as you want to be, and so am I.

Commentary on George's Story

George is a sweet, unpretentious, tender-hearted man. We have spent many hours together, and the more we hear about his story, the more we are amazed by his lack of cynicism. Even though he has difficulty trusting people who are new to his life, he still treats everyone with kindness and generosity. George has simple hopes for his future and does what he can to help others when he sees a need. You would be fortunate to have George for a neighbor.

When he was arrested for stealing soda cans, no one asked George for his motivation. Did he need money? Was something going on at home? Did he know it was wrong? Kids exchanged empty bottles for money all the time. If George had been from the "right side of the tracks," his offense probably would have been laughed off. His actions could have been interpreted as the demonstration of a creative entrepreneurial spirit. Since George's parents were poor, he was prosecuted and sent off to a juvenile correction facility. No one cared that George admitted his guilt for his offense. Adults didn't look at George as an equal. They looked at him as a bad kid. That was George's first experience with felonism. Unfortunately, it was not his last.

When George was arrested a second time, he had already been tagged. The police watched him, not to give him support or make sure George had what he needed to walk down a better path. They wanted to catch him doing something else for which they could arrest and punish him. If he had not been arrested for selling soda bottles to their owner, George's word may have held more weight when the woman in the woods made her accusations. It's difficult to believe a strong teenager could attempt to rape a woman and leave absolutely no evidence, but it seemed logical to the felonists in his life. If George and his parents had insisted on a trial, he probably would have been found innocent due to absence of evidence, but you can't blame them for not taking the risk. If his jury had been stacked with felonists, he probably would have been sent away for several years—at least until his twenty-first birthday. In today's political climate, it is likely that George would have been charged as an adult and received a much longer prison sentence.

George's counselor at the boys' home presented his third encounter with a classic felonist. For clients who are in denial, helping them see the truth about their actions is vital to healing, so on the surface, it was a good treatment goal. However, getting clients to a place where they overcome their denial without causing them further anguish can only be accomplished by creating an emotionally safe environment. Pushing George to confess, and shaming him when he didn't, may have been a good tactic for an interrogation room but not a counseling session.

Since George had never attacked his counselor before, it can be assumed that Ms. Counselor's fear of a pending attack came from wearing felonism-tinted glasses. We speculate that Ms. C felt justified in calling security for her safety, but we would like to ask Ms. C two questions: "How do you expect innocent people to react when they are being pressured to lie and admit guilt? What could George have done differently to convince you of his innocence?" That is one of the problems with felonism (all prejudice really): almost no tools exist to wrench felonism from the hands of those who hold to its propaganda.

Quitting school in the ninth grade could have been seen as a signal for help. It was probably illegal at the time, but no one noticed or cared enough to intervene. The pregnancy of his fourteen-year-old sister was another signpost of distress within George's home. Still, no one in this small community seemed to be alarmed. If there had been a place where George, or any member of his family, had felt emotionally safe enough to request assistance, he may have been able to finish school.

You might ask, "Aren't his parents the people who should be held responsible?" Absolutely. Until their children became adults, George's parents were responsible for him and his siblings, but they just were not very good at it. In fact, George saw Dad2 as a terrible father. Considering the alcohol and domestic violence detailed in the story, you may agree.

Although George's parents were responsible for his initial delinquency, we maintain that "innocent" bystanders in the community also had a responsibility to assist George and his family—at least the children. Even if community members were not legally responsible, the community shared in the negative consequences of George's misguided childhood. Had he been supported, George could have finished high school. That would have let George get better training for a stable job and possibly a more established adult life. Not only would George and his family have benefited, but his community would have been a little bit richer from the taxes he would have paid and the contributions he would have made to the local commerce. When anyone in a community goes to prison, the community is diminished; at the very least, everyone loses from the forfeiture of the prisoners' potential earnings.

Throughout George's childhood, he was a conqueror. He overcame paralysis as well as physical and sexual abuse. In adulthood, he continued efforts to be a loving member of society after several betrayals by the people who should have protected and loved him, but George knew his limits. He knew losing custody of his children would bring him to his knees, and it did.

It would have been wonderful if George could have sought help from professionals during the time of his emotional distress instead of leaving town, but why would he? He had no evidence that counselors would be any different from Ms. C, and there was plenty of evidence that officials in the local government had no intention of helping a guy with three convictions and little formal education. Leaving his biological and step children and the wife he loved was the most difficult act he had ever performed. At the same time, it may have been his most heroic act. Moving away may have saved the lives of Wife2 and those who had been willing to support her sexual abuse of their daughter. It is reasonable to believe that his actions ensured that his daughter would not receive further abuse as a tool for attacking George. Like millions of others before him, George turned to alcohol and drugs to deaden the pain of his grief and justified anger.

Even today, after years of sobriety, George has no memory of where he went or how he made a living during the first two years of life without his family. After reading his story, a felonist may want to conclude that George was a terrible person and was guilty of every accusation hurled at him. Hopefully those readers will accept these two years of misery as evidence that he really is a law-abiding person. There are no records of George committing any crimes during this, the darkest period of his life. When he did commit a crime (reselling soda bottles and burglarizing unoccupied houses), he owned up to his guilt. Only George and the woman he was accused of raping know for sure whether he was innocent of the charge. He says he was, and the way George has conducted himself before and after those accusations supports his claim.

In 1998, George went before the Board of Probation and Parole. The purpose of holding parole hearings for people with sex offenses is a mystery to us. Even when such prisoners have successfully completed treatment programs, they are rarely given parole. Because everyone knew he would be denied, we were surprised when George left his hearing in a happy mood. His cheerfulness was explained when George told all his friends, "Linda Polk [co-author] called me a 'human being.'" From his childhood on, and especially in prison, George had become acclimated to the demeaning messages of dysfunctional people. This slight validation, the title of human being, gave George great joy. Oppression is like that: It often convinces the oppressed that their subservient position in life is appropriate and inescapable.

Even the great abolitionist and orator, Frederick Douglass, held to such defeatist thoughts for a time in his life.[140] Just like Mr. Douglass's elation when he first heard and understood the concept of abolishing slavery, George was enthralled to learn that someone from the **freeworld** proclaimed him to be more than a prison number.

Can there be anything more tragic than the creation of an environment where staff members (such as in Renegade's Story in Chapter 12) have to remind themselves that prisoners are human beings, and where prisoners see such an endorsement as a joyous event? How can we justify sustaining institutions where such a pattern is perpetuated? There must be a better way to ensure the safety of our citizens. Why do we continue dropping people into this human cesspool that we call prison and expect positive results? Do we honestly believe the splash back will not cover those who feed these human septic tanks with the same stench?

Oppression against people with sex offenses began in 1994 when Mr. Timmendequas was proven (through DNA, fibers, hair, and other physical evidence) to have raped and murdered a beautiful seven-year-old child, Megan Kanka. Mr. Timmendequas had been arrested two previous times for sexually assaulting young girls. While incarcerated, he had admitted to forcing two infants to perform oral sex on him. According to our extensive research, there was no follow-up care to help Mr. Timmendequas deal with his perverse thoughts. His last incarceration before murdering Megan lasted six years. He was released against the recommendations of one of his counselors who predicted Mr. Timmendequas would commit more sex offenses.

Acknowledging that Megan Kanka's death might have been avoided if Mr. Timmendequas' incarceration had been longer, the New Jersey legislature passed a series of laws that created the Sex Offender Registry, required neighborhood notification when someone with a sex conviction moved into a neighborhood, and demanded life in prison without the possibility of parole for repeat sex offenses. The compilation of these laws became known as Megan's Law.[141]

The original Sex Offender Registry laws were written to protect children by preventing recidivism by pedophiles. The American Psychological Association identifies pedophilia as a mental health issue that requires treatment as well as the application of criminal codes when it is acted upon.[142] Implicit in their statement is the fact that some people are sexually aroused by children, but they do not act on these impulses and should not be prosecuted. Unfortunately, if a person with pedophilia who has not acted out discloses their urges to a counselor, they will be in danger of the counselor reporting such revelations to the local law-enforcement agency. Every state has statutes requiring notification to child services or police departments if they believe a child has been or will be harmed.[143] A client mentioning sexual thoughts toward a child could easily put a counselor into "cover thy own ass" mode to keep themselves out of trouble even if the client never acts on their thoughts. Such situations inevitably destroy the client's chance for healing while plunging them deeper into mental darkness.

Joseph Russo is living proof that thoughts can lead to incarceration. In 2013, Mr. Russo was held in solitary confinement for a month and then arrested. His crime? Mr. Russo called the police and told them he had thoughts about hurting local school children. These thoughts had been occurring for over a year, but he had not acted on them.[144] While police praised Mr. Russo for calling them, they charged him with threatening acts of terrorism.[145]

Had Mr. Russo been given long-term treatment in a secured mental health facility that treats clients like valuable people, he would have a physically and emotionally safe place to go if these thoughts reoccurred. At this point, we seriously doubt Mr. Russo will seek help in the future— assuming he is ever released. How can he trust an institution that labeled him as a terrorist after asking for help with his macabre ruminations? While we praise the Fairfield Connecticut police department for protecting the public from potential danger, we wish they had found a solution that did not include burdening Mr. Russo with a criminal record for which he is not guilty. This is one more situation in which a short-term solution—probably motivated by a blending of felonism and a desire to protect the community—could have devastating consequences.

Connecticut is not alone in their practice of blindly applying felonism to protect society. Many government statutes and policies are written with good intentions but end up being the basis for control struggles and the promotion of felonistic attitudes. Can you spot the felonism hiding within the following segment of the Tennessee Code?

"The registration of sex offenders, the public release of specified information about certain sex offenders . . . and public notice of the presence of certain high risk sex offenders in communities will further the governmental interests of public safety and public scrutiny of the criminal and mental health systems that deal with these offenders."[146]

Public safety is desired, but it is not accomplished by government systems that expose private information on public sites. While this legislation calls for "certain" people with sex offenses to be on the registry, no distinction is made regarding who will be excluded, so even people with misdemeanor level convictions can be placed on the same list as serial pedophiles. No consideration is given to research that would identify the probability of an individual's rate of recidivism or the amount of healing an individual has obtained through therapy.

Furthermore, publically identifying people who are recognized as needing mental health treatment on public registries is a direct violation of HIPAA (Health Insurance Portability and Accountability Act) laws. According to these laws, "... demographic data, that relates to: the individual's past, present or future physical or mental health or condition..." are considered protected and not to be shared without consent from the individual.[147] Psychiatrists and physicians can be fined up to $1.5 million and spend a year in jail[148] for sharing such sensitive information about mental conditions, yet state police as well as state and federal investigative bureaus are required to make such information public without consent from the people on the registry.

Clearly, we need a total transformation of the Sex Offender Registry laws. Legislators on all levels have failed to recognize that these registries violate federal law in several ways. First of all, registry laws require citizens to provide information that could be used against them. In a case we will view in more detail later, Galen Baughman was required to report his most intimate sexual thoughts, even masturbation practices, to prison officials if he wanted to avoid further incarceration. That information was used to determine if Mr. Baughman would be civilly committed for an indefinite period after his sentence was completed[149] These are violations of the Fifth Amendment which says, "... nor shall any person be subject for the same offense to be twice put in jeopardy of life or limb; nor shall be compelled in any criminal case to be a witness against himself, nor be deprived of life, liberty, or property, without due process of law . . ."[150] Furthermore, many states now require registrants' driver's licenses and state identification cards to signify the holder's conviction. When credentials are required to cash a check or enter a government building, these citizens are immediately identified as less than worthy of the same status as citizens who do not have these identifiers on their IDs.

Legislators say this is not punishment and does not cause harm. Would you feel punished if you were forced to repeatedly testify against yourself, to tell the world you were a reckless driver after getting a speeding ticket? We wonder if some legislators would have preferred a tattoo across registrants' foreheads? Maybe they feared this would be too obvious of a connection between felonism and the antebellum practice of branding slaves who had run away.[151] This idea may seem farfetched, but it's not if we consider that legislators in several states require certain people convicted of sex crimes wear electronic monitors on their ankles for the rest of their lives.[152]

A second reason to overhaul sex offender laws is that they do not protect the public as we demonstrated in the commentary for Dean's story (Chapter 6). A 2008 study published by the U.S. Department of Justice found that Megan's Law does not have any effect on reducing sex crimes; in fact, there is evidence that they make the public less safe because the stress and isolation may encourage pedophiles to seek out children.[153] Therefore, the tremendous expenses and strain these registries impose upon law-enforcement agencies are not justified.[154]

Every three to twelve months, every state must update the information on these registries. Proof that this burden is overwhelming was documented in Chicago, Illinois. During the first three months of 2014, the Chicago Police Department turned away over 600 people who were trying to register or update their information. The police department did not have enough staff to meet the daily demand. They also turned away another 300 individuals due to registrants' lack of required identification and/or money ($100 annual fee). Through no fault of their own, each person who was not able to register within the timeline set for them could be arrested and held in jail for 364 days and 23 hours, and some were.[155]

According to the Justice Policy Institute, each state has spent an average of about $12 million to implement sex offender registries. Once the registries are running, they take about two thirds of that amount annually to maintain.[156] Wouldn't we be better off putting those funds into prevention and/or reconciliation programs?

What's the motivation for ineffective registry laws that violate HIPAA rules and zap millions of dollars from tax-funded programs? We believe the main motivation for expanding registries is to manipulate voters into believing politicians who promote these policies will protect them. When politicians convince constituents they can resolve a safety concern with registry legislation, they ultimately increase their political power. Registry laws say their intention is to keep children and communities safe, but it appears little consideration is given to the effectiveness or consequences of these rules. It is as if politicians have noticed a fire in the kitchen and sprayed every inch of the house with flame retardant rather than address the cause of the flames and take reasonable steps to prevent future fires.

Registries do not provide the true stories of people like George, who has no history of harming minors, yet all are assumed to be a threat to children. George loves children and has never acted in a sexual manner toward any of them, yet he is not allowed to patronize public libraries, attend school performances, or enjoy public parks without special permission because his name is on the registry. George pays taxes for such services. How can he, and the 760,000[157] other men and women on the registry, be barred from public facilities while being taxed to fund them? Most registrants are also banned from voting, so their input is not considered by politicians. Are these not violations (taxation without representation and paying taxes for services which are denied to the payee) of the very principles on which America was founded?

Felonism is at its worst when it comes to the treatment of men and women who have been convicted of sexual crimes. Due to misinformation, the public has approved of these harsh, ineffective measures. The masses have accepted laws that mirror the Black Codes of the mid-1800s when Blacks were severely restricted in where they could work and live. Today people with sex convictions can be relegated to live in the less comfortable parts of town and banned from a multitude of jobs. In some places, they are almost excluded from towns due to restrictions blocking their admission to certain areas of residency within a given number of feet (1,000 to 2,500) from a school, church, park, or other location where children might congregate. A good example of this was demonstrated in Miami, Florida. From 2006 to 2010, over 100 registrants were forced to live under the Julia Tuttle Causeway due to lack of housing that met registry restrictions.[158] Even today, probation officers in Miami are requiring parolees to live in public places, such as parking lots, because their families cannot afford or find housing that meets city and county restrictions.[159]

In 2011 the Office of Justice Programs found that the majority of people committing rape were white men in their mid-thirties.[160] Through those convicted of sex crimes (mostly men of racial minorities), we can observe the extension of racism into felonism. These two forms of oppression follow similar patterns: the creation of laws to corral a given population, the persuasion of public opinion that this oppression is necessary to protect women and children, and the acts of a few entrepreneurs and politicians who happily preach their distorted gospel as a means of securing their current and future power and social status. America's wealth and standard of living has increased a great deal since the successes of the civil rights movement began in 1955. This fact alone is proof that racism is wrong. Why would we now believe felonism will improve our lives if racism only worked to diminish America's progress?

Even though registry laws were passed long after his conviction, George was required to register with the TBI within forty-eight hours of his release and every three months since that day. Of the twelve years since his release, George has only had one negative encounter with a law-enforcement officer. As he described in his story, George did not have transportation to check in with Ms. M, his TBI case manager, at the appointed time. George called on the day of his appointment and explained that he would have a ride the following day. When Ms. M told him to wait until the next month to sign in, George told her he would come next month but that he would also be in her office the next day. George had never been late before, and he had never missed paying his fees. Still, Ms. M found it necessary to reprimand George in the middle of a crowded lobby, yelling in a loud and demeaning voice that if he was ever late again, she would put him in prison and throw away the key. We wonder what would have happened if George had followed Ms. M's instruction and waited an entire month to meet with her.

By statute, the worst punishment Ms. M could have administered was eleven months and twenty-nine days in the local jail. That is a pretty severe punishment for missing an appointment, but since George had a sex offense, Ms. M's threat may have become a reality if she knew which strings to pull. All across America, laws are being enacted to allow the "civil commitment" of those who have sex convictions.

According to the ATSA (Association for the Treatment of Sexual Abusers), twenty states have approved the civil commitment of people with sex offenses who did not receive life-without-the-possibility-of-parole sentences. After a prisoner's sentence is complete, these states can hold them in secure facilities for indefinite periods.[161] According to a ruling from the 1997 U.S. Supreme Court ruling, Kansas v. Hendricks, protections from double jeopardy and ex post facto rights do not apply to people with "habitual sex offender" labels, *and* states do not have to provide mental health treatment for such individuals during their civil commitment.[162]

Looking back at America's past, we are greatly concerned that these civil commitment laws will eventually be applied to a wider segment of society. In some regions, legislators have already expanded registry laws to include people convicted of methamphetamine use, murder, and not paying child support.[163] Along the same vein, in 1970 the federal government passed a series of laws intended to prosecute and imprison the top bosses of organized crime.[164] Today, RICO laws are used to arrest elderly adults whose grandchildren were accused with gang activity (i.e., selling marijuana to an undercover police officer).[165]

While we support long-term treatment for women and men who struggle with urges to sexually offend others, we are concerned that felonists have and will continue to abuse these laws just as they have done with RICO laws.[166] As part of plea agreements, some defendants are intimidated into agreeing to civil commitment after their sentences are completed. In one egregious case, Galen Baughman was not allowed to have attorneys or an expert witness present during the state's assessment to determine the necessity of civil commitment. As Mr. Baughman's case demonstrates, some prosecutors believe it is legal to deny defendants the right to present evidence in their own favor.[167] Thankfully, Mr. Baughman won his case, but he's one of only a few to win a civil commitment case. Ms. M's threat to put George in prison "and throw away the key" (even though George does not live in a state with civil commitment laws for people with sex offenses) is just the type of abuse we fear.

Felonism has harmed George since he was a teenager. It has harmed his children by forcing them to live the latter part of their childhoods and early adulthoods without him. Local and state governments also make sacrifices for felonism by having to pay someone to update George's picture, vehicle, housing, and employment information four times per year. By placing George on the Sex Offender Registry, felonism has caused unnecessary emotional distress to a number of people with whom he and Lynn used to associate. Now multiply that loss by the 400,000-plus men and women on the registry who are not active pedophiles, and you can get an inkling of the damage America is enduring at the hands of felonism. George has worked hard to heal himself of the emotional wounding he received as a boy and young man. He practices daily the tools he learned in anger management classes, the sex offender treatment program classes, and life in general. The least we can do is validate him as a human being and treat him with the respect he has deserved all along.

Chapter 8

Jamesha's Story: Childhood Interrupted

You have it easily in your power to increase the sum total of this world's happiness now.

How? By giving a few words of sincere appreciation to someone who is lonely or discouraged. Perhaps you will forget tomorrow the kind words you say today, but the recipient may cherish them over a lifetime.

—Dale Carnegie

You could probably say I come from an unblended family. Of my mom's six children, I am the youngest and the only one to live away from Mom since the early days of my infancy. My unofficial adoptive father, God-Dad, must have been Mom's friend when I was born, but somewhere along the way that changed. It probably happened as the result of God-Dad's multiple efforts to legally adopt me. Mom would not relinquish her parental rights, so it never happened. What did not change, until the terrible day I learned about felonism, was my relationship with God-Dad. I lived at God-Dad's house almost my entire childhood, well, sort of. See, Mom never had the money to get a court order allowing God-Dad to be my guardian; maybe she just didn't want to mess with judges more than what was already necessary for a person living in poverty. Regardless of the reason, I could not attend school from God-Dad's house.

Every morning he would drop me off at my mom's house where I would join my five siblings on the bus ride to school. After school I would get off the bus and wait at Mom's house until God-Dad picked me up later in the evening. This arrangement always caused problems for me that other people in my family didn't understand. God-Dad was able to give me better clothes and a better place to live than Mom could, but that just made my sisters jealous and bewildered when I told them I would rather live in the same house as them. To this day I don't understand how six children in a house can be that much more work or expensive than five. I guess Mom never read *Cheaper by the Dozen*.

The day I learned about felonism was a hot day in August; I remember because it was the third day of my fifth-grade year. It seemed like a normal day until we all got off the bus, and I saw my oldest sister coming to meet us as the bus rolled away. That never happened. It wasn't a great neighborhood, but I didn't need an escort. Then I saw something that really confused me. All our furniture and possessions from our apartment were sitting on the curb. That's when Sis told us what had happened. Earlier in the day, Mom had made a phone call for my step-dad about some kind of drug deal. It turned out the person on the other end of the phone was an undercover police officer. Eventually we learned that Mom was sentenced to nine months in jail, and my step-dad got five years. Apparently the entire neighborhood knew because they were on the street taunting us about being evicted as a result of my parents' arrest. That was my first experience with being seen as a second-class citizen, and it was the beginning of the worst year of my young life.

Just as our furniture was out on the street, so were we. All six of us children, including my two pregnant sisters, had to move, immediately. Someone decided we would all live with my grandmother in her little two-bedroom duplex, and she was not happy about it. Being pretty upset with Mom, Grandma let us know we could live in her house, but she would not take responsibility for our food, clothing, nor discipline. Mom was to be replaced by my oldest sister for those responsibilities. Grandma lived in a different part of town, so the move meant we would change schools, and I would not be allowed to live with God-Dad.

During the previous four years, I had been a very good student, but fifth grade turned foggy for me. Ambivalence followed me like an imprinted baby duck. All day long my thoughts centered on my new, chaotic home life. From the reactions of our neighbors before we moved and Grandma's disdain over our invasion of her home, I understood it would not be good if people at school found out Mom and Dad were in jail. No one in my family had to tell me it was a secret.

Having the mind of a fifth grader, I told everyone Mom was on vacation. That lie didn't play very well five months after arriving at my new school. After all, who goes on vacation for that long? But it was the best I could think of at the time. Fear of what might happen if I got caught in my lie about Mom being on vacation always lived in the back of my thoughts, but it was better than what would probably happen if I told the truth.

I don't know if my teachers knew about what had happened to our family, but I didn't trust them enough to ask. On the outside, I made sure to look like a normal kid. That would keep people from prying into my personal business. On the inside, I was in great turmoil. Fifth grade was the first and last year in which I made Ds on my report card. I've earned a place on the Honor Roll almost every grading period, and I even graduated from high school a semester earlier than my peers. While school was an emotionally scary place that year, I looked forward to attending because it provided the best food I received all week. Those two meals a day weren't always what I wanted, but it was better than walking around with a growling bear in my stomach.

The worst part of that entire year was that I had no one to talk to. I still loved my mom, and I needed to talk about that. Grandma obviously didn't sympathize, and my sisters were still mad at me for having what they perceived to be a better life than theirs. They had lived with Mom's drug use for years and were angry with her for using and for getting arrested.

On the three occasions we were allowed to visit Mom during her incarceration, I was elated, but there was no one to talk to about the joy and anger I was feeling. A lady from the state came to Grandma's house one time to make sure we were in school. Because she already knew about Mom being in jail, I thought she would be a good person to talk to about my feelings. I asked her to come back and see me. Even though she said she would, I never saw her again.

On the rare occasions that I got to talk with God-Dad (I usually had to lie to a teacher and say I was calling my "real" dad), he just said mean things about Mom. Maybe God-Dad thought he was preventing me from following in Mom's footsteps since the things he said were true, but all he did was hurt my heart and make me feel even more emotionally isolated. Every day of those nine months when Mom was incarcerated, I wanted to run away from home. On the many occasions when I just couldn't pretend that nothing was wrong, the best I could manage was to hide in the bushes that separated Grandma's house from the lot behind her duplex. To this day, I don't think anyone in my family knows about my hiding place or how much I hid my suffering.

I have always been a strong person, and that year made me even stronger, but I have paid a heavy price for that strength. The world just does not look the same anymore. I still can't talk with God-Dad or most of my family about what happened, and I can't talk about it with myself without a flood of tears rolling down my face. Life is better for me now, and I am grateful for that, but I think my comeback could have happened with much less pain if there had been a way to talk about Mom's incarceration.

Based on what I now know, I'm sure there were other fifth graders yearning for the same thing, but we never found each other. Maybe if people saw the real effects of prejudice against people with felonies and their families, kids would be safe to talk about their feelings, even at school, and the world would be a better place for everyone.

Commentary on Jamesha's Story

According to a 2008 report by the Texas Department of Criminal Justice, over 7.3 million children in America have an incarcerated parent.[168] Of those children, only 12 percent of their fathers and 14.6 percent of their mothers report weekly, face-to-face visits with their kids.[169] The incarceration of a parent is just as devastating as death or divorce to many children, but few schools or facilities provide direct assistance to kids in this situation. During Linda's (co-author's) twenty years as an educator, she worked in three states and six different public schools. As far as she could determine, none of them provided support groups for children of incarcerated parents. On the rare occasions that she heard talk of a student whose parent was incarcerated, it was usually to explain the child's negative behaviors rather than offer support and understanding for the trauma they endured.

Since her retirement in 2010, "Sesame Street" has launched a program that helps parents and children talk about the incarceration of a loved one.[170] It is wonderful to see some parts of our programing related to children are moving in a more positive direction. When schools follow their lead and create emotionally safe environments for children of incarcerated parents, we predict our educational systems will improve and graduation rates will sharply increase.

Aside from public ridicule, secrecy about parental arrests is also motivated by fears that parental rights will be terminated. In 1997, President Clinton signed into law the Adoption and Safe Families Act (ASFA), which requires the termination of parental rights when a child has been in state custody for fifteen of twenty-two months.[171] The positive intention of this law was to hasten adoptions for children who would never return to their parent's home. Exceptions are allowed, for situations where a child lives with a family member while in state custody or when the state does not care for the child, but many parents are not aware of these exceptions. Parents only know that most prison sentences average about fifty-seven months,[172] and that court-appointed attorneys may not be trusted (when allowed) to assist with custody matters. After all, they didn't prevail in the parent's criminal case.

In one respect, Jamesha was fortunate in that her mother's sentence was only nine months, but it would have been helpful if Jamesha and her sisters had been given one or two options regarding their living arrangements aside from living with a grandmother who did not want six extra children in her small, two-bedroom duplex.

We can only speculate about the reason Jamesha's case manager never returned. Maybe the local child services agency did not have the resources to assist her, did not care about her welfare, or was too unorganized or understaffed. Regardless, without that second visit, how could the child services agency know whether or not Jamesha and her sisters were having their emotional, educational, health, and housing needs met during their mother's incarceration?

According to several research studies identified in the Urban Institute Justice Policy Center's 2008 study, Jamesha's emotional response to her mother's incarceration was fairly typical. Children of incarcerated parents will either internalize their feelings (resulting in issues, such as depression, disordered eating and sleeping, and emotional withdrawal), or they will externalize their emotional upheaval in aggression, developmental regression (reverting to behaviors from years ago, such as bed-wetting, baby talk, and an excessive need to be held), and acting out through behavioral problems.[173] Shamefully, when these behaviors disrupt instruction in the average public school setting, isolation and/or punishment are more common than counseling and identification of the origin of the child's outburst.

We contend that America's educational system is not in decline because classrooms are filled with bad teachers. It's because so many students and parents, especially families living in poverty, perceive school staff to possess the same felonistic attitudes as prison staff and other members of the criminal justice system. A student who remembers the degrading treatment showered upon their parent by a police or correctional officer subconsciously believes it would be a betrayal of their parent(s) to cooperate with people whom they perceive to have parallel status. In many instances, felonism creates a bind for public schools. Children (and parents or family members) do not trust school authorities enough to reveal the real source or their negative interactions. Since most teachers have had few experiences with the criminal "justice" system, they do not suspect the root cause of sudden changes in a child's behavior. Instead of suspecting incarceration, they often attribute these changes to drugs, hormones, or some other issue. When an educator correctly guesses the cause of a student's distress, there is a high probability that the student will refuse to confirm their parent's incarceration out of feelings of shame or embarrassment, or loyalty to parents in the midst of a felonistic society. In the minds of many students, suffering in silence is far better than betraying a parent, even if the parent is causing them pain.

Research has shown that incarcerated parents benefit from regular visitation with their children. Benefits may include lower recidivism (i.e., fewer victims), increased parental self-esteem, and increased parent involvement upon release,[174] but prison visits benefit the child too. A 2011 study by Cornell University revealed that regular prison/jail visits impact children in the following ways: "[They] decrease the feelings of loss [and] of separation, help dissolve fears or fantasies about prison by seeing it firsthand, and encourage discussion of the current situation, thereby addressing issues that could lead to shame or fear."[175] Despite these identified benefits, guardians of children with incarcerated parents rarely assist with arranging regular child visitation to prisons/jails.

When visitation does occur, fathers who have never been suspected of sexual abuse toward children are often not allowed to hold their children. Visitation areas are rarely large enough to accommodate more than 25 percent of the jail or prison population, and little consideration is demonstrated toward creating an environment conducive to parent–child bonding. When they visit in a Tennessee prison, children of all ages are often expected to remain seated throughout their visit (unless being escorted to the vending machine or bathroom), which could be as long as eight hours.[176] Furthermore, a child displaying emotional outbursts can easily result in the termination of a family's visit. These outbursts could be used as opportunities of instruction, ways for families to improve their dynamics; instead they are used to shame children who express their emotional devastation. Even though Tennessee has adopted the Children of Incarcerated Parents Bill of Rights (identified at the end of this chapter), there seems to be no consequences for facilities and agencies that do not abide by its rules.

Jamesha has beaten the odds, but she has not yet overcome her past. While she spends a great deal of her time mentoring younger children living in public housing, Jamesha believes she needs counseling for herself. She feels stuck, even after graduating early from high school and achieving a high score on her ACT. However, she is determined to have a better life than those of her siblings. Notwithstanding her success, Jamesha, like all children of incarcerated parents, is an unintended victim of her parents' convictions.

According to psychologists Ross D. Parke and Alison Clarke-Stewart, the lives of all children whose parents are or have been incarcerated will be negatively impacted in a way that puts them at risk of depression, poverty, drug and alcohol addiction, and a host of other debilitating issues.[177] It is logical to predict that as long as inmates, their children, and other family members are undervalued in America, and as long as felonism is legally institutionalized within government policies, the coordination needed between families, schools, police departments, children/family services, and prison/jail staff will remain absent, and our children will continue to suffer.

Children of Incarcerated Parents Bill of Rights

1. I have the right TO BE KEPT SAFE AND INFORMED AT THE TIME OF MY PARENT'S ARREST.

2. I have the right TO BE HEARD WHEN DECISIONS ARE MADE ABOUT ME.

3. I have the right TO BE CONSIDERED WHEN DECISIONS ARE MADE ABOUT MY PARENT.

4. I have the right TO BE WELL CARED FOR IN MY PARENT'S ABSENCE.

5. I have the right TO SPEAK WITH, SEE AND TOUCH MY PARENT.

6. I have the right TO SUPPORT AS I STRUGGLE WITH MY PARENT'S INCARCERATION.

7. I have the right NOT TO BE JUDGED, BLAMED OR LABELED because of my parent's incarceration.

8. I have the right TO A LIFELONG RELATIONSHIP WITH MY PARENT.[178]

Chapter 9

Jay & Lori's Story: Family Betrayal

To forgive is to set a prisoner free and discover that the prisoner was you.

—Lewis B. Smedes

Jay's Part of the Conversation

Hello. I am Jay, and I am going to share with you my experience as a convicted felon, for it is similar to those of many who have served time and then returned to the **freeworld**. I was incarcerated for a serious crime. I hurt many persons whom I loved and shall regret this always. Since confessing to my offense (first to myself, then my family, and eventually a judge), I have returned to the rational, loving thinking I used to have many years ago. I will say this, not in my defense, but as a fact, that the old saying "It takes two to tango" holds true here. I could have removed myself from the caustic environment. Instead, I let my stubborn side rule, and over this I more than stubbed my toes.

When I first went to jail, I knew I had to keep my spirits up because I had been a correctional officer. Experience had taught me that staff and incarcerated individuals would take advantage of me if they could. After a long negotiation, beginning and ending with my guilty plea, I was sentenced to 75 percent of a twenty-five-year term in prison. On the day I went to prison, a thought jumped into my mind; "Free at last, free at last! Good Lord, G-d Almighty, I am free at last!" Here I am, entering prison for a huge part of my future, and I am thinking "Free at last!" It came from my relief in knowing the family situation which had gripped me by the neck for so many years and influenced me to commit a horrible offense had finally ended its reign over my life. This insight helped. I was strengthened to dig in and do what I needed to do. I was determined to return to the way of thinking and behaving I had practiced before giving all my power to my wife. I had allowed myself to be taken down a path I knew in my soul was wrong. My first step in recovering myself was to process what had happened: For a time, I thought the path I took was right. I should have listened to my soul, but I had betrayed it.

Prison was a mixed bag for me, though overall, I had a decent existence during the eighteen years of my incarceration. I made good use of the time by recognizing my wrongs and doing what I could to correct my behavior. Although there were issues in prison, I believe I handled them as well as I could.

My faith was respected most of the time, and I made a few life-long friends. At times when I was able to perform mitzvah (favors) for others, I helped with what I could, such as setting up the library. With that task, I got to learn the Dewey Decimal System. Eventually, I did return to the kind of person I was raised to be, before I committed my crimes.

While incarcerated, I needed medical help for my heart. For several years medical professionals neglected my heart problems until I had rectal bleeding.[179] Then, they panicked and rushed me to the outside hospital, where the doctor found out how bad my heart was. He made sure that I received the operation I needed. Back at prison, one of the doctors told me my medical records were absent of documentation indicating a heart problem. I guess the two heart-valve replacements I received from the **freeworld** cardiologist had cured me and taken prison doctors off the hook to provide further treatment! This was my assumption anyway. Many prisoners are given one aspirin for serious conditions, such as broken bones or high fevers, so I think my assumption is a fair one. Plenty of times I witnessed medical neglect and was threatened with violence for voicing my concern, but I did survive.

Faced with the prospect of my release, a few weeks before I left prison, I needed to deal with some items. Where was I going to live? How would

I support myself? Knowing I would be emotionally vulnerable when I first stepped out into the **freeworld**, I realized returning to the city where my ex-wife lived was not a good idea, although that was the only place in the state that I had ever called home. Fortunately, I had some help, for which I am grateful. The prison chaplain worked with me to find a place. One facility he found was a Christian halfway house. Because I am Jewish and practice my faith and culture, this was something he had to clear with me. I thought about it, and decided it would be interesting for me to live there for a while.

One of my friends from prison, who had gotten out earlier, and his wife (I'll call them Carl and Dawn) had offered me a place in their home. Thinking it would be better for me to begin this new journey independently, and knowing they lived near my old hometown, I declined their invitation. The Christian halfway house that I transitioned to was a large building with bedrooms, dining and cooking facilities, and a chapel. Most of the residents there were homeless. I would have liked to have had a job as soon as I arrived, but my age, health, and record were huge detriments to overcome. Those three issues greatly limited what I could do and where I could work. The men were friendly and did not intrude into my space. I guess they know what it is like to find one's way when options are few. Eventually, though, I learned to find my way around, and where important places were.

The Social Security office was important to me. I was sixty-two years old and had to consider if I should wait three more years for a larger check, or begin receiving a monthly income immediately. The meager finances I had were dissolving, so I opted for the early check. I am lucky, as it did take care of what I needed, but not much more.

In the halfway house I had some responsibilities. One was working in the clothing room, where donated clothes were processed to be sold. This helped with the facility's up-keep, such as buying food, attaining medical help, and paying for utilities. The conditions of my parole allowed me to go anywhere I wanted and meet with friends outside of the halfway house, even female friends.

Even though I had not been in the company of a woman for many years, I chose not to involve myself romantically when I first left prison. I did not want to push my luck. I knew the stresses of establishing a romantic relationship while learning to navigate this new world could make me vulnerable to falling back into old patterns. To say I was gun-shy is an understatement.

Carl and Dawn lived within 100 miles of the halfway house. Visiting them was tempting, but I needed more time to consider the consequences of going near the town I came from. I wanted a quiet life and knew it was up to me to make that happen. A staff member of the halfway house and his girlfriend, who worked for the city, invited me to share an apartment with them, but I declined their offer too. It was wonderful to have options after so many years of incarceration, but for the moment, I wanted to serve. Some of the men in the halfway house seemed to benefit from my counsel, and I enjoyed seeing their progress.

That changed about a year after getting out. I was beginning to grow wary of some of the practices at the house. This was especially true after the night I attended a worship service led by the director of the program. The regular minister was late, so the director performed his duty. I stopped by the door to listen. The minister, seeing the Star of David decal on my hat, went into his conversion spiel. I asked him if he had a New Testament Bible on hand. I borrowed it and turned to the verses which supported my understanding of why a Jew should not convert to Christianity. Handing the New Testament back to the director, I thanked him and went on my way.

The next week I saw the director again. When I wished him a good day, you should have seen the look of fear in his eyes! He thought I was going to what, circumcise him? Then the director told me one reason he had welcomed me into the halfway house was the hope he could convert me. That conversation put me to thinking. Would this environment eventually trespass on my soul? Was the facility going to start discriminating against me now that they knew I had no intention of converting? I didn't want to stay to find out. The next time Carl called and repeated his invitation to live in his home, I said OK.

While change is difficult for me, I became comfortable in my new home. Carl and I had spent several years as cell mates, so we got along well. Since I had started my Social Security, I was able to contribute toward my living expenses in their home. Thanks to sharing the expenses, I had more than enough money to take care of what I needed, so I saved enough to buy a simple computer. This allowed me to continue my long-time practice of studying Jewish history and reach out to new acquaintances. Since I had a driver's license, Carl and Dawn lent me their car on occasion. Not only did I enjoy trips to the store, but I even started going on occasional dates. By now prison was about two years in my past. I had been in the **freeworld** long enough to know that I would no longer betray myself for the sake of another.

In prison, I spent most of my time at a co-ed prison and had a female friend there. With plenty of time on her hands, Jan was studying to convert to Judaism. She had been abused by her late husband and felt that when she got out, she would do better in a religion where women were afforded more respect. I did not feel Christianity was less respectful to women than Jewish tradition, but she had her experiences. I respected her perspective and was happy to correspond with Jan regarding her potential conversion. We became good friends there and even talked about marriage. Shortly after my release, Jan was granted parole. Because her sentence was life with the possibility of parole, Jan would remain on supervision until she died. Jan did not want "to weigh me down" (as she saw it). I got a letter saying she loved me, but that we could not create the life we discussed while inside. I was sad for a while, but life went on.

As old as I was, I still wanted some interaction with decent women, so I registered on some dating sites on the Internet. One woman I met at a coffee shop sat and listened to me talk. I felt as if I was being judged during our entire conversation/my monologue, although I said nothing about my past. Maybe she had Googled me after setting the date, but was just too polite to cancel? Anyway, she just sat there in silence, so I will never know if her thoughts were critical or just elsewhere.

After encountering another woman via an Internet dating sight, we agreed to meet at a restaurant. Since she had not mentioned it, I was surprised to see her and her sister. Not being a suspicious person myself, I wondered for a long time about what they were thinking. Surely they could not have wanted what I thought they might have wanted—me? Anyway, they were nice women. We had a nice time, but it turned out to be a one-night stand without benefits.

One of the dilemmas I always worried about was when to tell someone about my past. I will never know if these ladies knew about my incarceration before we met or if they just didn't see me as a fit for them. Relationships with women can be very confusing, and it isn't any easier when you have been incarcerated in the past.

One night Carl asked me to drive a neighbor into town. I had met the young man who lived down the street but never been to his house. I accidentally knocked on the wrong neighbor's door. A woman, I will call Ms. C, had a surprised look on her face, as if Attila the Hun were standing on her steps. Ms. C yelled for me to stay right where I was as she left the room. Seconds later she returned with a gun pointed directly at me and said she had been expecting me to come to her house with ill intentions. I later learned that Ms. C's sister had informed her of my past incarceration. Ms. C ordered me to stand right there while she called the police. Feeling uncomfortable about having an angry stranger pointing a gun at me, I wished her a good evening and walked away.

Identifying my correct destination, I proceeded to pick up the fellow needing a ride and take him about twenty-five miles into town. I was surprised to find five police cars waiting for me when I returned to Carl's house. After showing them my license, revealing that I was on parole, and explaining that I had simply turned left instead of right, all was well.

We didn't know it at the time, but this meeting had been brewing in Ms. C's mind for several months. After learning about my past, Ms. C obtained a picture of me, and allowed her mind to create a fear-based, fictional scenario involving my violent intrusion into her home. She was loaded for a bear, but she didn't realize that I'm just a cuddly puppy at heart. Eventually, Ms. C accused Dawn of forcing her family to move out of the neighborhood by allowing criminals to live in her home. Dawn went over to Ms. C's house and had a friendly conversation that helped resolve some of Ms. C's fears, but she and her family eventually sold their home and moved. The saddest part of that story is that Ms. C's fears had practically imprisoned her and her daughter in their home for almost two years while everyone in Carl and Dawn's home held good intentions toward all the residents in the neighborhood.

After a few months of posting on a dating site, I came across an interesting person. Lori's post said that honesty was a turn on for her, and lies would result in an immediate end to the relationship. When I read that, without thinking, I stood up, pointed at the screen, and said; "That is my girl!" As it was, we both were looking for an honest person to have as a friend.

Things were slow at work one night, so I started a chat with Lori—who had become my favorite distraction. That night, for the first time, she sent me her phone number, and I called her right away. Forgetting that my phone plan had limited minutes, we talked for quite a while. It took me over a year to pay that bill off, but I would do it again.

After meeting Lori in person and realizing what a treasure she was, I was in constant agony over when to tell her about my past. Maybe it would be better to keep it to myself because I had already been rejected by most of the ladies I had dated after making this revelation. Besides, I was no longer that man. Years of therapy and self-examination had given me the tools I needed to make better choices should I ever find myself drowning in a dysfunctional relationship.

With dread in my heart at the potential of losing Lori, I told her all about my past. I told her everything, while wondering in the back of my mind whether she would still accept me when I stopped talking. Misinterpreting her tears, I resigned myself to releasing this wonderful woman from my life. When Lori told me she was not crying about my crime but about what I had gone through, I started crying too. If anything, my honesty only strengthened our relationship. We have been together and in a strong loving relationship ever since. Unfortunately, Lori's decision to stay with me has cost her dearly.

After a few months of dating, I moved into Lori's home. As Carl helped me move, and even as I was unpacking, he asked if I was sure. Remembering my past troubles, Carl assured me I could move back with him and Dawn if things did not work out. I was confident that this relationship would remain centered on love, even though my new living conditions had me sleeping on the couch in the living room. This was necessary because Lori's adult son and disabled brother occupied the remaining bedrooms and we weren't ready for me to move into her room.

Between my social security check and income from a part-time job, it occurred to me that I might be able to make amends, to demonstrate my remorse about the past, by offering a little money to my ex-family. Knowing it was not wise, and illegal, to make this offer myself, I contacted an attorney and asked that he relay my desire to contribute a token payment to assist my family. Still in her dysfunction, my ex-wife (Mrs. X) jumped on this by attempting to sue me for pretty much everything I had. Since I was under no legal obligation to assist Mrs. X, I withdrew my offer, Mrs. X having convinced me I made a mistake by trying to help.

Months later, Mrs. X called me and tried to get money from me again.

Answering that phone call caused a bit of a problem. Lori heard my side of the conversation. She got on the phone and let Mrs. X know where she stood with her. I was a little embarrassed, but also grateful that Lori stood by me. More than six years later, we still stand by each other.

As I write these words, Lori, her brother, and I have made a comfortable life for ourselves. Her brother is very sick. Even with the pressure she has been under, Lori has been an angel. I love her very much, and thank the Almighty for her, and for her brother, who is one of the most ethical persons I have met. We came from opposite sides of America and met in the middle. We are of different faiths, but work closely together to help and support each other. All is going as well as we can hope for, and I thank G-d for this. Amen.

Focusing on the positive parts of my re-entry to society may have led readers to believe that my return from prison was easy. It was not. How can I place the love and anguish of my heart on paper? I will always miss my original family, but I know that I have no control over them. I would love to seek their forgiveness and find a way to restore our relationship, but my previous attempt proved this to be impossible. Maybe one day they will reach out to me, and we can heal together. In the meantime, I have a new family, made up of good people who accept the truth about me and look at me as I am today.

To some, parts of my story may even come across as unrealistic. Few people who have undergone post-prison life find it to be as easy as what you read above. So what happened? Did I really have it as good as I show here? Truth is, I had my hardships, before, during, and after going to prison. They came about through wrong decisions, and wrong resolutions that I could have broken but did not. It has been about nine years since my release, but my past still haunts me daily. I emphasize that the worst issues I have ever faced were consequences of the choices I made as part of a dysfunctional family.

I did things that caused separation from my immediate family, and from my siblings. In her last letter to me over twenty years ago, my sister asked, "What have you done to me?!" I now see that betraying myself led to the betrayal of others. It was a viscous cycle, in which almost every adult in my immediate family participated. They are not responsible for what I did, but I pray they will not hold me accountable for what they did in withdrawing from me and each other. Only one friend stuck with me all of these years, and I will always be grateful for his loyalty.

Lori's Part of the Conversation

My first verbal conversation with Jay was the night before I actually met him. We had discovered each other online, and he asked me out to dinner for the following evening. I refused because I had undergone knee surgery a few weeks prior. I wasn't ready to go out yet, as I still limped a little. I told him I wasn't saying "no," just "not yet" and gave him my phone number. No sooner had I hit "send" on my keyboard than my phone started ringing. It was Jay. That was the night of his very large phone bill. I agreed to let him come to my house the following night after his work. At that time, Jay had a full beard and walked with a determined stride as he moved toward me. I'm five feet short, and Jay is six feet tall. My first impression of Jay? "My God, he's a freaking mountain man!"

The first time Jay came into my home, he met my dogs. Jay was thrilled because they are half wolf and half husky. He has always loved wolves but never thought he would be welcomed by them as part of the pack. My dogs accepted Jay instantly. They are excellent judges of character: If my dogs don't like you, you had best be leaving my house.

My older brother, Roy, lived with me for seventeen years before I met Jay. From the first time Jay came over, they talked like old friends. Between Roy, the dogs, and my intuition, I suspected I had a keeper. Roy and Jay came to love and respect each other like brothers. As I write this, it is six days since my brother passed on. Jay is as wounded by Roy's passing as I am. He has been my rock during this time.

After a few weeks of seeing each other every day, we knew each other well enough to move in together. He was warned by his friends that we were moving too fast. I know they had Jay's best interest at heart, but six years later, we still move in tandem. On occasions our lives will have what we call, "A fly in the ointment," and we started out with a big one.

That fly was my youngest son, who I'll call Bill. Although it was none of his business, Bill looked into Jay's background and decided he didn't want Jay in my house. Bill, who had lived under my roof (mostly at my expense I might add) for thirty years, gave me an ultimatum, "Either Jay goes, or I go." When I told Bill I didn't do ultimatums, he left. Jay had told me at that time that he would much rather leave than cause a rift between Bill and me, but in my eyes, Jay didn't cause the problem, my son did.

Things were quiet for a few months when another fly appeared. This time it was Mrs. X. I think she had learned that Jay was in a happy relationship, but who really knows one's motive for maligning another person? Mrs. X calls, begins berating Jay, and demands Jay pay her money for their grown daughter who still lived with her. Then she asked to talk with me. I think she meant to let me know what a terrible person I had chosen as my partner. I set her straight, and that was that. There's no more fly in our ointment.

Two years after we met, circumstances arose that caused me to lose my home. We were looking for a place to rent when the realtor told us that Jay and Roy could buy a house under their names, and that's where we still live today. It's a little quieter than it was when my brother was here; we're trying to adapt.

People at this stage of life usually bring baggage from their past along with them. I was no exception. I had been married twice and lived with another man for twenty years when I had him leave. My second marriage, to Ted, was the one that would have caused me to become a felon had my plan succeeded. When we had been married about three years, I found out that Ted had been stealing from me and defrauding my whole family. Feeling shamed before my family, I was enraged and wanted to kill him. In that moment, I truly wanted to see him dead.

Ted had a rifle in the house, and I told my thirteen-year-old son (the oldest of the two boys) to load it for me because I understood almost nothing about guns. I knew if it was loaded, I could pull the trigger, and that was all I needed to know. I sat in the stairway in the foyer and waited for Ted to come through the front door. As Ted entered a while later, I aimed it at him and fired. Ted backed out of the door as quickly as possible, and I pulled the trigger again. Lucky for me, my son didn't want to lose his mother, so he had left the safety on. There but for the Grace of God, and my very clever son, I did not become a criminal that day. This was my first born, and I never doubted his love, nor he mine.

I share this to help readers understand that we are all susceptible to criminal actions during times of extreme emotional pain. Sometimes split-second decisions when we are at our weakest points determine the outcome of events that forever transform our lives. I'm not making excuses; I've made many wrong choices in my life and adversely affected those I love most. I have been forgiven my mistakes, so I can do no less for others.

Now that I have given a glimpse of who I was decades ago, I can assure you I face life much differently now than I did then. Let me tell you a little something about Jay: he's a very intelligent man, compassionate to a fault, kind, loving, and supportive. No he isn't a boy scout. He's just a great person who would do anything to help someone in need. He's so easy to love. God bless him. His only fault is that he's a bit of a klutz. If that's the worst I can say about Jay, and it is, then I have no complaints.

Jay has made one omission in the telling of his story. He has accepted the blame and the consequences for his incarceration, but his wife should have taken responsibility for her part in that fiasco. At the time of his arrest, Jay did not involve her to protect his children. He hoped the children would be better off with one parent than with none. I disagree, but these events occurred before my time. I suppose even then, he put their needs before his own. Jay and I have made a life for ourselves, and we are very comfortable with each other. I only hope this gives hope to those who are re-entering society. As for society itself, more compassion and understanding are what we should all strive for.

Commentary on Jay and Lori's Story

It is often said that everyone in prison claims they are innocent. That hasn't been our experience in talking to hundreds of prisoners over the years, and Jay has confirmed this.

What about people suspected of a crime who don't confess? Media reports of confessions made to fellow prisoners seem pretty common. Modern crime shows depict confessions obtained by prosecutors who "hire" an inmate with promises of reduced sentences or dropped charges if the **snitch** wears a wire and finesses a confession from men and women who stubbornly insist on proclaiming their innocence. Unfortunately, this practice is not always fictional. It occurs when prosecutors have little or no evidence to convict their suspect. Rather than thinking they may have arrested the wrong person, some investigators and/or prosecutors reach into their bag of dirty tricks to make sure they get the conviction they want.

Knowing such manipulative tools are at the disposal of prosecutors, wisdom would dictate that people in jail loudly proclaim their innocence when asked about it by cell mates, but this is a tricky proposition. Admitting to being a law-abiding citizen increases a prisoner's vulnerability to predatory cell mates. However, making false claims of criminal activity to create a façade of toughness, possibly protecting one's self in jail, can hurt them in court. Much to Jay's credit, he confessed guilt to his crime even before law-enforcement officials were aware of them.

Once a prisoner has survived incarceration and been released, halfway houses have the potential for becoming their next stumbling block. The first halfway houses in America were founded in New York City and Chicago around 1896 by Maud Ballington Booth. Hope Hall 1, in NYC, and Hope Hall 2, in Chicago, were so successful that halfway houses were quickly adopted by public prisons. Both private and public halfway houses were originally designed to heal men released from disease-ridden prisons and assist them in obtaining employment when they were ready.

Today's halfway houses are run by nonprofit and for-profit companies in some states and are owned by the government in others.[180] Requirements vary for each establishment, but most of them charge between $100 and $150 per week to share a room with two to five other residents. The stated goal of most halfway houses for returning citizens is to reduce recidivism by assisting newly released prisoners who are on parole with adjusting to the outside world. Some halfway houses exclusively serve people coming from mental health and/or addiction treatment facilities, some solely accept newly released prisoners, and some serve both. Since half of incarcerated individuals were convicted of drug charges,[181] and about 40 percent of violent crimes are related to alcohol use,[182] participation in follow-up treatment programs, such as AA (Alcoholics Anonymous), NA (Narcotics Anonymous), and group therapy, is often mandatory for residents.

As in Jay's case, religion can also play a dominant role in halfway houses and missions. These nonprofit facilitates do not receive federal funding (usually) so their "pray to play" requirement must be accepted as a condition of residency. The attendance of religious services is mandatory. Such facilitates see themselves as offering "the chance to study the Bible" with the hope of proselytizing residents, with little reverence given to any religious abuse that residents may have experienced in their earlier years.[183] Since converting new belivers is the goal of most faith-based facilities, residents such as Jay, who have no intention of converting, are in precarious positions. They can betray themselves and act as if they are accepting the teachings of that establishment. Such an act would increase the returning citizen's status and almost guarantee continuing services. Residents can also chose to speak their truth, as Jay did. While openly rejecting the halfway house's religious teachings may not result in immediate expulsion, the ridicule/judgment initiated by staff and residents could motivate them to leave. Once Jay publically professed his refusal to practice Christianity rather than Judaism, he no longer felt welcomed. Fortunately, Jay had options when he needed them. That is not true for many returning citizens.

Since Jay's family abandoned him when he was arrested, long-term homelessness could have been his fate if he hadn't developed a good relationship with his cell mate. Thankfully, Jay's parole conditions did not ban him from associating with other returning citizens, but it is quite common. This policy may have good intentions, but it denies the fact that the only hope for many returning citizens resides with those who have shared the same shoes. Another lucky break for Jay was that he and Lori did not have to rely on renting.

Throughout the late 1800 and early 1900's, restrictive covenants banned people of certain races, religions, or cultures from renting or owning a home in a given area. Even after the practice was deemed unconstitutional by the U. S. Supreme Court in 1948, landowners united in contracts agreeing to refrain from selling or renting their property to Blacks, Jews, or other identified individuals for a given period of years.[184] These covenants existed as late as 1988 when George and Laura Bush purchased a home in Texas that contained such a covenant. The Bushes probably didn't know they were prohibited from selling their home to a Black family (because the addendum was part of the platting or mapping documents, not part of their deed), and there is no indication they sought to act on this prejudicial band.[185] We mention it to demonstrate the smooth transition from racism into felonism in our life time. Although the name has changed, the practice of banning a given segment of society from renting in certain areas is legal once again. Not only are individual structures forbidden to many returning citizens, but entire sections of various communities have enacted laws excluding individuals with any type of sex offense. You probably remember this from George's story.

When the Anti-Drug Abuse Act of 1988 was passed as part of the War on Drugs, its intention was to rid government housing of drug dealers and their activities.[186] Eight years later, President Clinton expanded the mandate to prevent anyone with one legal strike against them from ever obtaining assistance with public housing. His initiative also resulted in giving public housing authorities access to criminal databases to determine the criminal history of applicants and residents.

These housing policies, combined with others, seem to imply a desire to see ex-felons in a state of homelessness. Although they did not apply to Jay, policies that prevent returning citizens from living with family members residing in public housing also reduce their chances of success.[187]

Severing family ties further, legislators and law enforcement officials have created regulatory practices that allow prisoners to be housed without consideration of proximity to family members.[188] State and federal prisons often place prisoners in facilities several hundred miles away from their closest family members. Parents and spouses who make tremendous sacrifices to relocate to a town close to their incarcerated family member are often given no consideration by prison authorities. Prison administrators are free to move inmates to any location as often as they wish, irrespective of the sacrifices made by a prisoner's loved ones.

This practice disregards various studies from the 1930s to present times which have concluded family interaction should be considered a primary treatment plan for felons. Remaining in contact with three or more people outside of prison while incarcerated creates an average success rate of 70 percent during the first year of parole. This same study showed that half of felons who received no visits while incarcerated returned to prison within the first 12 months of release.[189]

One government-funded study by Dr. Edward J. Latessa and Dr. Christopher Lowenkamp at the University of Cincinnati identified important discoveries regarding effective programs that reduce recidivism.

Of their two main findings, the first is a bit logical—don't put low-risk returning citizens in the same program as high-risk returning citizens. Such grouping actually increases recidivism of the low-risk individuals and wastes money on a program they didn't need,[189] yet Bob, Skai, and Renegade's stories consistently indicate this study is ignored

Their second finding is a shocker. For individuals at high risk for repeating past offenses, punishment, talk therapy, grief counseling, and Twelve Step programs, among others, are not effective. What has been proven to work are programs led by people with integrity (unlike the half-way houses Austin lived in) that focus on cognitive therapy, and "behavioral strategies, such as role-playing and practicing new behaviors."[191] These programs work for low-risk individuals too, but only if they are in homogeneous groups. Doctors Latessa and Lowenkamp emphasized the importance of administering a program with high integrity to reduce recidivism by as much as 16 percent for high-risk participants.[192] That may not seem like a big reduction, but out of 1,000 potential victims of recidivism, that could mean 270 fewer people get hurt. Though the government paid for this research, we have seen little evidence that its findings are being implemented by halfway houses, jails, or prisons.

An obstacle to having high-integrity programs is finding staff members who are not felonists. We have witnessed counselors advise prisoners departing on parole with words like, "Just get a trailer and park it outside the gate. That way you won't have to go so far the day you come back." We also know of halfway house owners who begin their orientations for returning citizens with statements such as, "I can have you sent back to prison with the snap of my fingers, so don't cross me." Rather than increasing the probability of compliance, such statements put an emotional wall between halfway house staff and residents.

In traditional classrooms, the relationship between teacher expectation and student success is so strong that the phenomenon has been given a name, the Pygmalion effect.[193] The idea is that students will meet the learning expectations of their teachers, whether they be high or low. The work of Doctors Latessa and Lowenkamp supports the idea that returning citizens are also influenced by the expectations of the professional leaders in their midst. It is logical to assume that hiring felonists to staff prisons and halfway houses is counterproductive. Since we would not willingly hire a school full of teachers who expect children to stay ignorant, let's not hire felonists to monitor prisoners or assist with the re-entry to society of people with felony convictions.

Preventing recidivism is a community project, but it appears felonists prefer to place all the responsibilities for housing, clothing, food, employment, and child care on the shoulders of the person who has just paid for their offenses with years of incarceration. The felonist's view may seem fair to some, but it is not a realistic strategy for keeping our society safe. This research confirms that any halfway house placing a greater emphasis on exercising power and / or making money (and many of them do) than supporting the re-entry of their clients will not have success in helping people transform themselves into contributing members of society.

Jay witnessed years of medical negligence (even to the point of criminal neglect in some cases). Felonism seems to have created a pattern of medical professionals abandoning their Hippocratic oath when they enter the prison gates. Some would have us believe prisoners like Jay and Dean actually have it too good because prisoners are legally entitled to more medical services than **freeworld** people. This urban legend seems to be pretty widespread. On March 4, 2013, Kevin Mathews wrote an article for an online organization, Care2, about several people who had committed crimes in order to receive medical treatment that they could not afford. Yet, as Mr. Mathew's notes, overcrowding and the privatization of medical treatment in prisons has led to a decrease in medical support for the incarcerated.[194]

Another problem stems from the fact that most people arrested live in poverty-stricken neighborhoods where the health care they receive before and after incarceration ranges from minimal to nil. In 2003–2004 the U.S. Census Bureau conducted surveys/interviews of 14,300 scientifically selected prisoners to determine the level of physical and mental health care being provided in federal, state, and local prison and jail facilities. Not only did they reveal that incarcerated individuals received inadequate physical health care, but most of the prisoners with mental illness were off their treatments at the time of their arrest. Researchers concluded improvements are needed both in correctional health care and in community mental health services that might prevent crime and incarceration.[195]

According to another 2003 study, people who are or were prisoners comprised 35 percent of the nation's TB cases, 12 percent of hepatitis B cases, 29 percent of hepatitis C cases, 17 percent of AIDS cases, and 13 percent of HIV cases.[196] Concerns regarding these contagious diseases in an overcrowded, understaffed environment can be exacerbated by the high number of medical staff who believe prisoners are faking their illnesses.[197]

To make this more personal, we present a September 2007 report by *AELE Monthly Law Journal* that identified a multitude of lawsuits filed on behalf of prisoners who had died or claimed to suffer serious pain and disabilities due to lack of medical treatment. These suits identify a wide range of abuses, from jailers delaying contact with an ambulance service for a man who later died of a heart attack (even though the detainee had informed jailers of his heart condition upon admission), to prisoners being denied services because they did not show up for their last appointments (even though they had not been informed of the appointments nor was transportation arranged by the prison). In some of these suits, judges ruled in favor of prison staff who claimed ignorance of a prisoner's medical conditions. In other cases, judges revealed their own felonistic tendencies when they affirmed doctors' decisions even though prisoners were left in severe pain due to negligence. In one case, prison medical staff refused to order much needed diagnostic tests to rule out back injuries. Because the staff had seen the prisoner 17 times in three months and prescribed pain killers and muscle relaxers, the doctors were absolved of responsibility.[198]

As a whole, this summary of twenty-five cases demonstrates a pattern of deliberate indifference to many prisoners from medical staff simply because their patients had felony convictions. We recognize that some prisoners are not ideal patients, and some will feign an illness to receive attention or cope with the boredom of prison. However, people in the **freeworld** do that too. Such behaviors indicate unmet needs which should be addressed, not because they are prisoners, but because they are human beings.

If you agree with the felonistic claim that people should receive slight or no medical care while incarcerated, please consider the long-term consequences of such a position. How does a lack of mercy and compassion affect the social and family life of medical personnel who are allowed— or encouraged—to forsake their Hippocratic oaths? Will society not be negatively impacted when prisoners with serious medical needs, such a hepatitis C or bipolar disorder, return to society untreated?

Bearing in mind that all readers are in contact with returning citizens (even though you may not know it), let's turn this question around: If all men and women were treated with respect and with concern for the downward spiral that led them to incarceration, if they were valued enough to receive appropriate medical and mental health treatment, if they were supported and prepared for a successful life and then allowed to provide a healthy living for themselves and their families, wouldn't our entire population be safer, healthier, and more upwardly mobile?

When your children are eating at a restaurant, your spouse is shopping at a crowded mall, or you are watching a movie at a local theater, who would you rather see as a peer, a returning citizen who has been mistreated and abused for the last five (or more) years or one who received appropriate treatment to heal their emotional / mental issues? Under our current system, it will probably be the former.

Chapter 10

John's Story:
Racism or Felonism?

The difference between stumbling blocks and stepping stones is how you use them.

—Anonymous

Being a Black man with thirteen felony convictions makes me look pretty scary to people who don't know me, but I'm really just a fun-loving guy who only wants to provide for my family and play with my kids. While I don't like to use the race card, I think that if I had been born white, I wouldn't have any felonies because all my charges were related to drugs. It's really hard to resist the drug business after seeing guys make $2,000 a day for just standing around. The thing that's harder is seeing a white guy arrested for the same offense that I was doing—or worse—and watching him get slapped on the hand with a misdemeanor (if he even gets charged at all) while I catch a felony and jail time.

Just a few months ago I had another experience with a police officer that I felt was motivated by a racist attitude. I was driving to work and received a call from my wife. She was pregnant at the time, and something had happened that made her concerned about the baby's health. Her anxiety rubbed off on me. After turning around to get home, I was pulled over. The officer said he'd clocked me driving forty-five miles per hour in a thirty-five-miles-per-hour zone. It didn't seem like I was speeding, but I was distracted by concerns about my wife and coming child. When the officer came to the window, I was still talking with my wife. Both of us explained to him that she was pregnant, and we had reason to believe our child might be in danger. We needed to get her to the doctor as soon as possible. Rather than expressing concern for our situation, this officer focused on whether or not I had stolen the vehicle I was driving: Disregarding the fact that the logo on my shirt matched the logo on the side of the vehicle, his first question was, "Is this your vehicle?" After taking my license back to his patrol car, where I am certain he learned of my past convictions, the officer wrote me a ticket. Since our local chief of police publicly claims that his officers write tickets for only 16 percent of all traffic stops,[199] I can only assume my real offense was either driving while Black or being an ex-felon. Overall, though, I've made my peace with prejudice. I don't like every person I meet and don't expect everyone to like me. What I do expect is for men to treat me like a man because that's how I approach them.

I have found that people use my past mistakes to justify their disrespect toward me and greedy intentions regarding money. They never tell me to my face that they don't respect me, but their actions make it obvious. I'll tell you a story to show what I mean. A few years ago I got out of prison for the last time. I needed a job, so a friend hooked me up with a guy who owned a used-car lot. I'll call him Fred. Two or three people I knew told me Fred would be a good employer and would hire me in spite of my past convictions. Fred and I agreed that he would pay me minimum wage to work eight hours a day plus $35 for each car that I detailed for him.

It was hot that summer, but I didn't let the heat get to me. I'd rather work in air conditioning, but I was committed to work in any condition that would allow me to feed my family and legally put a little money in my pocket. Well, based on what others had told me about Fred, I thought he was an honest fellow, so I set about working for him to the very best of my ability. I made sure his place was spotless at all times. When the ground work was done I started on the cars. Some of those cars he took in for resale were downright nasty when I first saw them, but I had a system.

First of all, I used a bit of oven cleaner and a pressure washer to shine up things under the hood. Once the grease was gone and the motor sparkled, I took the seats, door panels, and dash boards out of the car so that I could remove the rugs without damaging them. Every part of the interior got the total treatment—cleaning, refurbishing, and polishing—to make them look brand new. Once every part looked and smelled just right, I put it back in its place so well that you couldn't even tell anything had ever been removed. If Fred was around when I finished a car, I would show him my work. He'd always say, "That's just the way I wanted it. Great work!" I put a lot more than $35 worth of effort into each car, but I was proud of my work and the results. It was also my way of letting Fred know I appreciated the opportunity he had given me to make an honest living.

Friday rolled around and I was really excited about bringing home a good paycheck for the first time in several years. It was not nearly as much as I could have made by selling drugs, but this felt much better. Knowing I had earned an extra $420 for detailing twelve cars above my hourly rate had me singing all day. But then the hammer hit. Fred informed me that according to his count, I hadn't detailed twelve cars, and the ones he did count had not been up to his standards. I couldn't believe my ears. It was a bald-faced lie and outright disrespect toward me, and he knew it.

If Fred and I had been in a prison setting that day, I would have had to beat him down, or get beaten trying, in order to maintain my respect on the cell block, and that is exactly what I wanted to do. Somehow I was able to maintain control during the time I had to wait for my wife to pick me up. Having just gotten out of prison, I certainly didn't want to go back inside, but it was not easy! Even today when I see Fred about town acting all righteous among his friends, I have to fight the urge to teach him a lesson about how to treat a man. Since I won't work for a man who disrespects me, that was the last day of my employment for Fred, but I do have to credit him with giving me a job and teaching me a valuable lesson: Some people who appear to be successful and good-hearted will use you if they can. Maybe I should have known Fred would cheat me. After all, he is a used-car salesman.

My job now is with a nonprofit organization. While I am thankful for their willingness to hire me, it frustrates me a great deal that I am not being paid what I'm worth. I value the way they acknowledge the good work I do, but that does not put food on the table. I can work forty hours a week and still qualify for food stamps for my family, which just seems wrong to me. That's why I've been on the lookout for a different job for over two years, but nothing has happened yet.

I do appreciate the honesty of those who are straight up about refusing to hire me because of my past convictions. Since getting out I have applied for numerous jobs that would help me get ahead and out of poverty. I'm always honest and check that little box asking if I have ever been convicted of a felony. On the rare occasion that I get the chance to explain that I will never go back to my past criminal behaviors, it doesn't seem to matter. The answer is pretty much the same, "We don't hire people with felony convictions." That policy is actually illegal, but I don't see anyone being arrested for doing it.

At least they don't lead me on like one company did recently. The boss at my current job knows a lot of people in town. The nonprofit he started forty years ago benefits our community in many ways, but they are and will always be on a shoestring budget. Like I said earlier, I appreciate their support, but they just cannot pay me what I need to fully support my family, or what other companies pay for people with my skill level and work ethic. A few weeks ago I was talking to the foreman of a company that supports my employer. I became excited when he said they were hiring new people, and that they hire ex-felons. I knew that if I could get on with this company, I would at least double my hourly wage, so I watched for a chance to talk with the owner of the company.

As it turns out, my boss, the owner of this construction company, and I were at an event later that week. Right in front of my boss, I repeated what the foreman had told me to the company's owner and asked what I needed to do to become an employee. When the owner told me to talk with him next month, it became plain to me that I had been misinformed by the foreman. After all, the foreman had been very specific about the fact that they needed to hire new employees immediately. I was being played a fool once again. An old prison expression explains exactly how I felt at that man's response, "Don't piss down my neck and then tell me it's raining." If a man has a prejudice against me because of my past, or because I am Black, I prefer the truth. It's much easier to handle than false hope.

I have been surprised by the lack of understanding from the people who refuse to hire me because of my past. When I'm working and earning a wage commensurate to the expertise and effort I put into the job, I am always happy. The idea of using or selling drugs doesn't enter my mind. That makes people around me safer and means the government will not have to help me with money to raise my kids. I'm a happy man when I'm receiving fair compensation for my work, and that happiness trickles down to my family and community. My wife is happy, and our kids do better in school when I'm able to come home, play with the kids, and help around the house rather than stress over how I'm going to pay the bills or find a second job.

I don't understand how the people who refuse to hire me, or the ones who will only hire me for "slave wages," think this will play out. Do they think that continuing to punish returning citizens for crimes we have already served time on will make us better people? Do they think they are helping us learn a lesson or making returning citizens more determined than we already are to stay out of prison? If we could have talked openly, I would explain to them that I decided to be the best man I could become long before coming to them for employment.

Maybe they could learn to understand that being afraid of people who have made mistakes is not profitable for anyone. Trust is a tricky thing, but unless we are willing to talk about finding ways to trust each other, or at least talk about why we don't trust each other, our distrust will keep growing. Even if we can't have an open discussion about our differences, I will continue conducting myself with integrity despite their inability to be honest with me or themselves. I may not have their money, but I know myself. I can hold my head up proudly as I walk away from their hypocrisy.

Before closing, I want to share with you the reason I am so determined to stay away from criminal activity and out of prison. The last time I was inside, my wife brought the children for a visit. We had a great time together. As usual, I couldn't believe how much each of the kids had grown, and I was astonished at how fast the visitation time flew by. It just reminded me of how much I was missing, but that was not the hardest part. At the end of our visit, I escorted my family to the gate, kissed and hugged everyone as long as the guards would allow, and started walking back to the room where the mandatory strip searches were conducted after every visit. All of a sudden I felt something on my leg and looked down to see one of my beautiful daughters clinging to my leg, crying, and pleading, "I want to go with you, Daddy!" Her little voice was so filled with heartache that even the guards were crying. That's when it hit me hard: These children deserve better, and that is what they are going to get. The emotions of that moment affect me to this day. It took all my strength to tell my wife to stop bringing the children to visitation, but I just could not put them through that emotional turmoil.

Recently someone asked me what tomorrow would be like if felonism miraculously disappeared tonight. I told her I would have a great job tomorrow, conflicts would be reduced because people would be on the same page, and those of us who have socially isolated ourselves as a result of being treated like outcasts would start to fully contribute to society. The best part of that miracle would be the knowledge that when my children's hearts are broken, I can stay right there with them and help make it better. That fear of returning to prison on some trumped-up charge created by a felonist would no longer filter my thoughts. I would truly live in peace.

Commentary on John's Story

Our supposition in Chapter 1 that felonism is replacing racism (and other isms), is supported in John's story as well as by testimony at a U.S. Equal Employment Opportunity Commission (EEOC) hearing on November 20, 2008, where staff attorney Laura Moskowitz stated, "We believe that the confluence of these factors—increased numbers of Americans with criminal records, the racial disparities in the criminal justice system, and employer practices that screen out applicants with a criminal record—disproportionately exclude minority applicants from employment."[200]

John's remark that he would probably have no felony convictions if he had been born white is also substantiated by a 2009 Human Rights Watch report based on FBI records.[201] Even though reports show equality between the races when it comes to drug use, 2.8 to 5.5 percent more Blacks are arrested than whites. Conviction rates and lengths of sentences are higher for Blacks and minorities too.[202] According to an academic review of scientific studies in 2005, people of color receive sentences about ten percent longer than their white counterparts, depending on the type of offense. This trend was consistent in federal and state courts.[203] The

2007 study by the American Sociological Association (ASA) Research and Development Department states:

The most severe impacts of these outcomes have been experienced by young Black males, who bear a disproportionately heavy burden at all stages of the criminal justice process. They are stopped and searched by police, arrested, sentenced, and incarcerated at levels far beyond their representation in the general population.[204]

This ASA study does confirm that some segments of the "judicial" system are free of racial bias, but how is John going to overcome the assumption that the local police are racist when a police officer is more concerned about establishing car ownership than the health of his unborn child? Maybe it is an urban legend that police officers will escort speeding cars to hospitals during medical emergencies, but if John had been white or free of felonies, wouldn't the life of his unborn child have at least been given greater consideration than vehicle ownership?

According to the EEOC, John is correct in stating that it is illegal to refuse to hire a person solely based on criminal history. In the press release on January 11, 2012, the EEOC commented on Pepsi Beverage Company's agreement to pay the $3.13 million it was fined for past discriminatory practices, which we discussed earlier in the book. They stated, "The use of arrest and conviction records to deny employment can be illegal under Title VII of the Civil Rights Act of 1964, when it is not relevant for the job, because it can limit the employment opportunities of applicants or workers based on their race or ethnicity."[205] Potential employers are mandated to consider the following:

—The nature and gravity of the offense or conduct,
—The time that has passed since the offense or conduct and/or
   completion of the sentence; and
—The nature of the job held or sought[206]

These EEOC guidelines are not arbitrary. A 1994 study by the Bureau of Justice presented evidence that returning citizens who have lived outside of prison for seven or more years are no more likely to reoffend than a person who has never been incarcerated. This research also demonstrated that the older a person is, the less likely they are to reoffend.[207] Following these EEOC guidelines indemnifies employers from accusations of employment neglect in the event that the employee with a criminal history commits a crime while on the job. Allowing for these facts, and our own experiences, we believe employers who demonstrate loyalty to returning citizens will be rewarded with excellent work from loyal employees. On the other hand, employers who demonstrate a felonistic attitude toward employees, such as the used cars salesman that hired John, will probably get what they expect from the employees they feel entitled to mistreat.

We believe the EEOC was correct to rule that carte blanche refusal to hire individuals with past convictions is evidence that felonism is often used as a cover for racism. Devah Pager and Bruce Western of Princeton University conducted studies in which white, Latino, and Black college students posed as applicants for entry-level jobs using the exact same resumes and qualifications with one exception. The white applicants admitted to having criminal records. Even though the minority students' applications indicated no criminal activities in their pasts, the Hispanic applicants were called back 14 percent of the time, and Black applicants 10 percent compared to the white applicants, who received a callback rate of 13 percent.[208] From this we surmise that whites can obtain equal status to minorities in the job market by claiming a criminal history, but minorities have no way of obtaining equality to whites when they are looking for employment.

Long after adults have completed their prison sentences, economic punishments continue. While speaking to a committee meeting at the EEOC, Stephen Saltzburg, a professor at Georgetown University, stated, "Ex-offenders fortunate enough to find employment can expect an 11 percent reduction in hourly wages and, at the age of forty-eight, this same ex-offender will have earned $179,000 less than if he had never served any time."[209] If we assume this amount covers a thirty-year work history, returning citizens are earning about $6,000 less per year than their peers. That extra $500 per month could make a big difference in the life of a father trying to feed his children or a mother buying clothes for her children.

Ultimately, society pays the highest price for felonistic hiring practices. The Commission on Effective Criminal Sanctions (CECS) reports that returning citizens who remain jobless during the first year of release are three times more likely to return to prison, yet 60 percent of returning citizens are unemployed during their first year out.[210].

Knowing employment is important to reducing recidivism, government programs (funded by tax payers) teach valuable job skills to prisoners while they are incarcerated. At the same time, legislators and corporations have created thousands of laws and policies that restrict success for ex-felons. Some estimates say there are 50,000 laws that create collateral consequences for returning citizens.[211] Continued prejudice against returning citizens almost guarantees the creation of new victims as well as a squandering of taxes. Not only are training funds used for prison programs wasted when employers refuse to talk with returning citizens about their pasts, but employers hurt themselves by not hiring the qualified workers they need to conduct business.

Returning citizens seeking employment can be further victimized by inaccurate records from the FBI. Mr. Saltzburg identified a report for the Attorney General's office which states nearly 50 percent of their records are incomplete or inaccurate.[212] If felonism were not a prevailing attitude within the government, wouldn't this problem have been resolved long ago? This is a prime example of how felonism hurts almost everyone involved. Employers lose, returning citizens and their families lose, and potentially new victims lose. Who wins? Companies and individuals who increase their wealth and/or political power from the prison industry? In reality, no one wins.

Chapter 11

Red's Story:
Folly Created by Hypocrisy

The foundation stones for a balanced success are honesty, character, integrity, faith, love and loyalty.

—Zig Ziglar

Before the start of WWII, I was born in By-God West Virginia and given the name Red Frizzel (not my real name). By the start of the Korean War, a judge decided I was of age to make a good soldier. See, I'd gotten caught breaking into a grocery store. The judge made sure our coal town community did its patriotic duty by sentencing a bunch of us kids from the poor side of town into the Army or Marines. I see I'm getting ahead of myself, so let me back up just a tad.

I'd been an honest guy all the way up and into high school. Life was good and got even better when I met Mary. She turned my world upside down. I was flat out in love. Mary's father was a big wig in the coal company where my dad worked—along with almost everyone else in our town. Dad didn't like the idea of me being with Mary, nor did her father. I'm sure they thought I was trying to marry above my station. Some may have believed I was trying to use Mary to advance my social status, but none of that was true. We just loved each other.

Back then, education was not as important to future employment as it is today, so the school let me work instead of going to class. During my senior year of high school, I was working at a neighbor's farm during the day. After baling hay and performing other chores under the hot son, I worked the third shift in the cold, dark mines. I aimed to save money for Mary and me to get married. It was a lot of work, but we were happy, and our dreams of living on our own, not dependent on either set of parents, thrilled both of us.

Mary's father was a powerful guy. When the local store was broken into, I was immediately accused. There was no evidence against me because I didn't commit the crime. I'm not even sure the store was robbed. Eventually the charges were dropped, but her father's plan had worked. Mary and my dad saw me as a crook. Dad beat the hell out of me while repeatedly yelling, "No Frizzel is a thief." Convinced that I was a criminal, Mary was whisked off to college, and I never heard from her again. That was the end of Red Frizzel, the man who believed hard work paid off. I was now Red Frizzel, the man who lived for himself. Sure, I still had a tender spot for kittens, children, and folks who proved to me that they had integrity, but the rest of them were fair game—to be used by me before they could ambush me.

Being a heartbroken kid, I reasoned that if I was going to be treated like a thief, I might as well benefit from it and act like one. I broke into the store (the only one in town). The finger was pointed at me again, but this time I pled guilty in front of God, the judge, and my family because it was true. The Korean War was in full force at the time, so the judge gave me a choice. I could continue my third-shift coal mining job for no pay—as a resident of the West Virginia State Penitentiary—or I could enlist in the United States Army. Since the Army put me in a shooting war that led to me being a POW, I was incarcerated after all. It was just the beginning of a long list of betrayals in my life. I had always prided myself on my honesty, and still do, but in this one area, I decided to allow myself an exception. I never pled guilty again.

After the Army, I kicked around the big city of Chicago, Illinois. In the early '60s it occurred to me that between By-God West Virginia, Korea, and the Windy City, I was sick and tired of cold weather, so I moved to Florida. Sticking to my hometown's definition of who I was, I started robbing Piggly Wiggly grocery stores in Florida and Louisiana. It was good money, and it beat robbing banks. I knew there wasn't as much money in Piggly Wiggly grocery stores as there was in banks, but FBI agents and federal prisons awaited those who were caught up in bank heists. Also, FBI agents were more aggressive in their searches for bank robbers, whereas the local law was easier to outfox.

Eventually, I got busted in Florida and was sentenced to life in the Florida State Prison. With good behavior, I could be out in twenty years. Talk about an education, I got one! The main thing I learned was that Florida prisons can break just about anyone. The guards were brutal, sick psychopaths and got paid to practice their antisocial behaviors. They would beat prisoners, set prisoners against each other, use rape as a form of punishment, and employ prisoners to perform violence against other prisoners. The entire system was intent on demonstrating power and control. Despite the word "corrections" in the name of most prisons, they had nothing to do with rehabilitation.

As I saw it, there were two ways to survive a Florida prison: 1) be mean and tough enough to be of value to the guards, or 2) become the minion of a religious organization. My friend, Jack Murphy, picked option 2. I picked option 1, but I never got anywhere near as sadistic as the guards. Florida guards seemed to have no sense of right versus wrong. They would beat mentally damaged prisoners and put them in cells with **booty bandits** who were much larger and stronger. Rape was a constant threat to young prisoners and the mentally ill. Eventually, it seemed that the only way to beat the Florida prison system was to escape, so eventually I did.

About the time I had been inside for eighteen years, politicians started talking about making life sentences longer and making these new laws retroactive. Such an act was unconstitutional, but I had seen enough to know politicians didn't mind violating prisoners' civil rights if it got them more votes. Since I had worked my way into a trustee job, I was allowed a job outside the prison walls. Without endangering anyone's life but my own, I walked away one day and hightailed it to Alabama.

Being on the escape guaranteed that the only way I could make a living was through criminal behaviors. While at a Tennessee hotel, I robbed and accidently killed a man. I say "accidently" because I never meant for the man to die. It was my intention to hit him hard enough to make him pass out so I could get away, but he was not able to handle the blow. I was caught and found guilty of robbery and murder in Tennessee. Since I had two more years to serve in Florida (they didn't extend my sentence after all), I was extradited to Butler Prison in Florida.

There was a well-established rumor that the Florida State Prison property held the many unmarked graves of prisoners who had been caught trying to escape or doing something else to seriously embarrass a warden or guard. Knowing I was an escapee, the guards at Butler saw me as a person who had embarrassed them. They couldn't kill me because Tennessee was expecting me back, but they beat me pretty bad and threw me in the **hole** for several weeks.

After my Florida sentence was finished, I was transferred back to Tennessee (at the expense of tax payers). While I was there, the Bill Glass prison ministry show came to the facility. This is a huge business aimed at converting prisoners to Christianity. It's kind of like the circus coming to town. For two or three days, the yard was filled with entertainment and a collection of motorcycles and sports cars for the prisoners to drool over. For the "benefit" of the prisoners who resisted coming out to see their much-coveted vehicles, born-again Christians roamed throughout the units inviting guys who were minding their own business in their cells to "accept Jesus as their personal Lord and Savior." I was sure surprised to see Jack Murphy, my old friend at the Florida State Prison, walking around in street clothes. Jack tried to get me to see the Jesus deal, but that was never my thing.

Time went by and I came up for parole. My best friend in the Tennessee prison system is an old, hard-ass convict named Andy who is sort of like Jack. Andy found a spiritual connection and turned himself into a nice guy. I never could figure out their angles. Anyway, Andy's fiancée (now wife) spoke up for me at my parole hearing. I had told Linda I wouldn't do any more robbing, she believed me, and I was released. The fact that I was in my late sixties and had potential for creating a great deal of medical expenses for Tennessee probably had a lot more to do with the granting of my parole than Linda's support, but I'm still grateful for Linda's courage and kindness.

Now I have not changed my mind about society, but I have kept my word to Linda. On many occasions I've told Andy, "I love Linda. She is the nicest lady I have ever met, and if I were thirty years younger, I would fight you for her." Andy knows that's my way of saying "thank you." although I do wish I were thirty years younger.

When I first got out, I stayed with Linda until I got back on my feet. Some years later, Andy got out too. After I got old and sick, Andy and Linda made a place for me in their home. I'm seventy-eight years old now and near the end of my road. Andy has asked me if I have any regrets. I guess there are two, and they are related. First of all, I regret not being able to forgive the guards in Florida and Tennessee who were cruel to me and others. Don't get me wrong, there were a few guards who treated prisoners like humans. I'm even friends with a couple of them to this day, but they're in the minority. I can't forgive those guys because that would mean forgetting their inhumanity. In my book, anyone who says they forgive but don't forget is lying!

My second regret is never having the ability to let the world know how hypocritical America's "correctional" and "justice" systems really are. They dish out the harshest and unkindest treatment to our most vulnerable people: the old, veterans who could never get over the horrors of war, people of minority races, and the poor—all the while claiming to be Christians. As I understand it, Jesus taught love and forgiveness. I lay here about dead, but I can only see that religion is a load of BS. Religious folks lie every time they support the death penalty, convict innocent people, or dole out harsh treatment toward suspects and prisoners. Maybe if everyone knew the truth, things could get better.

Commentary on Red's Story

Red died in 2007 after leaving us with his story. In honor of his request, his ashes have been scattered over what he always called "By-God West Virginia" so that he could fly over the mountains to find his final resting place. Red harbored a lot of bitterness. He could not reconcile the way "bad guys" were treated with such cold-heartedness by the "good guys."

Red believed the worst thing one human could do to another was lock them up for decades next to the death house, then after many years, say, "Okay, today is the day you die." Red mentioned to Andy (co-author) that during the war, North Korean soldiers would put POWs in front of firing squads and fire blanks at them. He said the effect could drive a man insane. As gruesome as the North Koreans were, Red saw the actions of the Florida guards as worse. To Red it was a cut-and-dry case of the angels becoming devils while continuing to proclaim righteousness.

Things have not improved much in Florida prisons over the last thirty to forty years. On October 3, 2014, an article in the *Miami Herald* con-firmed Red's reports that the Florida Department of Corrections (FLDC) is a cesspool of violence and corruption facilitated by prison staff. George Mallinckrodt worked as a psychotherapist at the Dade Correctional Institute from 2008 to 2011. He filed many complaints of staff abuse with the FLDC. After reporting that correctional officers taunted, starved, and beat mentally ill prisoners for sport, Mr. Mallinckrodt was told by guards that he would not be protected from violent inmates. Just one instance of the abuse Mr. Mallinckrodt reported is the case of prisoner Joseph Swilling, who, during one anger-management session, showed Mr. Mallinckrodt the scars he had received from a brutal beating by guards. They had handcuffed Mr. Swilling in a hallway that was not monitored by cameras and repeatedly kicked and beat him. Mr. Mallinckrodt's com-plaints were ignored, and he was eventually fired, allegedly for taking long lunches and breaks.[213]

On July 7, 2014, the *Miami Herald* ran another article about four FLDC investigators filing a federal whistleblowers lawsuit. John Ulm, Doug Glisson, David Clark, and Aubrey P. Land's complaint alleges that "state prisoners were beaten and tortured, that guards smuggled in drugs and other contraband in exchange for money and sexual favors, and that guards used gang enforcers to control the prison population." These four men claimed those actions were either "tacitly approved or covered up."[214]

One of their major allegations centered on a twenty-seven-year-old inmate who was gassed to death by guards in 2010 for requesting medical assistance with his blood disorder over a four-day period. This incident occurred at the Franklin Correctional Institution in Florida,[215] expanding Red's claim of severe treatment throughout the FLDC and, we believe, demonstrating that severe forms of felonism are practiced at FLDC facilities as part of its culture.

In response to articles written in 2014 by the *Miami Herald* and other media, the secretary of the FLDC recently fired thirty-two COs. Twenty-three of those officers were fired for their participation in exces-sive force on a criminal level, which led to the death of two inmates in two separate facilities. No mention was made of charging any of these officers with murder, but the *Miami Herald* article quoted union officials as saying these officers were complying with orders from their superi-ors.[216] Secretary Crew (the man in charge of the Florida Department of

Corrections at the time) had made no statements regarding the termination of these employees, one of whom was Inspector General Jeffery
Beasley, who told Florida Department of Law Enforcement investigators
to stop asking him about the death of inmate Randall Jordan-Aparo, or
he would have their "asses." Unfortunately we are unable to obtain the
FLDC's investigation results on the death of Mr. Jordan-Aparo because
the list of forty-six inmates who died of non-natural causes does not
include his name.[217]

Even more disconcerting is the 2012 death of Mr. Darren Rainey,
which is on the list but has not yet been classified as homicide even
though evidence of a cover-up by the warden and two COs was publicly presented in July of 2014. The medical examiner has even ruled Mr.
Rainey's death as homicide. The fact that Mr. Rainey's skin separated
from his body when COs removed his corpse from a scalding two-hour
shower (in which he was locked inside as punishment for defecating on
himself) is evidence enough for most people that someone should be held
accountable, yet no one has been charged.

This system is too reminiscent of the antebellum South when slaves
were murdered at the will of their masters because our nation had been
lulled into virtual blindness regarding the atrocities of slavery by those
who profited from its practices. Back then, many citizens were outraged,
but law-enforcement agencies were not willing or able to prosecute the
inhumane treatment of Black men and women. For example, in 1811
Lilburne and Isham Lewis, nephews of President Thomas Jefferson, never
faced trial for viciously murdering a seventeen-year-old slave named
George.[218] Frederick Douglass mentioned the murder of three slaves in
which the perpetrators were never prosecuted,[219] and we are sure there
were hundreds more. It was not until the printing of *Uncle Tom's Cabin*,
depicting the heart-wrenching effects of slavery's cruelty upon individuals, that our nation began to come to its senses.[220] Today it appears prison
staff, and society as a whole, have blindly relegated people with felony
convictions to the status of property as well. As we have mentioned, the
Thirteenth Amendment, the very Amendment that made slavery unconstitutional in America, still allows prisoners to be enslaved[221] and generations of severe abuse and murder to be ignored.

Whether you believe the purpose of prison is to punish or rehabilitate,
felonism cannot be excused, even in a prison setting. People convicted

of felony offenses are sent to prison *as* their punishment. If you believe convicted individuals are sent to prison so that they may be punished (e.g., poorly fed, subjected to slave labor, raped, physical and mental abuse, etc.), please consider the consequences that come about when others witness that violence. In a study (funded by the U.S. Department of Justice) by Benjamin Steiner, PhD, and Benjamin Meade, PhD, "indirect exposure to violence contributed to higher incidence rates of misconduct for inmates."[222] This must be a causative factor in higher recidivism rates as well as in the endangerment of prison staff.

There is a great deal of evidence that prison staff members, especially COs, are also negatively impacted by the violence they witness *and* impose. In 2013 the Desert Waters Correctional Outreach, a nonprofit organization devoted to the wellbeing of prison staff, found that the longer a person was employed as a staff member, the greater psychological and physical distress they displayed.[223] On March 24, 2007, the *Denver Post* ran a story entitled, "Prison Horrors Haunt Guards' Private Lives." "You treat other people like you treat convicts."—this quote, which appears beneath the title, was made by a CO who suffered long-term effects after being savagely attacked by prisoners. During his interview with Bruce Finley, the ex-CO stated that since the occurrence, he only wants to be around his wife and child, but they do not want to be around him because he is miserable all the time.[224]

This CO's revelation that he started treating everyone he encountered outside of prison the same way he treated prisoners is revealing. It confirms a thought process that says it is okay to treat prisoners in a demeaning manner that is not appropriate for non-prisoners. That is felonism in its simplest form. The article explained that some prisoners throw human waste at the COs. Disgusting as such an act is, would it not be wiser to engage in some sort of treatment addressing the prisoner's motivation rather than increasing their anger with more violence and isolation? Could we not just recognize that while their behavior is disgusting, they are reactions to the conditions in their environment? It is parallel to Southern slave masters criminalizing slaves for stealing food when starving or criticizing them for running away when threatened with lashes or death. Why would we expect people placed in powerless and barbarous conditions to do anything other than rebel with any weapon within their reach?

Prisoners who have been placed in solitary confinement report to us instances where they invented outrageous behaviors as a strategy to deal with human deprivation. They felt that some human contact, even a beating, was better than isolation. Human beings are social by design. We need to connect with other people.

This fact was first confirmed by studies conducted in an orphanage by psychoanalyst Rene Spitz in the 1940s and 1950s. Dr. Spitz demonstrated that babies receiving nourishment, hygienic needs, and shelter, but no other physical contact from their caregivers, were severely handicapped for the rest of their lives. In fact, 37 percent of the children Dr. Spitz studied actually died after two years of the deprived conditions, and those who lived were severely mentally disabled.[225]

More recently, Dr. Stuart Grassian, a board-certified psychiatrist, interviewed hundreds of men in solitary confinement and found that a third of them were either psychotic or suicidal. He concluded that solitary confinement induces a "specific psychiatric syndrome, characterized by hallucinations; panic attacks; overt paranoia; diminished impulse control; hypersensitivity to external stimuli; and difficulties with thinking, concentration and memory."[226] Even though it is obvious that denying physical and social connection is severely detrimental to human beings, felonism allows prison administrators to justify this cruel treatment (which violates the Eighth Amendment's prohibition of cruel and unusual punishment[227]) and isolate over 80,000 prisoners for twenty-three hours per day on a daily basis.[228] There appears to be no consideration given to the long-term effects imposed on prisoners, the community to which prisoners are later released, or the prison staff administering and witnessing solitary confinement.

In his Denver Post article, Mr. Finley reported the words of another ex-CO, Gary Kapolites, who says, initially, he was proud of "cuffing inmates, inserting tubes up the noses of those on hunger strike, or enforcing rules when inmates refused to cooperate." Later in the interview he describes being the first man in an extractions team toward the end of his ten-year career at a supermax facility (the harshest of all institutions, where all prisoners experience long-term solitary confinement with minimal human contact).[229] As Mr. Kapolites ran up against the inmate with all his force, the prisoner collapsed like a "marshmallow." Even as his peers praised him for his valiant efforts in overpowering a defenseless man, all he felt was hollow. Mr. Kapolites says the job had become shallow, and after a while he felt as if he was experiencing sensory deprivation. In Kapolites' final assessment of his previous job he says, "[COs] are doing time too . . . A lot of them are not able to detach . . . Alcohol problems. Domestic violence. They have a propensity. The very things they are supposed to be against, they end up doing."[230]

Mr. Kapolites' statement is reminiscent of Frederick Douglass's argument that slavery is degrading to the master as well as the slave.[231] Human beings are not born to be hateful and violent. (If you disagree, we challenge you to identify even one infant who is treated with love that displays a penchant for violence.) Therefore, administering such hostile acts toward wounded people is not going to teach them better behavior. That's like trying to improve the palate of a person who doesn't like vegetables by continually pouring green, carcinogenic dyes into everyone's water supply. Instead of teaching that person to enjoy broccoli, it just makes everyone sick. Not only are prison staff members being polluted, but the emotional mud they consume at work infects relationships with their spouses, children, and friends. The Florida COs described in Red's story and the Colorado COs mentioned above are not unique; they are the norm.[232]

Lest readers believe these instances are isolated to a couple of states, we invite you to consider abuses that received international condemnation. From 2003 to 2006, fourteen Americans received disciplinary actions for abusing prisoners in Abu Ghraib, Iraq. Official reports are classified, and it is unclear exactly who ordered the abuse of prisoners, but the abuses were similar to those alleged by Red and other contributors to this book who have lived inside American prisons (sexual abuse, humiliation, and physical abuse).[233]

According to CBS News, the highest ranking official participating in these demeaning acts was Staff Sergeant Ivan Frederick. Before being deployed to Iraq, he was a prison guard in Dillwyn, Virginia.[234] Charles Garner Jr., said to be the ringleader of the abusers, was a civilian CO in Pennsylvania.[235] Could it be that the other soldiers involved in the Abu Ghraib abuses looked to these two men as experts on appropriate and normal incarceration techniques?

Americans and the world were outraged and humiliated when the Abu Ghraib abuses were exposed, so why do we turn a blind eye to these abuses the vast majority of the time when they occur in our own country?

Chapter 12

Renegade's Story: Illegal Friendships

Twenty years from now you will be more disappointed by the things you didn't do than by the ones you did do.

—Mark Twain

As a prison employee, I have always done my damnedest to remember that prisoners are people—real human beings. Between listening to the bravado of co-workers who believe in their hearts that prisoners are just a tad more valuable than cockroaches, and reading details about atrocities committed by some prisoners, their value can be difficult to see. Nevertheless, I sincerely believe all people are valuable and deserve to be treated with dignity and respect. That statement, and other things I will say in this chapter, will be distasteful to readers who believe prejudice against people with felony convictions and their loved ones is appropriate. In fact, felonists reading this chapter could cause the termination of my employment and the loss of my pension, so I am withholding and/or changing the names of places and people to protect my identity. You may judge me as a coward, but I see myself as acting with wisdom, removing ammunition from the hands of those who see themselves as my enemy.

To tell the full story, I have to back up and explain a little about my life before working for the DOC (Department of Corrections). I made my way into this world as the sixth child of two hardworking parents.

Dad was a logger, and Mom was a homemaker. It was back in the days when pretty much all wives were homemakers, even if they didn't have children. My oldest sibling was twelve when I was born and fifteen when Dad was hurt in a terrible accident. Thankfully, Dad is still alive today, but he has been in a wheelchair for over fifty years.

With Dad's income pretty much gone, Mom started working at any job she could find. Mostly she cleaned houses and church buildings, and the whole family helped. I remember Dad picking cotton from his wheelchair right along with the rest of us, but we still qualified for commodities. That was food (usually cheese and butter) distributed by the government to assist poor families and maintain price supports for farmers. We were somewhat ashamed to get government handouts, but I thought they tasted good.

By the time I was fourteen, I realized that to get clothing and other things I needed I had to work and purchase them myself. Mom just couldn't afford things like shoes and jackets. Lucky for me, we lived in a part of the country that usually stayed above twenty degrees in the winter. Doing odd jobs like mowing grass and delivering papers was part of my daily routine the entire time I was a teen. That didn't change when I went to college.

Dad must have told me 10,000 times that education was the only way to have a chance at life. I agree with him now, but I really questioned his logic for a while. I wasn't a great student in high school, but due to a series of fortunate events, a caring high school teacher, and a few supportive church members, I was able to enroll in a two-year college right out of high school and then a four-year college. Even with the Pell Grant, I had to work while in school. During my senior year, I held three part-time jobs, but I finally graduated with a BA in sociology/psychology.

After graduating, I took a job at a mall bookstore. I made $2.35 an hour. That was about the time a very popular book, *The Joy of Sex*, was released. I thought it was strange that the book was so popular because the community had a church on just about every block. Most people who bought the book also purchased a Bible. I never did figure that one out, but it made for entertaining speculations.

About the same time, two things happened that changed the course of my life. First of all, my boss cut my hours in half, and second, a prison that I had never heard of had a huge riot that burned down a section of the

facility and caused an exodus of prison guards. Practically starving from
my low wages, I went to the employment office downtown searching for
a job that would allow me to apply my degree and lift me out of poverty. I
saw a massive amount of jobs for "correctional officers" that didn't require
experience and paid more than double my current salary. Since I had no
money for rent, I moved in with my brother, who lived closer to my new
position. The drive to his house would normally take about two hours,
but my car had some sort of electrical problem that I couldn't afford to
fix. I could only drive for fifteen minutes before she shut down. After I
let her cool off for fifteen minutes, she was willing to limp back out on
the highway for another quarter of an hour.

In December of 1975, I learned the definition of "correctional officer";
it meant prison guard. Having never been inside a prison or even known
someone who had, I was pretty green. Lucky for me, I was put on the
third shift working on the prison ward of the state hospital, but I did
have a shift or two at the main prison. It was terrible. Overcrowding
was so bad that huge rooms were filled with bunk beds placed so close
to each other there was barely room to walk. It almost reminded me of
diagrams of slave ships in the 1700s. Even those accommodations were
not sufficient, so men were given blankets and told to find themselves a
spot on the gymnasium floor. It was no wonder they had tried to burn
the place down earlier that year.

Coupled with egregious overcrowding was the lack of staff. The DOC
was actually hiring hitchhikers passing through town and putting them
on the payroll with almost no training prior to being assigned to a post.
There were so few COs that prisoners were locked into dorm rooms at
6:00 PM and not let out until 6:00 AM. Accountability for the horrors
that occurred each night was non-existent.

Back then pretty much everybody smoked. Aside from making sure
no one escaped, my job as a CO at the hospital was to sit and smoke
with men who were dying or had been raped to the point of needing
emergency medical care. It was a small gesture of goodwill, but it was
about all I could do while staying compliant to policy. Sharing cigarettes
seemed to comfort some of the guys. I may have shortened my life by a
few years, but I will never regret dispersing this small token of support.

One guy, Jim, had been arrested with a friend for sleeping in a barn.
The prosecutor said they were attempting to steal, but the men were

asleep on a cold winter night when their presence was discovered. Jim and a friend of his had left New Hampshire a few months earlier. They were just young kids trying to see the country, but Jim had twice been convicted on some minor robbery charges before he left home at the age of eighteen. Because this was Jim's third conviction, he was given a life sentence as a habitual criminal and thrown into the dorm. Jim was raped so many times the first week that he landed in the hospital. All I could do was smoke cigarettes and sit with him as he suffered physically and emotionally.

I followed Jim's progress through the years and watched helplessly as he put himself into the service of a well-established prisoner who offered Jim protection in exchange for regular sex. In prison vernacular, he became a "**punk**." Jim also began working out in the gym. To ward off future rapes, or to express his anger for the past ones, Jim built a reputation as a notorious fighter. I think he developed some mental issues after spending a great deal of time in solitary confinement (as a result of his fights), but I know he became addicted to drugs while inside prison. Years later, Jim qualified for parole on two different occasions, but he had been so wounded by then that he couldn't function outside of prison.

There were bright moments when I witnessed prisoners protecting each other from predators and a few COs sticking their necks into dangerous situations. It was during these times that I realized many people gave up their lives in order to help others. It was also then that I realized this job was my calling. I didn't need to go to a foreign country to be a missionary. I could be a missionary right where I was and make a whopping $523 per month while serving. I was finally on easy street (in my mind), and able to perform a meaningful task.

My first month as a CO was pretty rough because I didn't get paid for four weeks. I had to learn how to use a gun, and I witnessed terrible cruelty. Although I met and worked with some great guys (there weren't many female employees back then), it didn't take long to understand that the only concern of some prison officials was the institution and their positions within it. Witnessing and imposing inhumane acts and conditions on prisoners was not a blip on their radars, and those are the people who rose to power. I decided early on to be as much of a renegade as I could without getting myself fired.

When I was hired, they said my degree qualified me to become a prison counselor as soon as a position became available. After my first year as a CO, a program opened designed for new felons between the ages of eighteen and twenty-five who were serving shorter sentences. The purpose of the program was to keep these young fellows away from the hardcore prisoners, give them the education they needed, and help them establish themselves as contributing members of society when they were released. It was hoped that keeping these young guys separated from men with long sentences would leave them ignorant about the finer arts of being a criminal. Federal money provided for this project. It came under the Title I Act and was used to hire teachers and counselors.

This program was educational for me too. I had never known—it'd never even occurred to me—that children were being used as punching bags, ash trays, and sex toys by their parents/family members. Some might say we were being fooled by these boys' whiny stories of victimhood, but the scars on their arms and legs where many cigarettes had been extinguished, or disfigurements where they had intentionally been pushed into hot stoves, were plain to see. A more complete story was illustrated by the broken bones and torn skin in private places described in their medical files. Over the last forty years, I have heard many people respond to my concerns about prisoners being raped or large numbers dying from AIDS with the statement, "They deserve what they got. It's their own fault they're here." I couldn't agree with that, but saying so would have endangered my position and blocked what little assistance I could sneak in from time to time.

I nicknamed the director of this new program "Trip City" because he was something else. After retiring from the military, Trip City embarked on a new career as a minister about the same time he was hired by the DOC. He seemed to have some real personality conflicts regarding both of these positions. I believe he invited every female teacher and office worker to have sex with him, which is probably why he was fired from his ministry position. In spite of Trip City's unprofessional behavior, we were able to help the majority of our charges escape rape, earn GEDs, and learn to make a living for themselves. I wish Jim (and many others) had been offered this program when he first entered prison. It would have made all the difference.

Life was really good for me during those initial years. My social life was expanding, I was making good money (or it felt that way compared to my past), and I knew I was making a positive difference in the lives of many people. One day my dad called and asked me to come home. A Rural Development Program was about to start in my hometown, and he was sure I could get employment. Most of my siblings still lived close to him and Mom, but I think he wanted to have all of us around. How could I say no?

Even though I wasn't working with incarcerated men in this new position, my education about the darker side of our society continued. Back then the police in rural areas considered things that happened within a family to be outside their jurisdiction. In my new position, I saw firsthand the hell the prisoners I'd met at the DOC had endured.

One of my jobs at the Urban Development Program involved a four-teen-year-old pregnant girl who desperately wanted an abortion. Her father demanded that she complete the pregnancy since it was his child in her womb. My job was to drive her the forty miles or so to receive prenatal care. Her home life was abominable, but I couldn't usurp the authority of the local police, who knew about her situation. Witnessing darkness parallel to what I had seen at the prison in my hometown was an eye-opener. "You really can't go home again" is the lesson I quickly learned after returning to my old community. Everyone had changed, including me. After seven months, a staff member at the DOC called saying he needed my help, and I was very happy to oblige.

It was good to return to my old life, but the program I had been so proud of, as well as the entire DOC, seemed to have disintegrated. The previous governor of my newly adopted state had been caught with his hand in the cookie jar. The work-release program at the time seemed to have no supervision. I think politicians and/or the prison staff were being paid to grant favors to prisoners or to look the other way as gross negli-gence, and criminal activity accelerated in the DOC. Whatever the cause, people with life sentences who were still practicing violent behaviors were allowed to work downtown, sometimes without any supervision. Lifelong rapists were roaming the streets when they were supposed to be in cells. Of course they resumed their favorite pastime, and instances of rape in that community increased.

The new governor was elected because he convinced voters he would protect them by being tough on crime, yet he immediately dismantled many of the positive programs in the DOC. The young men we had worked so hard to protect were moved to an adult prison. Along with sending these inexperienced fellows into a setting where they were preyed upon, that move exasperated the serious problem of overcrowding. Many of the "**freeworld**" teacher positions were eliminated and all the chaplain positions disappeared for a while. I was at an institution with 1,150 prisoners when all but three of the counselor positions had been eliminated. To compound the problem, the percentage of time prisoners were required to serve to complete their sentences was pretty much doubled. Men no longer received reductions in their sentences for good behavior, so violence soared. I remember one eleven-day period when three prisoners were killed.

Not only was violence between prisoners accelerated, but it seemed that COs stepped up their activities in the bullying department. They would learn the main triggers for the prisoners in their area and purposely push their buttons. Then the officers would have an excuse to put them in solitary confinement for days, weeks, and even months. No system of review existed to determine when people would be released from solitary, and there was really no system of checks and balances—no recourse for the many times when COs violated the law. We had a warden who used prison money to purchase a boat for himself while demanding food expenses for prisoners remain at 63¢ per day per prisoner. They ate a lot of corn soup, beans, and wheat porridge in those days, but it's not much better today.

Even now, I shudder when thinking about one particularly sadistic CO because of the way he treated Kent. A country boy from a small community, Kent had been convicted of killing a man by pushing him out of the boat they were using in the middle of a lake. There were no witnesses, and Kent always held to his innocence. I suspect putting Kent in prison was how the people of his hometown dealt with the fact that he was gay. It was the mid-1980s and misinformation about AIDS was everywhere. When the prison learned that Kent had AIDS, he was locked into a single-man cell on the mental health ward.

As a coping device, Kent captured a mouse in his cell and turned the creature into his pet. He found pleasure in caring for and training his mouse. It was a good way for Kent to pass his lonely days and keep his sanity. Then the sadistic CO I mentioned decided Kent didn't deserve to have this little shred of happiness. Right in front of Kent, the SOB CO stepped on the mouse until it died while howling with laughter at the obvious emotional harm he was causing Kent. This was one of the many times I mourned my lack of power and felt real pain for all these men with shattered lives.

Remembering the horrendous death Kent later experienced from AIDS, with little medical assistance or emotional support, has caused me to recall a group of selfish, hard-hearted nurses. In the early 1990s a new prison was opened for people with medical needs. Part of the design included dayrooms where prisoners could meet (if they were well enough to leave their beds). Seeking some distraction from their pain, prisoners would watch television, play cards, or just socialize.

Each dayroom was equipped with a television set, but the nurses kept taking the TVs back to their stations so they wouldn't miss their favorite shows. For a while the associate warden in charge of treatment would require the nurses to return the televisions to the dayrooms. Explaining that the sets had been purchased for the prisoners, and that the nurses had duties to perform which should consume their time did not put a dent in these nurses' belief that they were entitled to watch television while (or instead of) working. As soon as the associate warden left the unit, the televisions would "walk" back to the nurses' stations. Determined to solve the problem, the associate warden had all the televisions anchored to tables in the dayrooms. Not to be outdone, the nurses decided that having prisoners leaving their cells during the day posed a security risk. The nurses decreed that these dying men be locked in their cells for all but one hour of each day. Even though the motivation for that rule was totally selfish and insubordinate, it has endured for over twenty years.

Let's get back to the early 1980s. With conditions as overcrowded and neglected as they were, it didn't take long before a group of prisoners filed a class action lawsuit in federal court on the premise that they were being subjected to cruel and unusual punishment. The court rightly decided that the DOC was guilty and ordered a great deal of changes. Several prisons were closed and prisoners were moved into already overcrowded institutions while repairs were made in the worst facilities. Tensions grew even higher until, one day, prisoners held a sit-in. They refused to leave the facility to work in the fields that surrounded the prison.

Concerned about his reputation, Warden P did everything he could think of to intimidate the prisoners, but prisoner solidarity was the name of the game that day. Prisoners were demanding immediate improvements that had been court-ordered a year earlier. Agreeing to their conditions would be political suicide for the warden considering the mood of the government and most citizens. Warden P suggested a compromise: if ten men went to work their shift in the fields, he would authorize showers for everyone (not a daily event back then) and a return to cells. Twenty prisoners appeared to break ranks and agreed to go out into the fields, but instead of working, they set the fields, barns, and two or three of the new tractors ablaze. The protesters stayed right where they were for several days. Finally, the media broadcasted the situation. Prisoners who had been selected to speak for their peers were given airtime to describe the terrible conditions they were experiencing despite the federal order for improvement. Everyone went back to their cells and hoped for the best, but the status quo never really changed.

Two years later, while on my day off, I was called to come into work. For the last few days, prisoners had been telling me something big was about to happen in response to the state legislature's demand that prisoners start wearing heavy, striped jumpsuits made of a thick canvas type material—in the summer. The warden had chosen that day to say prisoners would not be served food unless they were wearing the new uniforms in the chow hall. When I arrived at the prison, all I could do was watch from afar as prisoners burned their new uniforms and spread fires to every combustible part of the compound.

The uniform change had been made in response to several escapes. The legislature passed a new law removing "**freeworld**" clothes from prisons and requiring uniforms. It was reasoned that society would be safer if prisoners escaped wearing recognizable uniforms because they could be identified more quickly. Legislators failed to recognize that escaped prisoners would kidnap or kill people for their clothes as their first order of business when absconding in the future, thus making the general public less safe. True to form, the prison administrators who approved the new uniforms did their best to use the issue as another way to humiliate prisoners and make their lives a little more uncomfortable.

It had long been a tactic of prison administration to blame men in **administrative segregation** (also known as protective custody—"PC" or "the hole") when the administration removed privileges for the entire institution or implemented harsher rules. The purpose of this tactic was to create division within the prison population. It's easier to control people who are fighting among themselves than people who are fighting the authorities. Since most prisoners were not aware of this strategy, they were always angry at this segregated group who seemed to be causing them so many problems.

Once in control of the facility, the more ruthless prisoners took men out of these segregated cells and savagely raped them. Although homosexuality does exist in prison, rape is often used as a tool of revenge, humiliation, and dominance more than a form of sexual satisfaction. When the riot was finally over (thanks in part to a few wise prisoners who prevented the murder of captured COs), I shared many a cigarette that week in my meek effort to provide comfort to those men who had been in PC.

I remember one kid in particular. While attending a nearby university, Ted was pressured into selling a few pills to an undercover policeman. He hadn't been much of a drug user himself, but Ted figured this was a way to connect with the "cool" group on campus. After the riots, we smoked quite a few cigarettes, but it didn't help him. Within days of his release from prison, Ted committed suicide. Such a bright, young kid, with so much potential, had been totally destroyed by that riot. If you ask me, the DOC and the state's political system, which allowed decades of abuse and neglect to fester and explode, must take a large share of the blame for that situation. We can't push people to their breaking points without enduring our own negative consequences.

Shortly after the riots, I received a call from an administrator at the very first prison ever built in our state. Mr. B asked me to transfer to his facility and become the classifications coordinator (the person who is supposed to decide in which prison and/or in which bed to place new arrivals). Since being a counselor for such a large number of prisoners was frustrating, I gladly agreed. I had a lot to learn, but I enjoyed the position enough to stay in it the rest of my career.

One of the things I liked about classifications was seeing all the programs that were added as a result of the riots. I was especially glad to see a treatment program designed for people convicted of sex offenses. However, despite the fact that the program was created by people with more degrees than me, I was able to identify several problems. The main flaw of this program was its exclusion of prisoners whose reading and writing skills were below the ninth-grade level.

It took a while, but I researched the IQs of the men in our state with sex offenses and found that most of them were near or below seventy. Just as I had suspected, these men's reasoning skills were limited. After sharing this information with a few peers, we started an informal program for the men who didn't qualify for the official one. If this had come to the attention of the administration, we could have been identified as insubordinate, but that never happened.

Contrary to the philosophy of the official program, our main focus was to teach the men simple social values. Many of these prisoners had been molested as children and felt this was normal despite society's reactions. When our students learned that it was not right to follow boys, or girls, into bathrooms or say certain things to children about their genitalia, they complied. After training a few hundred men and tracking them for close to twenty years, I am proud to say that only one of our unofficial "students" was convicted for another sex offense after leaving prison.

With that said, this new treatment program for men with sex convictions was great. Initially, Step 1 was a two-year program that focused upon identifying the origins and triggers of their deviant behaviors. Later steps worked on improving prisoners' self-esteem, developing empathy for their victims, and creating a safety plan to prevent future offenses if relapse was imminent. Because many people convicted of sex offenses are not honest with themselves, much of the work is conducted in groups where men are expected to identify dishonesty in their peers and then see it in themselves. It would be great if this program was offered to all prisoners for all offenses, but the program has been whittled down so much over the last few years that now it barely exists. The current program is provided a few hours a week and only lasts three months while the old one maintained hours similar to that of a full-time job and took several years to complete.

Two desperately needed programs that have never been implemented are" family living" and "relationship development" programs. It is so obvious that 99 percent of our prisoners come from dysfunctional homes. Many of them have parents who were incarcerated when they were children, and most of today's prisoners have children themselves. It depresses me when I remember the *many* stories men have shared with me about the abuses they endured as children. One man told me about being repeatedly sold for sex by his parents starting when he was twelve years old. Since that man has no model about what a loving family looks like, it is reasonable to think that some education—as well as counseling—would be helpful.

If we really want to reduce crime and have a safer society, let's teach all prisoners steps they can take to develop healthy relationships. I believe that even people with limited intelligence have fewer problems with anger and addiction when they are part of an emotionally healthy family. Just like most of the good programs implemented at the DOC, a healthy-relationship program would probably be destroyed as soon as it started showing signs of success. That sounds cynical, I know, but it's pretty likely. You can ask any volunteer who has had the audacity to make suggestions on how the DOC could improve: They are immediately banned from returning to any prison, and they are usually not told the reason for their expulsion.

When a man who had held AA meetings at two different prisons every week for twenty years started making suggestions to administrators about how certain people should be treated and how programs could be improved, this volunteer suddenly became a "security risk." Like I said in the beginning, some staff members are only concerned with the promotion of the institution and themselves. They see "inmate friendly" volunteers and staff members as threats and eliminate such people as quickly as possible—even if they have to lie or frame a person to remove them.

Several prisoners come to mind when I think about the good that could have been done by a family living program. Seeing all the loss of so many men with great talent, potential, and dreams, I determined long ago to spend as much time as I could sharing their stories and implimenting plans that would help these men have better lives. I remember Al, who had been raised in the South by his mother while his father lived in the North. Both of Al's parents were addicted to drugs, so it was no surprise to me that Al was in prison for stealing property to support his habit. Before his incarceration, Al was raising his two children. Their mother did not want them. Just like Al's mom, she was a street walker and a drug user.

Shortly after getting out of prison, Al called me in despair. His mother had taken his son on a trip to the store, but they never made it:

Al's mom made a side trip to a public bathroom where she murdered Al's son before turning the gun on herself. Maybe if Al had received a little more education about signs of distress in the family, he could have prevented this tragedy. We will never know. This was one time when I was very glad I had violated prison policy and given my phone number to a guy just before he was released. There is no telling what Al could have done if he had not been able to talk with someone he trusted.

Another prisoner whose ignorance regarding relationships caused a great deal of pain was Robert. When Robert was a toddler, he and his sister were taken to New Mexico by their mother. Later they were forced to return to their father's trailer in Georgia. While Robert was still a kid, his step-mom taught him how to give her sexual pleasure and please himself with cocaine. Since Robert was pretty young when he got caught burglarizing to pay for his habit, he was given probation instead of prison.

Needing to leave the environment he was raised in, Robert moved to Alabama without permission from his probation officer. Unfortunately, Robert took part of his home life with him, his addiction. Rather than stealing, Robert sold his body for drugs. By chance, Robert developed a friendship with a Church of Christ minister and was adopted by the church where his friend preached. For the first time since being taken from his mother, life was good for Robert.

Knowing he could trust this new family, Robert told them he had skipped parole in Georgia. Trusting the advice of the church members, and their promise to help him when he got out, Robert turned himself in and was given a three-year prison sentence. That's where I came to meet him. Along with several other prisoners, he was willing to come to my office on a regular basis and listen to me encourage and advise him.

Robert followed my plan for the first few months he was out on parole. While he waited for his case to be transferred to Alabama, he worked at a greasy-spoon chain restaurant and saved every penny possible. He made friends with his boss to the point that she was doing his laundry each week. I think she had a bit of a crush on Robert even though she was at least thirty years his senior.

Once again, life was good for Robert, but one day a woman from the local domestic violence shelter began working at his greasy spoon. Robert was smitten by Gina. Soon they traded nights in their halfway houses for trysts at cheap motels. Within three weeks, the $1,900 Robert had saved to start a new life in Alabama had been reduced to $32. To make matters worse, Gina left Robert's bed and came to work on the arm of another man. I named him Bruno because to me the name depicts the hulk of the man he was. Suddenly, it was over. Gina was gone, and so was Robert's money. But wait. When pay day rolled around, Gina called Robert crying and begging for his forgiveness. Seeing the error of her ways, Gina flung herself back to Robert's arms—just long enough to pick up the $600 paycheck he had received.

That was the breaking point for Robert. Even after his boss moved him to a different store so he wouldn't see Gina, Robert turned to the only soul-salve he knew for pain this deep, cocaine. Robert's parole was revoked, and he completed his sentence in prison. It is my hope that the end of Robert's story is good. True to their word, the fine church folks in Alabama picked him up the day he left prison, and I have not heard from him since. I'm taking that as a good sign.

A few years ago when a new governor was elected, he brought in a new commissioner. The man talks a good game, but since his arrival, many programs have been eliminated, staff turn-over has skyrocketed, overcrowding has increased, and violence within the prison has reached an all-time high. Classification coordinators used to be able to divide members of rival gangs into separate institutions. We used to have a core group of seasoned COs who knew from experience that it was better to treat prisoners with the illusion of honey than outright disrespect. Since so many of the "good" COs have left, by force or choice, we now have a surplus of young, inexperienced COs who leave orientation and begin their first day on the job with a "how many heads can I bust today?" attitude. Officially, the DOC only hires people with college degrees, but in reality, they will accept anyone with a GED and a valid driver's license. I'm anticipating the day when we go back to hiring hitchhikers.

Just like in the old days, the results of assessments that identify prisoners' needs are regularly trumped by the availability of empty beds. Sometimes the only way I can keep a prisoner out of a dangerous cell assignment is to state that he is unable to safely climb stairs. Another problem created by the standards of this new commissioner is a change in qualifications for help with addiction issues. If I had my say, anyone with a history of cocaine or methamphetamine use would have access to a drug treatment program. Currently, they don't qualify unless they have several felony charges related to drug use. Even if a new prisoner begs for drug treatment, he can't get it if alcohol or drugs were not part of his arrest record. So now, a drug kingpin who did not use the product he sold is required to successfully attend drug treatment programs (betraying himself and lying to appear compliant) while people who really need it are denied.

Corruption and inhumanity are alive and well in this newly "transformed" DOC. Last winter an edict was issued from the central office that all winter hats worn by prisoners must be white or gray. This meant men who had purchased black hats from the prison "store" (even if they had just made the purchase the previous day) would have to destroy their hats or bear the expense of sending them home and then purchasing new ones. One particular prisoner had a gray hat, but the CO in his unit thought it was the wrong shade. Two days in a row the prisoner was ordered to give his hat to the CO, essentially allowing it to be stolen from him. When the prisoner flatly refused, a group of five COs dogpiled the "offending" prisoner and removed his hat in front of all the other prisoners. In the struggle, one of the older COs hurt his knee, so the prisoner was charged with assaulting an officer, adding time to his prison sentence. There is no way such a blatant act of felonism contributes to prison security or the safety of society.

Before I close, I want to share one positive idea about how to help society and prisoners who are leaving after years of incarceration. Many men (and women) are abandoned by their families when they are arrested. Because current DOC policy prohibits staff members from socializing with prisoners after their incarcerations, many prisoners feel abandoned a second time when they leave their "prison family." Prisoners and prison staff members don't have great relationships, but it's often the only relationship returning citizens know. For the last twenty to thirty years, the only positive relationships they have known were with DOC staff and/ or other prisoners, but conditions of parole and prison policy usually ban their association with either group. While there could be some potential risks, I believe staff members and ex-felons should be allowed to continue supporting each other. If these relationships were permitted, and even encouraged, recidivism would probably be much lower. For example, if Robert had been able to consult with me when Gina entered his life, I could have helped him see the danger zone he was entering instead of hearing about it after his parole was revoked.

Contrary to DOC rules, I did keep in contact with another man who called asking for advice. Sean's son had just come out of the closet and told Sean that, with all his heart, he wanted to be a woman. While Sean couldn't help but see his son's effeminate features, this news was a tremendous shock. Sean said it was very difficult, but he took my advice and loved his son, just the way she was. Now Sean has two daughters, and he loves both of them. If I had followed policy and not accepted Sean's call, I'm not sure how he would have handled his son's news. People do strange things when they have no one to turn to. That's why we need relationship development programs.

I hope that, after reading my story and getting a better sense of what it's really like inside a prison, those of you with harsh views toward felons have softened. If you still believe whatever happens to prisoners is their own fault, if you believe prisoners should be treated as harshly as possible so they will not want to return, think about this famous statement: "Let he who is without sin cast the first stone."

Commentary on Renegade's Story

First we want to acknowledge the great courage it took for Renegade to share his story. Many argue that prisoners who complain about harsh prison conditions are not accepting responsibility for the harm they have caused others. For some people in prison or jail, that certainly is true, but in our experience many people in prison are just as honest as Abe Lincoln. If you have held negative attitudes toward prisoners who tell it like it is, we hope you were able to accept Renegade's story, which testifies to the fact that prisoners often have legitimate grievances.

Managing incarcerated individuals is a challenge. Prior to incarceration, their lives were so out of control that many of them committed crimes, such as embezzlement, assault, rape, offenses against children, murder, and other acts that hurt individuals and society. Yet, even prisoners with violent offenses can be redeemed and transformed into contributing members of society. Andy (co-author) is living proof of this. Some prisoners may be unable to mentally or emotionally return to society, but even these prisoners deserve to be seen as worthwhile human beings rather than mindless, caged animals.

It is easy to believe that rules will maintain safety—inside and outside of prison. The typical scenario for creating rules goes something like this: A prisoner uses the blade from a disposable razor to attack a guard, so a rule is made that prisoners can't use disposable razors. Then a prisoner conceals contraband in his beard, maybe drugs smuggled in by a visitor (although most contraband is imported by staff), so now a rule is made that prisoners can't grow beards. Since no thought is given to the consequence of implementing both rules, the administrators look like fools to prisoners and their family members (who often pay the fees for their write-ups), and all prisoners are now in noncompliance with policy because they cannot follow both rules. As ridiculous as this sounds, it happens.

Writing rules to ensure security in a prison is difficult, especially if you view prison as a place to punish people. As we saw in Renegade's story, using rules as tools for reacting to perceived problematic behaviors can easily lead to power struggles that have destructive outcomes. The situation degrades into a human game of "Whac-A-Mole," and just about everyone gets hurt.

When writing prison policies, it is important to remember that few prisoners remain in prison their entire lives. Do we want them entering our communities as people who can only follow rules when swift, severe consequences are applied, or do we want returning citizens who know how to live happy lives and who don't feel the need to hurt others? For people focused on life-long revenge, that is a difficult decision, but we invite you to consider a twist on Frank Sinatra's saying, "The best revenge is massive success."[236]

If you're a prison guard and the prisoner you watch over becomes a contributing member of society, haven't you won? Haven't you honored the person they hurt and limited the probability that this person will hurt anyone else? We believe returning citizens who have learned from their mistakes are far safer to be around than the person who has never been caught, or who has been emotionally or physically abused for their mistakes and not given the chance to learn to be better.

Let's consider the consequences of prisons that write policies based on the belief that prisoners should be punished: The administrations' hearts may be in the right place if they think punishment will motivate returning citizens to live a good life out of fear of returning to prison, but what are the long-term consequences of this philosophy? Let's use prison rules regarding friendship as an example. Pretty much every prison in America has a policy that reads something like this:

Relationships between DOC staff and inmates are forbidden. This includes, but is not limited to social, emotional, economic, romantic and sexual relationships. It includes inmates who are currently in custody, on probation or parole, and those who have been in DOC custody within the last one to three years. Social media relationships are also banned as are relationships with any family member of any inmate. (*Based on policies from several states, especially Alabama*)[237]

Renegade's decision to privately educate men who were soon to be released was a violation. His willingness to check on people he had seen every week for ten or twenty years, people he knew needed help understanding the "**freeworld**," could have been used as grounds for dismissal and the termination of his pension. No doubt the intention of such laws is to maintain uniformity and fairness while placing prisoners in a social "time out," but treating everybody the same is hard enough when watching over people you consider to be friends or peers. It is even more difficult when housing nineteen-year-olds with drug convictions and forty-year-old serial killers in the same facility. Do we really want to treat them exactly the same?

Aside from the absurdity of trying to treat everyone equally, this rule offends prison staff in two ways. It sends an underlying message that staff members are too gullible to prevent themselves from being tricked by prisoners. It also puts staff members in a vulnerable place. The simplest of acts, such as letting a prisoner know they will have a visitor when count time is over, can be perceived as a violation of this rule. Talking to prisoners about social changes, or helping them understand some new piece of technology they viewed on television, can be seen as "inmate friendly" and impact their employment records. Acting on ideas that could reduce recidivism, but did not descend from top administrators/legislators, is dangerous behavior for prison staff such as Renegade. Basically, this rule socially handcuffs prison staff as much as prisoners. How can COs maintain their normal sense of human connection while being so limited in their interaction with prisoners?

It is easy to see why Renegade had to remind himself on a daily basis that the men he was supposed to be helping were human beings. How would you react if a person you saw at work every day, or even a stranger, was wearing a watch and refused to share the time of day with you? Wouldn't you take that as an insult, a message that you are not worthy of their response? Now imagine that happened to you all day long, every day, for years. Wouldn't it change the way you interacted with just about everyone you met once you were judged worthy of being told the time of day?

Again, let's look at it from the staff member's point of view. Imagine you were not allowed to demonstrate the least bit of kindness to a select group at work at a factory or some other job setting. You couldn't inquire about their health, stoop to pick up something one of them dropped, share a joke, or relay the message when one of their mothers called to say she would be taking him to lunch. Could you maintain a healthy attitude toward the people who were banned from your positive inter-action, or would you develop a prejudice against them—out of habit if not thoughtful consideration? Wouldn't that eventually change the way you interacted with your family and friends outside of work as well as eliminate a positive work environment?

Life as a prison staff member, or a prisoner, would be much easier if one could become a robot upon entering the prison and return to their human life when exiting. Such a possibility would relieve Renegade of the deep sorrow he feels on a daily basis for the prisoners (and some staff) he leaves behind at the end of each day. Morphing into unemotional robots at work would prevent felonistic COs from abusing prisoners, such as Jim and Kent, who entered prison as fairly innocent kids. Complying with the rule that prohibits any sort of relationship between staff members and prisoners would be so much easier if everyone behind the razor wire were automatons.

But here's the thing: no matter how much it's denied, prison staff *and* prisoners are human beings. Both have the need for love, the desire for touch, and the need for social and/or sexual contact. Every prison has hundreds of policies, and many of them have destructive consequences for prisoners and staff members. From this one policy banning relationships, we begin to understand why so many COs transmute into brutal people, both inside and outside of prison and why returning citizens experience culture shock when they are released.

To help capture the emotional damage created by prison policies and attitudes that say prisoners must be punished, we share the following poem. It was written by a man during his confinement:

The Caged

It comes as a straight line of subliminal signal.
These are the things and stuff everyone should have; why don't you
  have them?
You must be less
Less loved, less cared for, less.
Oh it's sexy; everyone is doing it.
Everyone has it, you're less.

Less is the cooking pot of desperation.
Desperate to fit in and have it, stuff—the cool stuff.
Yet no desperation is as hot and palpable as that of forced separation
Separated from the things, the stuff, the person that consumes your
  every waking and slumbered part.
Desperation is a cold lonely stone thrown into the fiery chaotic heat
  of action.
The desperate create more desperation; it's called down and into
  being.
Waxed of their own not wanting, making it a certainty
They strike out to consume
To be fruitful
To be material
You're less
And so are consumed.

by Molmoc

Here we see the full, malicious circle of emotional violence created when prisoners are treated like second- or third-class citizens. Those who see themselves as oppressed can fall into the trap of believing the only way to become equal is by casting their oppressors into the role of being less worthy. Essentially, they become the mirror image of their oppressor, practicing the same wrongs that they were trying to overcome. Is there any way out of that pattern other than obliterating the premise (felonism) upon which this oppression is founded?

A sad demonstration of this felonism's effects on COs recently made national news when three COs from Attica State Prison in Warsaw, New York, pled guilty to a misdemeanor charge of gang beating a prisoner. This beating was not unique, but the outcome was. It was the first time New York prison staff members had been given criminal charges (gang assault, conspiracy, and tampering with evidence) for the non-sexual beating of a prisoner.[238] The 2011 beating of Mr. George Williams was vicious, and the cover-up was atrocious. The reduction of these felonious acts to a misdemeanor level indicates something troubling about the culture of the prison and its surrounding population. Oppressive prison employees who commit crimes are seen as less responsible than the prisoners they guard. Fearing the consequences of losing a trial (because the jury pool would come from a town where most of its citizens either worked at Attica or had family or friends who did), Prosecuting Attorney Green reluctantly negotiated a plea deal.[239] The estranged wife of one officer who pled guilty did a great job of summarizing the effects of the prison environment on its staff. She said, "He was a very calm, laid back, easy going, and fun person to be around. There is right and wrong, and I think he forgot that."[240]

Overall, the outcome of this story is bittersweet. If the officers had been convicted, years of solitary confinement would have been their only hope for escaping acts of revenge from prisoners. Having personal experiences with years in solitary confinement, we see their escape from such hell as a blessing. The bad news is that these men were only banned from working in New York prisons. If they have not learned from this experience, it is possible these men will seek and receive employment as COs in different states and continue their violent behaviors under the protection of their uniforms. We hope they receive healing instead.

As we stated above, little thought is given to the long-term human consequences when policies are created for prisons and jails. Some consideration seems to be given to the few remaining Constitutional rights of prisoners, mostly the right to avoid cruel and unusual punishment, but as the anecdote above shows, in practice, even that right is denied on a daily basis. Thanks to the Supreme Court ruling on Sandin v. Conner (1995), prison administrators have carte blanche authority to obliterate just about every pretense of civil rights among prisoners. As long as administrators aim to punish, the desperation created by prison policies will continue to hurt people who are inside and outside the razor-wire walls.

Before men and women are able to leave prison in a better frame of mind than when they entered, not only will policies and rules have to change but also the attitudes of those who create and implement them. If we want the high rates of domestic violence, divorce, addiction, and suicide among COs and other prison employees to decrease,[241] we must make this transition. When we are sincere about our desire to significantly reduce the number of new victims at the hands of returning citizens, we will transform our rationale.

Renegade will be the first to tell you that kindness to some people has its risks. He has helped one or two prisoners who mistook his support for vulnerability and weakness. In these situations, Renegade had no recourse because asking for help would have exposed his "inmate friendly" behaviors. We are so proud of Renegade for maintaining a willingness to help others while accepting that there may be negative consequences. Even with his refusal to accept an attitude of felonism, Renegade knows he has been emotionally damaged by his job. We still see him as a bit of a hero.

Chapter 13

Rick's Story:
Deceived by a "Friend"

All the world is full of suffering. It is also full of overcoming.

—Helen Keller

Taking my buddy's offer to make a few extra bucks over thirty years ago turned out to be a *very expensive* decision that I'm still paying for today. It was the decisions and acts of my "friend," a certain prosecuting attorney, and a "legal" system dominated by felonism which really fucked me up. In 1985 my life seemed pretty good. Even though I was practically a kid, I had already experienced nearly every state of America as a cross-country truck driver. But Darrel Smith's life seemed even better than mine. When he asked me to help him with hauling a few stolen goods, I agreed. Although technology was not near as sophisticated back then as it is today, it was not long before the Feds came knocking on our door. Now, my mamma had raised me right (even if I'm not perfect), and I hold honesty in high regard, so when I was arrested, I admitted to my illegal activities and accepted my consequence without bitterness or anger. I had no one to blame but myself for receiving a six-year sentence in the federal pokey.

About three years into my sentence I was called to the visiting gallery one weekday. Concerned that there might be a family emergency, I was almost relieved to see two men in suits awaiting my arrival. They introduced themselves as FBI and began asking me about a fellow I had never heard of. They wanted me to testify against Darrel and say Darrel had killed this man (I'll call him Sam). Sam had been missing ever since Darrel and I had been arrested. Apparently investigators had no leads regarding his demise. Before that interview, I had never heard of Sam, and that's what I told the investigators. My ignorance was not what they wanted. Reminding me that Darrel had snitched me out on my current charge, they tried every angle they could think of to get some sort of evidence against Darrel, but I just didn't have anything to tell.

Keeping their mission in mind, these fine, upstanding FBI investigators drove from Memphis, Tennessee, to the federal prison in Atlanta, Georgia, and falsely informed Darrel I had told them all about Sam's murder. Using their best intimidation trick, they offered Darrel a deal: if he testified against me, they wouldn't give him the electric chair. Darrel took the deal. The next thing I know, I'm being charged with murder in the first degree and assigned a public defender.

During my trial, the prosecutor continually badgered me to make a deal for a lighter sentence by confessing and testifying against Darrel. He even told me my wife had signed a sworn affidavit against me and would take the stand to assist him in my prosecution. Fran (not her real name) and I had recently divorced, so we hadn't talked in quite a while, but I was sure she also knew nothing of Sam or his disappearance. Years later, when I was able to hire an attorney and get copies of the court records, I discovered that Fran's testimony matched mine, so the prosecutor knew Darrel was lying on the stand when he testified against me. Even though questioning witnesses in court with the knowledge that their answers will be false should cause the disbarment of attorneys, this prosecutor did not seem to mind. I also discovered that the gun used to kill Sam was not in the prosecutor's possession, even though he had tried to scare me into a confession by saying my fingerprints were on the murder weapon. Eventually the jury believed his incorrect theory about the cause of Sam's death, and I was wrongfully convicted to life with the possibility of parole. My theory of the case is that the prosecutor and investigators who participated in my conviction viewed Darrel and I as scum of the earth since we had federal felonies, which gave them license to use illegal and unethical methods to keep us incarcerated for as long as possible.

When my federal sentence was complete, I was transferred to a state prison. About thirteen years into my sentence, I received word that Darrel had cancer. Knowing that he was about to meet his Maker, Darrel decided to tell the truth about Sam's death. He wrote out a complete confession, exonerating my ex-wife and me of all allegations. Darrel affirmed that I was not present when Sam was killed and had no involvement in planning or implementing the murder. He also confessed that he had thrown the gun used to kill Sam into the Ohio River shortly after murdering him. Darrel had his statement notarized by a prison official, who has agreed to testify that Darrel was of sound mind and not coerced when he wrote his confession.

Forgetting that our "justice" system viewed me with disdain because I had honestly confessed to my first—and only—crime, I foolishly believed my release from prison was imminent. Nine years ago I hired an attorney who presented Darrel's confession to the judge who had convicted me. Apparently he is a *very* busy judge because he still has not made any type of ruling as to whether or not this murder charge will be removed from my record. While my attorney is making progress, it is evident that the system is rigged against my success.

During my time in prison, I occupied myself by working hard and staying away from troublemakers. That's not easy, but I had learned my lesson from associating with Darrel. Even for prisoners who try to do the right thing, that environment is pretty nerve-racking. An example of that stress can be seen in a situation I witnessed not long before my release. A guard on our unit, who was known to bring in drugs, cell phones, and other contraband for a select group of thugs, was approached by a prisoner I'll call Barry. Having built up a bit of a prison fortune, Barry asked this corrupt guard what it would cost to bring in a few things for him. I think Barry must have just fallen off the turnip truck because he didn't understand that approaching a stranger about participating in an illegal activity would make him look like a snitch. (Relationships must be developed before making important deals, especially illegal ones.) And you certainly do not make such a move in a place where others can hear your conversation.

After Barry returned to his cell, the guard called up two prisoners— two of his partners in crime—and told them Barry was getting too noisy. The officer said he was going to leave the unit for a while and expected them to handle this problem of excessive noise. It wasn't long before our unit was free of staff and the sounds of fists slamming on skin and bones rang out from Barry's cell. Since it was two on one, the beating was quick, and the thugs had time to take showers before the guard returned. I guess they wanted to make sure the guard could "honestly" say he could not tell from appearances exactly what had happened to Barry. Although I felt awful for Barry, I was pretty confident that reporting this incident to anyone at the prison would be useless. Considering what happened to Barry, I knew there was a good chance that I would have been treated with a similar beating at best, or to a permanent dirt nap at worst if I were to report what I had seen.

Living with the threat of and continually witnessing violence affects even the strongest of individuals. I remember the first day I got out on parole. My family took me to a steak house for a celebratory meal. Not only did I find it impossible to sit facing the wall (with my back exposed to the strangers in the restaurant), but I experienced a steady feeling of dread that someone might notice the sharp knives placed within my reach. In prison such an incident would result in a serious write-up and time in solitary confinement. It took me about two years to emotionally disconnect from the pressure-cooker life of my past twenty-five years, and I am still more vigilant than the average man.

Prejudice against me from people outside of prison started even before I was released. My sister told the parole board that she would provide me a place to stay and everything I needed to get on my feet for as long as I needed, but the Board of Probation and Parole (BOPP) had other plans. Even though I had never failed a urine test for drugs or alcohol, nor were these contributing factors to my offense, the BOPP determined that I needed to be in a halfway house the first ninety days of my freedom so I could attend treatment classes.

My wonderful mom found a suitable place in a city about 140 miles from her home and paid a $500 deposit to reserve a bed for me. Although the company she paid was on the list given to her by the prison, it was not on the list of approved facilities with the BOPP. Despite the refund policy being on her side, Mom never received a refund of her down payment. I'm pretty sure the owner of that halfway house, like many houses, has low regard for felons and their families but does not mind using them to line his own pockets.

Unlike many of the guys in the halfway house I ended up attending,

I was lucky to get employment and a drivers' license within two weeks of my release. Although my $120-per-week rent was supposed to ensure the staff assisted me with these things, I was pretty much on my own. They did help me obtain a birth certificate, but that was scary. On my first weekday out, a bunch of us loaded into the van for various destinations. After a short drive downtown, the driver turned and told me to get out, go into a tall building I had never seen before, present the papers he had given me, and buy a copy of my birth certificate. It may seem silly to most people, but being dropped off alone in a strange place unnerved me after having been locked up for twenty-five years. I'll bet everyone in that office wondered why my eyes were as big as moon pies. The next week, with the help of a fellow halfway house resident, I was able to obtain my driving permit and eventually my license.

In time I acquired another commercial driver's license (CDL), but that was a fiasco. Although I did everything correctly to pass the skills test, the examiner made up petty excuses to fail me. After my second attempt, I called my lawyer, and the third time was a charm. I can't help but believe the examiner knew about my felony conviction and wanted to keep me from a good salary. She need not have bothered. I soon learned that most of the good trucking companies refuse to hire drivers with felony convictions, and the really good ones won't hire drivers with murder convictions.

That same week that I earned my CDL, I took advantage of a reference given to me by a fellow prisoner before leaving. His dad had a company that cleaned large buses, the type used by big-name country music stars, and he was willing to give me a job right off the bat. Since driving and repairing diesel engines was my real passion, I eventually found a great job running the night shift of a large trucking company's diesel shop. I'll call them GE for Giant Eagle, but that's not their real name. The first two weeks I worked the day shift so I could learn company policies and give them time to hire an assistant. Within days of working the night shift as head of the shop, I was called into the office and told I was being fired for lying on my application. Knowing that I had been totally honest, I was baffled.

For at least eighteen years of my prison experience, I had worked for a prison company called TRICOR, and that is what I put on my application. During the first fifteen plus years with them, I was at one prison, and I had a certificate to prove it. A bit over three years before my parole I was moved to a different prison but continued to work for TRICOR. When the human resource department at GE's corporate office first contacted TRICOR, they were only told about my last assignment. Even though I presented proof of my employment, and TRICOR confirmed my eighteen years of employment, GE stood by their original decision. They inferred that a conspiracy to falsify my employment history had occurred. I lost a great job. We may never know, but I sincerely believe that if I did not have a criminal record, I would still be working for GE.

Along with costing me financial/career opportunities, felonism has played a part in my relationships with women. If your view of men getting out of prison comes from television or movies, you probably think we all run right to the brothels the day of our release. That's really not how it was for me or most of the guys I know. For men with a record, interacting with the wrong woman can land us back inside before we know what hit us. I knew how to relate to women before my arrest. I was twenty-seven at the time and had been married several years, but things had changed. For the past twenty-plus years, the only women I had seen were guards who used men as their sex toys or talked to them like they were scum. Logically, I knew there were plenty of women who did not follow the prison-guard model, but how was I supposed to know what dating behaviors were acceptable versus unacceptable after all these years?

The very first day I was out of prison, my ignorance of changes in the **freeworld** embarrassed me in front of my family. My brother filled up the car with gas and just started to pull away. Immediately I shouted for him to stop the car. I had no intentions of returning to prison for stealing gas the same day I got out. Once everyone stopped laughing, they told me about debit cards. Who knew? Apparently everybody except me. So I was really concerned that some other change regarding social interactions would not only embarrass me but get me into trouble. Later that day, my family took me to a department store to get supplies. Once again I was embarrassed and intimidated when the woman in front of me started a friendly conversation. In prison, you don't talk to strangers outside of a new cell mate. Random conversations usually mean there's a problem. Mom assured me that this stranger was just being friendly, but it still took a long time before I could engage in a conversation with an unknown woman.

To deal with my discomfort in the **"freeworld,"** I ignored my feelings of awkwardness toward female interactions and worked as much as possible. When I wasn't working, I spent time with my family. For the first two years of my freedom, that worked well, but it got old. Knowing I needed help, I eventually asked for it. On a chance meeting, I ran into a friend who had been inside about the same amount as me but had gotten out a few years earlier. He was married before leaving prison, so I asked his wife for help.

She didn't know any single women our age who were looking for romance, so she suggested I try a website. After a few months of resistance, I followed her advice, and it worked. Although I didn't include my years in prison on my profile, I did tell women within two or three dates about my past. From the very beginning, I maintained the attitude that if my past pushed them away, it would be okay. Most of the women had no problems with my past. After dating for a while, we would realize we didn't match and end the romance on a friendly basis.

One lady I dated taught me to stick with my decision to reveal my history within the first three dates. Becky and I emailed and talked quite a bit before actually meeting face to face in a public place. Sparks flew so brightly in that parking lot that the grocery store could have used us for their security lights. Our mutual attraction was so strong that I didn't think my past would be an issue. When I told her about it on the fifth or sixth date, she confirmed my reasoning and said my past did not change anything between us.

We met in the fall and continued seeing each other on a regular basis into the winter. Becky went to my mom's house with me for the family's Christmas celebration. Everyone in my family was happy to meet her, and we had a wonderful holiday. My sisters even gave Becky presents. It seemed only natural when spring rolled around that she invited me to a cookout with her family.

We arrived just as Becky's brother and sister-in-law pulled up. I thought it was a little odd that they walked into the house without Becky introducing me, but maybe they were in a hurry. Then Becky bolted to the house and left me standing at the car. Immersing herself in her family, Becky kept her distance from me and busied herself with one person after another. No one offered me a drink or food. No one spoke a word to the ex-con invading their space. After two hours of being the elephant in the room, I intercepted Becky and told her I was leaving. With a huge smile on her face she said okay, not ever mentioning that we had ridden together to this event. I left knowing my spark for her was totally extinguished.

When I called Becky the next day, she acted as if everything were fine. After I contrasted my experience with her family and her experience with my family, she apologized but still minimized the situation. Although she didn't come right out and say it, I was sure Becky was ashamed to be with me around her family. I can only surmise that felonism runs deep in her family roots. Becky was probably surprised to hear that I was not angry. I had given her no reason that I know of for being a felonist, and I made sure to continue that trend when we hung up the phone. I sincerely hope she finds a man with whom she can share all her thoughts and fears, and I hope the same for myself with a good woman.

Some readers might think I should be angry at Becky or Giant Eagle, but that's just not the way I want to live. Life has bumps in the road for everyone, regardless of their criminal history. No matter what your history, some people will always consider you inferior to them. Someone recently asked me what I would say to people who see felonism as a valid prejudice and who believe all felons should be oppressed for the rest of their lives. My reply: "Just one wrong word or move in front of a vengeful person could have you walking in my shoes. If that happens to you, will your attitude remain the same?" I met many people while in prison who should not have been there, but they were. After experiencing the worst our society has to offer, I spend every day being thankful for the life I now have. Hopefully, I will never have to live under a bridge or eat from a dumpster like some ex-cons do, but if that is in my future, it will still be better than life in prison. I hope you never have to find out for yourself.

Commentary on Rick's Story

Exiting prison can be a culture shock for returning citizens who have spent more than seven or eight years inside. Many men and women share Rick's ignorance of new technology even though they may have seen television shows and commercials displaying such advances. For people who entered prison in the 1980s, witnessing a person use a cell phone can be like walking into a Star Trek episode. We once heard a man tell about how he cried the first day he got home and witnessed his wife walking around the house with a phone next to her ear but no cord attached to the wall. She was talking as if there was a person on the other end of the phone. With no experience to contradict his assumption, he believed he was witnessing his wife have a break with reality. Even more disconcerting to returning citizens was the multitude of people walking around in public with ugly black ear adornments talking to themselves. Just hearing the word "Bluetooth" on television does not mean a returning citizen will recognize the device when they see it.

Experiencing perplexing new realities on the first day of one's release, and in the weeks that follow, can darken the joy of freedom. Even the toughest returning citizen can be filled with fear when they realize they cannot flush a toilet because it is missing a handle. They begin to question their ability to adjust when they are confounded by the simplest of tasks. Rick was fortunate to have family members willing to educate him, but they were unaware of the non-technological challenges he faced. Becoming accustomed to knives, silverware, keys, and a host of other items that are considered contraband in a prison setting can illicit feelings of discomfort and dread. Many returning citizens who have served long sentences find themselves forgetting to close doors on houses or cars for several months after release because this is not something they ever did while in prison. We know of men who've stood outside their work facilitates, frustrated that no one inside was opening the door. These men were so conditioned to listen for the electronic buzzer signifying the unlocking of the door from a remote location that they had forgotten they could open the door themselves.

These lapses in understanding probably appear humorous to most readers, but to a felonist, they are occasions for shaming or belittling the returning citizen. Because avoiding shame and re-establishing one's place in society are such high priorities for people experiencing the stress of re-entry, it is easy for them to behave in ways that appear to be overreactions by people who have not been to prison. For example, making a derogatory remark to a returning citizen who is causing delays at the Red Box could develop into an explosive situation. In the prison environment, ignoring disrespect brings a heavy price. The most minor consequence would be a reduction in social status. As a result, most prisoners are pretty civil to each other. For instance, prisoners don't cut in line unless they have mental issues or want to start a serious conflict. Some people who have never been to prison could take a lesson from returning citizens on this topic.

Returning citizens may also carry residual anger from the disrespectful, unfair treatment they received prior to going to prison. Returning to the **freeworld** could easily trigger nameless anger or anxiety associated with the last time they were "out." It's like returning to the curve in the road where you experienced a head-on collision after months of recuperating in the hospital. The trauma of an unfair trial or sentencing that was easily suppressed while dealing with the trauma of prison life can reemerge when prison life is ended. This was not the case for Rick because he was incarcerated when his unjust murder conviction occurred. However, recidivism may be reduced for some returning citizens if these emotional struggles are identified, accepted as normal, and treated whenever they occur.

If you read the commentary on Austin's story, you already know that the conviction of innocent people usually stems from one of three sources: perjury, faulty witnesses, and prosecutorial misconduct.[242] Rick and Austin's cases were influenced by the double whammy of perjury created by prosecutorial misconduct. In Rick's case, he has not been able to overcome that one-two punch even though he is paying an attorney rather than using a public defender. His attorney has met great resistance in acquiring the court records needed to clear Rick's name. His experience is not unique. Since 1989, as of this writing, 1,625 Americans have been exonerated, according to the National Registry of Exoneration. On its website this organization emphasizes its belief that only a fraction of those innocent of the crimes for which they have been convicted are identified. Forty-three percent of those wrongful convictions were related to inappropriate conduct of prosecutors. They are adding about 200 new exonerations per year to their current list.[243]

According to the Center for Prosecutor Integrity, incentives for prosecutors to reach into their bag of dirty tricks include "the gratitude of victims, favorable media coverage, career promotions, appointment to judgeships, and the allure of high political office." Although these rewards are enticing, it may be that the virtual absence of negative consequences for unethical and illegal behavior by prosecutors, or, as the Center puts it, "a culture of prosecutorial infallibility,"[244] is the most alluring.

A combination of twenty federal and state investigations between 1963 and 2013 identified 3,625 offending prosecutors. Of those offenders, sixty-three (1.7 percent) were publicly sanctioned but only fourteen (0.3 percent) of those 3,625 were actually fired or disbarred. In fifty of those sixty-three cases, the most severe "punishment" was the requirement of the prosecutor to pay for the cost of the disciplinary hearing conducted to investigate their misconduct.[245] Even when proven to have knowingly put an innocent person in prison, prosecutors are not sued or held accountable as criminals.

Another trick up the sleeves of police and prosecutors is the practice of piling on charges. For example, a person may be charged with armed robbery and the possession of a firearm in the commission of the same offense. In a July 13, 2012, video by "Religion and Ethics Weekly," the civil rights attorney Harvey Silverglate professes his belief that the practice of prosecutors stacking up charges that are not applicable in order to obtain convictions "has reached the point of becoming 'ingrained' into the process."[246] According to Harvard Law Professor Alan Dershowitz, prosecutorial misconduct is "rampant," and AJ Davis, an American University professor, says the practice is "pervasive."[247] Such observations by high-ranking judicial experts give credence to Rick's statement that angering the wrong person can cause just about anyone to land in prison.

Rick did escape one form of prosecutorial misconduct because he is not Black. Research has demonstrated a pattern of national, systemic racism among prosecutors in America. According to a 2015 article by M. Marit Rehavi and Sonja B. Starr in the "Journal of Political Economy," Black men make up 6 percent of the population, and 35 percent of the federal prison population[248] while 95 percent of prosecutors across our country are primarily white, especially in communities where prosecutors are elected by the populous rather than appointed by the executive branch.[249] Because prosecutors are able to establish charges based on police reports, they have a great deal of power. Prosecutors, not the police, are the ones who determine whether charges are worded in a way that triggers mandatory minimums. They are the ones who stack charges and set sentencing ranges that give juries the impression a defendant is really a monster. Rehavi[250] and Starr's extensive research demonstrates that Black men are charged more often and receive sentences nine times harsher than those of their white counterparts who are convicted or plead guilty to the same severity of crime and have similar levels of criminal histories.[251]

Aside from the tremendous cost of human suffering created by this disparity, Rehavi and Starr calculate that some startling economic tolls are being paid for prosecutors' racial prejudice. If just the disparity in mandatory minimum sentencing were to disappear today, 8,000 federal prisoners would leave prison immediately. That would create a savings to federal tax payers of $230 million per year. If equality were applied to all Black men in prisons and jails across the country, not only would monetary savings be tremendous, but a great deal of community strife could also be resolved.

The important question here is, "Why do we allow this in our country?" America was established on the principles that a person is innocent until they are proven to be guilty in a court of law. Defendants are to be given due process rights and a jury of their peers. The jury is to be given complete and truthful information to make a fair judgment. American courts have never applied these principles perfectly, but currently there is nationwide corruption within this process.

It is not our intention to say there is a mastermind conspiracy among prosecutors, or people who control them. We understand the reasoning behind the judicial system granting immunity from prosecution to segments of our executive branch (prosecutors in particular) so that they are free to perform their duties. It is our intention to shine a light on the fact that corruption exists within our system and that much of it seems to be fueled by felonism. If Rick had not been identified as a felon for transporting stolen property, we seriously doubt Darrel's false testimony would have concluded with Rick's erroneous murder conviction.

Just as Becky was not honest with Rick regarding her changed feelings toward him, felonists are not being honest regarding their lack of belief in redemption for men and women with felony convictions. If felonists who control the creation of policies requiring lifetime shame and isolation for all people convicted were open and honest, wouldn't they make the consequence for all felony convictions life-without-parole sentences? As a society, it seems we no longer practice the belief that people can pay for their offenses and start anew—unless that accused is our child or spouse.

Some argue that people getting out of prison have not changed. They point to high recidivism rates to affirm their biased belief. Let's consider a few more facts. Today it is difficult to meet your basic needs when you leave prison with a $30 debit card in your pocket, a prison ID as your only form of identification, and few prospects for employment that will pay a living wage. If you were facing homelessness and starvation for yourself, and possibly your family, and perceived all legitimate means for earning money to be outside of your reach, what would you do?

It is our experience that most returning citizens can be trusted and deserve a true second chance. They don't deserve limits on employment, housing, and social status, nor demands of conformity to a given religious practices in exchange for support. We invite you to find out for yourself. Engage in conversations with returning citizens, revealing your genuine concerns regarding their applications for work. Introduce yourself to neighbors who have felony convictions. Invite returning citizens to community or church activities that you attend with the understanding that declining your offer does not mean they are rejecting you. Following these suggestions will not only lessen your own fears, they will probably thwart any plan(s) being made by a small minority of returning citizens to exact revenge for about being ostracized, thus increasing the safety of yourself, your family and your community.

Chapter 14

Skai's Story: Looking from Both Sides

If you wish to know the mind of a man, listen to his words.

—Anonymous Chinese Proverb

I have lived on both sides of the fence. As a child, I told people my dad worked out of town because the truth, that he was a federal prisoner, wasn't safe to share. As an adult, I have worked inside a maximum security prison. What have I learned? Racism and felonism exist on both sides. These experiences have shaped me, molded me into the very private person I am today. While I have no shame about my past, sharing my story is not easy. The pattern of secrecy that was required to protect my family is not easily released. No, we weren't in any kind of witness protection program. We were just regular people, a blended family, coping with some stout discrimination. Since those biases still exist, I'm not willing to expose myself with details that have the potential to victimize me again. With the exception of my name, the names of others in my story, and the name of my home state, the events I share are totally true. Hopefully you will learn through me that prejudice can be overcome if that is what you choose for yourself.

Daddy and I have always been close. He didn't live with Mom and me, but he has always been a big part of my daily life. There were a total of nine children in our family, but Daddy was never too busy to answer the phone, listen to childhood worries, or spend time on "playdates" with me, his oldest daughter. He was a successful business man, but first and foremost, he was Daddy. He protected us, educated us, fed us, clothed and housed us, but most of all, he loved us. Thank God, he's still around to share that same love with his grandchildren! Us kids called him "The Two-Hour-Speech Man" because he loves to share his wisdom with us. Daddy doesn't lecture us or talk down to us, but he does make sure we understand the gems of wisdom he is bequeathing to us with the hope that our roads will be smoother than the one he's traveled.

"The Day of Infamy" that lives in my mind didn't happen during WWII but during my eleventh year of life. I was in middle school and had just attended my first pep rally. Daddy and I had a "date" to go to my school's basketball game, our first. Since Daddy had never missed one of our planned activities, it never crossed my mind that I would miss the game that night, but I did. The first damper on my excitement came when I called him after school. Daddy didn't answer the phone. That was very odd. He always took my calls, even if he was just going to say he was busy. After several more calls, Daddy did answer, but he sounded irritable when he told me he'd be at my house soon. The clock moved past our appointed time to meet, and I began to worry. Mom saw the look of anxiety on my eleven-year-old face. She too knew it was unusual for Daddy to miss a date and to not answer my calls. Before we could call him again, the phone rang. Thinking it was Daddy, I answered, but Donna (my step-mom) was on the phone, and she asked to talk to Momma. I was supposed to hang up my end of the landline, but I didn't. I don't know why, but as soon as I heard Donna say, "They got him," I knew exactly what she meant.

Mom rushed me out of the house, and we met Donna at Daddy's house minutes later. It was a disaster! Everything in his house was broken. There seemed to be no rhyme or reason to much of the destruction other than a demonstration of anger toward Daddy. Stuffing had been yanked from every piece of furniture and scattered everywhere. The control panel for the central heat and air was smashed off the wall. Broom and mop handles were severed, and they even broke the ladder that went to the attic in an obvious display that told us one thing. If Daddy was home when this happened, he must be badly hurt.

As it turned out, Daddy noticed the police at his house before they noticed him. Learning from the clerk at the nearby convenience store that the police had been showing his picture to people in the neighborhood, Daddy went straight to his attorney's office. He learned that two brothers in town who were big-time drug dealers had mentioned his name. Daddy turned himself in that same day (saving us kids from witnessing his arrest). It seemed like these brothers had opened the phone book and read every name they could pronounce.

By the end of the day, the police had arrested more people on drug charges than had ever been arrested in the history of Missouri. The *only* thing they took from Daddy's house, apparently thinking it was evidence against him, was a picture of Daddy and me standing in front of the limousine he rented for my last birthday celebration. There was no evidence against him of any drug dealings other than the word of two terrible men trying to trade their freedom for Daddy's conviction.

Daddy called the next day and put us all at ease. He said he'd be out soon, but in the meantime, Donna and my grandmamma could come visit him if they wanted to. Having discovered that the jail staff was prejudiced against Blacks, Daddy told Donna to come alone. As much as he wanted to enjoy the love of his children during this terrible time of his life, he refused to let us be exposed to their mistreatment. Besides that, jail visits were awkward since they were conducted between thick glass partitions. Soon enough, Daddy was moved to a federal prison, and we filled our weekends with long car rides to spend precious hours playing board games and sharing the Krystal hamburgers we were allowed to bring for lunch. Even today it's a family joke that Daddy always cheats at checkers, but I've never caught him.

During those years of weekends with Daddy, I learned several hard lessons. Grandmamma and Donna prepared us to face people who might be prejudiced against us by Dad's conviction. Their main instruction was to say Daddy was working out of town if anyone at school were to ask. They didn't want anyone who thought they could take advantage of Daddy's absence to start snooping around. Frankly, I thought Daddy's housing arrangements weren't the business of people outside our family, so I never discussed family matters at school, although one boy at school knew. He was my boyfriend, but he was also the brother-in-law of a man who was incarcerated at the same facility as Daddy. Those weekend trips to prison were a little more crowded when we all went together, but they were still fun.

It was during those visits that I learned the importance of keeping my distance from people who are not following the law. I talked quite a bit to one guy who was just eighteen when he was arrested. Marco had been hanging out in his neighborhood when a couple of undercover cops approached. When they asked about purchasing drugs, Marco said, "Don't pull up on me. I don't do that. Go talk to those guys down there." Once the fellows at the end of the street were arrested for selling drugs to the undercover cops, they came back and arrested Marco for not reporting illegal activity.

Marco was such a sweet guy with mountains of potential to do great things in this world, but now he has a felony conviction slamming the doors of opportunity in his face. I also learned about several women who were serving longer sentences than their drug-dealing boyfriends just because they were driven to a deal or let their fingerprints get on the money they were asked to hold for brief periods of time.

Daddy held tightly to hope that his case would be resolved soon, and he made sure that his family did the same. In the early days of his incarceration, Daddy repeatedly told me he would be home for my high school graduation. Momma says that all through my graduation ceremony, my eyes kept drifting upward. I knew Daddy wasn't able to make it, but that didn't keep me from continually scanning the audience, subconsciously hoping for a miracle. Along with hope, Daddy made lots of "Two-Hour Speeches" centered on my marrying a good man and the importance of never dating a drug dealer. I thought I followed his words to the T, but that didn't protect me as much as I thought it would.

When I did marry, I picked a great guy. Anthony worked two jobs and was never in trouble with the law. We were happy together, especially on the day our son was born. That day had a double blessing because it's the day Daddy was able to come visit me after completing time in his work-release program. My hope was fulfilled the day Daddy got to hold his first grandchild in his arms on the very day of Anthony Jr.'s birth. Just a few months later, our joy was overshadowed by the death of my husband's little brother. There are lots of conflicting stories as to the motivation and circumstances, but the short story is that his eleven-year-old brother was shot dead, and no one was ever held accountable.

Something drastically changed in Anthony that day. For the first time since I had known him, Anthony drank a lot and was private about his coming and goings. I know he was trying to cope with the loss of his brother, but the overall result was the threat of one of my biggest fears in life. One year after our son was born, Anthony decided to ride around with six unsavory fellows who had bad intentions. Just like with the death of his brother, details of the events that led up to Anthony's arrest are sketchy. I now know these men had planned to rob and kill someone, but I have no idea why. Only Anthony and two other men were caught. At least, they are the only ones serving prison time for the events of that night. Anthony refused to testify about what happened. It appears the police had no evidence against him because it took six years of Anthony wasting his days in jail for him to be convicted. Anthony escaped the life sentence given to the other men but was given a twenty-year sentence, thus fulfilling my earlier fear, that my child would grow up surrounded by the prison culture.

To help readers have a better understanding of my life, it would probably help to reveal that Anthony Jr. was born with Down's syndrome. Prenatal services had warned us that something was wrong with his development, but I was only twenty years old, and Down's is pretty rare in African American families. I was in denial before and after his birth that Anthony Jr. was anything other than perfect. We told everyone that even if he was born with arms growing from the top of his head, we would love him deeply. Before we left the hospital, one well-meaning nurse told me she was sorry for my tragedy. While I understood she was trying to be sympathetic, not for one second have I ever experienced Anthony Jr. as anything other than a gift to us from God. At the age of seven, Anthony Jr. still melts my heart every time he wraps his little arms around my neck. *Many* days, he is the reason I keep going.

Without financial support from Anthony, it fell on me to support Anthony Jr. and myself while bearing the expenses of staying in a relationship with my husband. Transportation costs were bad enough, but if we wanted to talk on the phone, I had to pay $1.50 for each fifteen-minute conversation. That expense doubled about three years into Anthony's incarceration and has the potential to triple if the Missouri Department of Corrections (MDOC) decides to move him to a facility further from my home. One of the maddening things about the phone system is that many phone calls get disconnected—without warning or explanation. Even though I request refunds for the minutes we're cut off, no compensation is ever given. I have to pay $3 whether the call lasts one minute or fifteen minutes. Global Tel Link says they only disconnect calls when they detect a legal issue, such as three-way calling, but that is not why our calls are terminated. Since there is no way for me to prove our calls comply with prison policies, they get to keep my money, and there is nothing I can do about it.

Because I didn't want to be a burden to my family, I had to get a good job while still in the whirlwind of Anthony's arrest. It had to be a job with a medical plan, a living wage, and regular hours that would allow me to meet the demands of being a married, yet single, mother. Even before Daddy was incarcerated, I had been interested in law enforcement. Being a police officer or an attorney may still be a part of my future. Who knows? Wanting to understand more about what Anthony and Daddy experienced, I applied to work as a correctional officer (CO) with the MDOC. Since he had not been convicted, Anthony was not in the MDOC system at the time, so there was no conflict of interest. I was a bit concerned about what Daddy would think of my new vocation, so I actually didn't tell him for a while. Daddy didn't react the way I thought he would. He was proud to hear that his daughter was a CO, and of course that gave him plenty of material for new two-hour speeches.

After a three-week orientation and over ten years of visiting inside a federal prison, I thought I was prepared for my position as a CO, even if I would be working in a maximum security male facility. Maintaining a professional demeanor was important to me. Respecting prisoners and seeing them as human beings was also a priority. On my very first day, I learned that some COs did not share my concerns. It was one of those rare days when minimum security prisoners were allowed to hang out on the yard, participate in sporting events, and enjoy a cookout. Seeing that I was blocking the queue where men had lined up to get their food, I stepped aside. My good manners were met with instructions from a veteran CO: "They're just inmates. You don't have to move." After interacting with a few more of my peers, I discovered this lady displayed a middle-of-the-road attitude. While some COs wanted to help prisoners as much as possible, others came to work each day in the hopes of being "victorious" in a physical or mental conflict with a prisoner.

Daddy had been right about racial prejudice being rampant. I worked on this one unit that was designed to be an incentive/reward for prisoners' good behavior. Men who had complied with policies, not gotten any write-ups, and been good workers were allowed to move to Unit 6 where they had special privileges. Twice a month they were allowed to purchase food (with their own money) from a restaurant willing to deliver to the prison. They were allowed to work in jobs that took them outside the building, and for a while they were allowed to purchase electronic games from a pre-approved list, sold by a pre-approved company, to entertain themselves during those long days in their cells.

Ms. Eunice was the manager of Unit 6, which meant she had control of who did and who didn't live in that unit. Time and again, I witnessed Ms. Eunice practice her racial prejudice against Black inmates. One time she arranged for a white prisoner who had recently tried to attack the warden (a clear violation that disqualified him to live in a privileged unit) to move to Unit 6 by transferring out a Black prisoner who had committed no infractions. Ms. Eunice made no attempt to hide the fact that she wanted Unit 6 to be filled with white prisoners even though over half of the institution was occupied by Black inmates.

The result of Ms. Eunice's follies was the destruction of a good program. The more she stacked the unit with men who did not qualify, the worse the Unit became. When unqualified prisoners continued breaking rules, everyone on the unit was punished by the removal of privileges. Several men tried mentoring new cell mates, but their best efforts did not overcome the negative effects of Ms. Eunice's blatant disregard for policy. I tried to override her destructive influence by reporting Ms. Eunice's policy violations to her superiors, even the warden. While my supervisors agreed that she was repeatedly violating policy, they instructed me to keep quiet. They assured me something would be done sometime in the future. It never was.

In an effort to tell both sides of the story, I must say that some prisoners could be very irritating and petty. These prisoners would work themselves into a total frenzy over the smallest of issues, like having pudding missing from their food trays, or being given a different brand of soda

from what they had purchased from the commissary. Along with screaming insults, they would file grievances over such trivial things. The worst
unit to work in was the one where men were locked up twenty-three
hours a day. Though it never happened while I was there, prisoners in
the hole had a well-earned reputation for throwing urine and feces on
COs. A great deal of these behaviors probably arose from the fact that
the prisoners on this unit had untreated mental issues, and the COs had
no training in the needs of people with mental health disabilities.

Many prisoners mistook the least sign of kindness for weakness. One
of my duties when I first started working as a CO was to walk around
the pod and physically count the number of inmates in each cell. In the
unlikely event of an escape, counting prisoners at certain times of the day
would give the MDOC a guestimate about when an escape occurred.
I had been warned that prisoners would test me, so I was not shocked
when I saw prisoners masturbating as I walked around the pod counting
everyone. Taking the "ignore it and it will go away" approach did not
work, so I tried the opposite. Reasoning that men were choosing to save
their self-satisfying activities for my visits outside their door, I began
giving them write-ups. They responded with a sharp increase in their
masturbatory activities. With remorse I discovered the one thing that did
work, public humiliation. Loudly joking about the microscopic size of a
man's penis (even when it was not true) seemed to magically make those
penises disappear from my sight. I hated to treat them so badly, but in
that environment, it was important that I let everyone know I deserved
to be treated with respect.

The first six months of my time as a CO were pretty rough. Until
arriving at work, I never knew whether I would be assigned to the maximum security, to death row, or to the honor units. Throughout that time,
I was careful about what and how I spoke to everyone. "Yes, sir" and "No,
ma'am" appeared in just about every sentence of mine. It didn't matter if
I was speaking to a superior officer, co-worker, or prisoner.

Keeping my sense of humor was also vital to my strategy of teaching
others how I expected to be treated by them. Sending mixed messages to
anyone was not an option. While others were willing to take short cuts,
disobey policies, or sweep problems under the rug, I was determined
to maintain professional conduct. Eventually I was assigned to the job
of unit secretary. Along with handling all the paperwork generated by

other staff members and prisoners (minutes on meetings, daily reports, discipline reports, commissary orders, etc.), I was also the liaison between the unit manager and prisoners. While something always needed to be done, the work was manageable, and I enjoyed the stability of working at the same unit every day.

Habitually fixing things that aren't broken, and refusing to fix things that are, seemed to be a cultural norm at the institution where I worked. Staff leadership seemed to be absent from the top down. Of the wardens I worked under, none of them put in full eight-hour work days. The commissioner did not visit the prison while I was there, yet men and women in these administrative positions made major program changes. One time they decided to change the procedure during meal times. Instead of opening cells so that the entire pod could go to the chow hall if they wanted to (meals were not mandatory), we were instructed to escort these 200 men one tier at a time. No reason was given for this change even though it caused more work and stress for COs.

I often wondered if it was their intention to create confusion, more work, and less safety for prison staff members, but I'm smart enough to know that voicing such a thought would have been employment suicide. When prisoners demonstrated total noncompliance, even violence toward COs, there was very little that could be done by lower level staff members such as myself. The commissioner was under political and public pressure to reduce violence within the prison. It was cheaper to keep the appearance of a peaceful facility by forbidding the issuance of serious write-ups that were deserved than by providing treatment to prisoners and training for staff. It was very discouraging to witness the same consequence (low level write-ups) for beds that were made improperly in the minimum security units and daily assaults on officers in the max units.

When it became evident that Anthony would be moved to the MDOC, I shared that information with my supervisor, two wardens, and an institutional investigator. I was delighted to hear their expressions of concern and offers of support because I had been worried about being fired. As it turns out, lots of MDOC staff members have incarcerated family members. To reduce the temptation of helping someone escape, prisoners' folders are flagged with requirements that they be excluded from prisons where family members work. One bad policy regarding staff–prisoner family relationships is that they cannot visit family members for four years after resigning. Based on assurances from the commissioner's office, I am hoping that this policy will soon change because I am very concerned about the effect a four-year ban will have on Anthony and Anthony Jr's relationship.

After three years of fervent prayers for protection before starting each shift as a CO, I accepted a job offer to work in a totally different field. Since I had never received any type of warnings or disciplinary actions, and I had given prisoners the type of respect and treatment I had hoped for my father and husband, many people were sad to see me leave. It wasn't until after leaving that work environment that I realized the negative effect it had on the way I now interact with the world.

One big change is that I seem to have a sixth sense when people are walking up behind me. Just like on my graduation day when I was unaware of my continual scanning of the audience for my father, I now look automatically over my shoulder and at reflective objects in all directions to stay aware of people who might approach from behind. My skin has grown thicker, and I hold my privacy in higher regard than I used to.

After listening to many horror stories about why different men became incarcerated, one more thing has changed in me. I share this in hopes that it will help others. In social settings, it is important to take every decision seriously because one bad choice in a moment of foolishness can change a person's entire world. Thank God I have my wonderful, loving son to keep me grounded. Anthony Jr. is my weakness and my strength. If I have anything to do with it, he will never participate in the pattern of generational incarceration that afflicts so many children whose parents are incarcerated. Hopefully it will not be your destiny either.

Commentary on Skai's Story

Skai (pronounced Sky) is a courageous and unique woman! She is the only person we have ever met who willingly worked inside a prison for the purpose of better understanding her father's experiences and preventing her current and future children from following in his path. We pray her open-mindedness is contagious because we believe broadminded thinking has a negative relationship to felonism.

Long before the conviction of Skai's father, authorities treated him as if he were sub-human by disrespecting and destroying his personal property. We do not know when this trend began, but today it seems many law-enforcement officers justify ripping the upholstery out of cars[252] or scattering all the items in a closet across the floor as part of their search efforts. Pre-conviction prejudice also receives assistance from the media when the names and faces of people who are arrested for serious crimes are plastered across our television screens and presented as guilty long before a jury trial or plea bargain.

Several unscrupulous but clever companies are cashing in on the presence of pre-conviction felonism in the workplace. These companies publish mug shots on the Internet and in local print papers of all people who are arrested. No follow-up is made to identify which arrestees are convicted versus which should not have been arrested. These companies create serious problems when an adult is looking for work and their potential employer finds their mug shot in a Google search. Many people arrested but not convicted are paying hundreds of dollars simply to have these companies remove their mug shots.[253]

Prejudice prior to conviction is not a problem unique to Missouri (or whatever state Skai lives in). We have a friend in Illinois who suffered some pretty severe consequences after looking inside the window of a house under construction in his neighborhood. Tom was charged with criminal trespassing and held in jail for several days. The absence of evidence against Tom, even after his home and vehicles were subjected to destructive searches, as well as the fact that he had a good reputation in the community, did not dissuade detectives from insisting that Tom was casing the house for a future robbery. Tom's claims that he was looking for remodeling ideas did not make sense to them. Eventually, Tom was bullied into accepting a plea and paying steep fines for his curiosity. It seems to us that the felonistic attitude of the police in Tom's case was enacted long before he surrendered to their pressure.

A far worse demonstration of pre-trial felonism occurred in 2009. In Ferguson, Missouri, Henry Davis was arrested on September 20th of that year because he had the same first and last name as someone who was wanted by the police. He had attracted police attention by pulling over on the side of the road during a terrible storm. An officer ran his plates and immediately arrested Mr. Davis. After it was established that he was the wrong person and was not wanted by the police, he was told he would still have to stay the night. Mr. Davis—denied access to a nearby mattress—was told to sleep on the concrete floor in a one-man cell. When Mr. Davis protested, at least four police officers beat him and then charged him with property damage for getting blood on their uniforms.[254]

Another account of blatant pre-conviction felonism is apparent in the case of Judge Elizabeth Coker. As a District Judge in Texas, she had a practice of texting prosecutors with questions (and other assistance) during trials proceedings that they could ask witnesses. Her texts indicated Judge Coker was focused on assisting prosecutors in obtaining convictions.[255] Within days of resigning her judgeship to avoid prosecution, Ms. Coker announced that she would run for the Polk County Criminal District Attorney's Office in 2013. She referred to her practices as a judge (without directly mentioning her illegal behaviors) as proof that she would be tough on crime.[256] We wonder, is Ms. Coker the only judge who has ever thought of using technology in a prejudicial manner against those who claim innocence, or is she the only one to get caught? By the way, the man Judge Coker was trying to convict was found innocent by a jury.[257]

The problem with applying felonism to suspects is that it destroys the Constitutional principle that those charged with a crime are innocent until found guilty by a jury of their peers.[258] If law-enforcement officers and judges are not going to respect this founding principle, we must wonder what rule of law is governing our country. How can America count itself as a civilized nation if every person suspected of an offense has the potential to not only lose their civil rights to due process and a fair trial but to be physically beaten if they complain?

We heard about a woman who supposedly got into her husband's boat and floated around the lake while reading a book. A forest ranger approached and asked to see her fishing license. The woman respectfully responded that she didn't have a fishing license because she was not fishing. Her only purpose for being in the boat was to enjoy nature as she read. To her surprise, the officer explained that she would be arrested because she possessed all the equipment for fishing and was in a "No Fishing Zone" of the lake. Using the officer's logic, she informed him that when they arrived at the police station, she would be pressing charges against him for rape. "Lady," the officer exclaimed, "I haven't touched you or even gotten into the same boat with you!" "Well, that's true, Officer," she replied. "But you have all the necessary equipment."

Though we laughed the first time we heard this joke, it is not funny when the principle is repeatedly played out in legal system. It seems our society has indeed made a subtle shift toward convicting people for having the equipment even if they have not committed any violations. Laws are said to be created and enforced to protect citizens, but it often feels as if the true motivation is to win an invisible control struggle.

Here are two examples: According to federal law U.S. Code § 863, citizens can be arrested for owning or transporting "drug paraphernalia" even when no drugs are present.[259] In most states, drivers can also be arrested for having empty alcohol containers in their vehicles—even if they have no alcohol in their bodies.[260] Lord help you if a stray container or someone else's joint is discovered under the seat or in the trunk of your car when you visit someone in prison.[261] Depending on which Department of Corrections facility you are visiting, your visitation privileges will be suspended (if not permanently terminated), and you will face criminal charges.[262] It does not matter whether you borrowed the car from a friend or the car rental company failed to clean out a beer can from under the seat. While the law prohibits the *intentional* transporting of contraband onto prison property, it has been our experience that prison personnel and police officers have a history of reading minds and overriding proclamations of ignorance.

In researching death rates for those incarcerated, we came across a U.S. Department of Justice report that seems to support our premise that felonism is applied to those suspected of committing felonies. In fact, this study may indicate suspects receive the brunt of the felonists' blows. The report, entitled "Mortality in Local Jails and State Prisons, 2000–2012—Statistical Tables," categorizes the locations and causes of the 42,966 deaths reported by jails and prisons submitting voluntary reports.[263] Almost twice as many prisoners who had not yet been convicted died from illness, suicide, and unnatural causes than those who had been convicted.[264] While these statistics are wide open for interpretation, they do cause us grave concern for the condition of American jails. Considering these facts and the condition of his home prior to his arrest, we fear Skai's father would have been subjected to grave brutality if jail officials had not known he had legal and family support.

Skai had to present a façade to people outside her inner circle regarding the problems her father was having. Can you imagine what it was like for a pre-teen to keep this tragic event at the top of the list of "things I can't talk about at school"? Because her father's case was so sensational, some teachers may have known about his arrest, but none ever approached Skai with empathy or concern. Thankfully she never had a teacher like Andy's (co-author's), who asked, "Why should I waste my time with you? You are just going to wind up in prison just like your Dad."

There are no official records regarding how many children have incarcerated parents, but 2.7 million is a common estimate.[265] Guess how many school districts have programs to assist these children in dealing with this trauma? Almost none as far as we can tell. The school district in which we live has no official program for children of incarcerated parents even though they serve almost 93,000 children. In 2010 Linda (co-author) personally interviewed most of the government and nonprofit agencies in the Nashville, Tennessee area who served children of incarcerated parents at that time.

Sadly, only one agency had a program specifically for this group. Yet, even though their program was part of a nationally known agency, with a multimillion budget, their program met once a month for about three hours, had no set curriculum, and provided no specific training for the mentors of children whose parents were in prison. We found it odd that this program met during one of the two times in a week when children might be allowed to visit an incarcerated parent. Especially troubling was the lack of any efforts to ensure visits between children and their incarcerated parents. Is this really the best we can do for our children?

Before closing our commentary on Skai's story, we want to address the pervasive attitude of felonism within America's prisons. Hopefully by now you've seen that nonviolent offenses, mostly related to drug use, are behind many arrests.[266] We understand that sowing bad seeds in life will usually reap negative rewards, but reform options that do not disrupt families or abuse prisoners can be applied, especially to people who are controlled by addiction or commit a crime in an attempt to escape poverty. Cruelty toward non-violent prisoners is a socially accepted, system reality. Who among us hasn't joked about prison rape references or jokes? Just as people with active pedophile tendencies are drawn to work in daycare centers, people with masochistic tendencies are drawn to work in prisons. The only difference is that those in the latter group are more likely to be promoted rather than incarcerated for practicing their aggressive impulses. Skai's father and husband deserve better.

On June 6, 1788, James Madison (nicknamed "Father of the Constitution and fourth President of the United States[267]) referenced orator Patrick Henry, who suggested that "licentiousness has seldom produced the loss of liberty; but . . . the tyranny of rulers has almost always effected it. Since the general civilization of mankind, I believe there are more instances of the abridgment of the freedom of the people by gradual and silent encroachments of those in power than by violent and sudden usurpations: but on a candid examination of history, we shall find turbulence, violence and abuse of power, by the majority trampling on the rights of the minority . . . This danger ought to be wisely guarded against."[268]

Doesn't it seem that the wisdom of these two men, whose vision gave birth to our nation, has been ignored? Under the guise of forcing citizens to live righteous lives, mountains of laws have been written to criminalize licentious behaviors. It may seem that these laws have righteous motivations, but we all know about corrupt brokers in every segment of our government who have written or enforced anti-drug, anti-alcohol, anti-gay, and anti-prostitution laws while participating in the very acts they publically tried to eradicate. We believe James Madison's statement agrees with the premise of this book, Abusers of Power trample on the rights of an identified minority for very selfish reasons.

Portugal has demonstrated that trying to control individuals' pursuit of happiness through drug use does not work. In 2001, the Portuguese government decriminalized drug use. Since that time, Portugal has benefited tremendously. Poverty has reduced, drug addiction is down, treatment is up, the spread of AIDS has drastically reduced, and police corruption has almost been eliminated.[269] How different could Skai's childhood have been if the same thing had happened in America? We can't help but believe that drug policy reform that focuses on treatment far more than incarceration would benefit millions of America's families.

Rather than searching for ways to support life, liberty, and the pursuit of happiness among all people, government officials have violated President Madison's warnings and focused on trying to legislate morality. Many of our laws are based on the false belief that the incarceration of "bad" people will make us a safer, better nation. It only took 227 years, or seven and a half generations, to fulfill Mr. Madison and Mr. Henry's nightmare, for in many ways, felonists have usurped our government and weakened our nation.

It may be that some prisoners can never return to their true nature, that loving nature they were born to. That was the opinion many people had about Andy (co-author) before, during, and after his incarceration. Some people *are* out of control, narcissistic in their every move, and unconcerned about who they harm in their pursuit of happiness. In these cases, our laws approach these people in one of four ways: kill them (the death penalty); take responsibility for their care until they die (life without parole); release them only to see them harm other innocent persons (life with parole or flattening sentences), or help them find redemption, as Andy did. It was not the prison's mission to assist his healing. Linda was told by one commissioner of corrections that rehabilitation was not the responsibility of the TDOC. Healing was Andy's choice in spite of the way he was treated in prison, but healing could become the result of incarceration for most prisoners—if we want it to be.

Many people in prison are angry. Whether their anger is at themselves or others, their anger is intense and justified. We are not saying their anger-motivated behaviors are justified, however. We believe all people are good on their first birthday. It does not matter if we become separated from our goodness by mental illness, neglect, or abuse; that goodness remains deep within our cores. Abusing and isolating angry people will rarely assist them in returning to their true selves, but identifying and healing the pain that exists underneath can achieve miraculous results.

Even people with the lowest self-esteem know on some level that they deserve to be treated respectfully and allowed some degree of control over their own lives. When this control is denied, a struggle begins between the person who wants control and the person who does not want to be controlled.

Linda (co-author) has demonstrated this principle many times with groups of teenagers and adults by asking pairs to gently put their hands together, palms touching. Then she asks a designated person in each couple to apply pressure and push against the other person's hand. As a natural instinct, the second person always begins to push back, often applying more pressure than that being exerted on their hand. If left unchecked, an innocent activity such as applying pressure to move the hand of another person can lead to conflict.

How much worse do we make our society when power-seeking people tell others which behaviors are legal within the confines of their own homes when all adult participants consent and do not harm anyone?

Looking back at Skai's experiences we see that when COs with felonistic attitudes have no reason to oppress prisoners (because the prisoners are complying), they create issues to demonstrate control. Skai's revelation that prisoners with minimum security ratings are being written up for things like improperly making their beds is just one example.

We suspect Skai never had feces or urine thrown at her because she treated prisoners with as much respect as she could in that setting. She did not initiate or participate in the control game to the extent that feces hurling was the only tool left in the prisoners' arsenal. We also suspect many COs don't recognize the part they play in reducing prisoners to such vile actions. They probably label the prisoner as evil and deserving of whatever mistreatment comes to them. However, lack of awareness of the maniacal control struggle between prison staff and prisoners does not keep society from suffering the natural, negative consequences logically unfolding around us.

As we have shown in the commentary of others stories, it is not uncommon for prison staff to take the emotional damage of their work home with them. Many COs abuse themselves with alcohol or drugs, become depressed, or use violence to solve conflicts with family members and friends. No matter how righteous our intentions, we will never be excused from the natural, negative consequences of abusing each other. Let's follow Skai's lead and find a better way to support ourselves. We can invent better ways to recognize and correct each other's mistakes and misdeeds. Just as we now look back on America's history and wonder, "How could so many people have justified making a living by enslaving others?" our descendants will be mystified by the inhumane ways we treat prisoners today.

Chapter 15

Susan & Stacy's Story:
Behind the Walls Dreams Do Come True

Whatever you do may seem insignificant, but it is most important that you do it.
—Mahatma Gandhi

R ecently I was asked if I would tell the story of how I met two of the most important people in my life, my husband and a dear friend. For over thirty years I have been a so-called "true crime" buff. I have read about and watched hundreds and hundreds of true crime cases. Never once did I suspect that maybe the defendant(s) didn't deserve to be incarcerated or could be in the process of being wrongfully convicted. Like the majority of the **freeworld**, my train of thought went something like this: "If they're locked up, it's for a reason, and society needs to throw away the key!" All of that changed in early 2010 when I heard about the case of Teresa Deion Harris in Tennessee.

I knew five minutes into the story that something just wasn't right. None of the pieces fit, no matter how hard I tried to put them together. Deion, as she's known to her family and friends, was charged in 1993 with first-degree felony murder, convicted in 1994, and sentenced to life without the possibility of parole (LWOP). Deion did not commit the murder, and this fact was not argued; she only witnessed the crime! The nagging question of how this happened to this young, twenty-three-year-old girl, along with *why* she was sitting in a prison with a life sentence, wouldn't leave me alone! *Never* before had I even thought of writing to an inmate. That was taboo to me. However, I did write to her, and much to my surprise, she wrote me back immediately. Deion and I began writing back and forth several times a week. After four or five months, I asked Deion if I could visit her. I soon got on her visitation list and finally went to meet this woman. I was completely unprepared for the loving and wonderful lady I met!

Over time we became more like sisters than friends, sharing all of our inner thoughts and secrets. We also discussed the crime and why she was innocent of felony murder. Deion would tell me that even if she were to come home today, she couldn't stop fighting because another person still sat in prison with the same sentence as hers. Just like Deion, Stacy was innocent of felony murder. This was one of her two codefendants, Stacy Ramsey, who was also charged, convicted, and sentenced under the draconian felony murder rule and is sitting in a Tennessee state prison all for witnessing the crime. She told me how Stacy had refused all help from the **freeworld** over the years; how he didn't get visits like Deion did, and how he was all alone. She asked me to please write to him, for which I told her she was crazy! I was still trying to come to the realization that I had written to *her*. Taking on a second prison pen pal was too much of a stretch for me. But once Deion asked me that first time, she never let up. She begged, she nagged, and she pleaded, "Please write to him. If anybody can get through that wall Stacy's built up around him, it's you, Susan!" After two months of this, I relented and wrote to Stacy. Never in a million years did I expect to hear back from him. Stacy had previously refused help from Deion's husband when he tried to reach out to him, so why would I be any different?

One week later, I opened my mailbox and was in complete shock; there sat a letter from Stacy! I was scared to open it, thinking he was going to tell me to leave him alone, and how he didn't need nor want my help. I read the letter so fast I had to re-read it several times. I kept thinking that I must have read it wrong. Stacy said he would love my help and that he appreciated my letter. Before I knew it, Stacy and I were writing to each other every single day. I would open my mailbox, see that day's letter, and get the worst case of tingles you can imagine. Because of the honest communication we had through our letters, I knew what a loving and caring man he was. Within months, I was somehow falling for this man I had never met or spoken to over the telephone. Not once did the thought ever occur to me (or matter) that he was in prison serving LWOP. After I finally convinced myself to push my own feelings aside and just help this man, I got a letter from him telling me that he was falling in love with *me*. Never in my life have I done such a huge happy dance.

Because I was still visiting Deion each weekend while all this was going on with Stacy, she encouraged me to come off her visiting list and get on Stacy's. In Tennessee you can only be on one inmate's visitation list at a time unless multiple inmates are part of your immediate family. Of course I refused. Deion had been my friend long before Stacy came into the picture. Once again she harped, begged, and pleaded. Finally she said the words I'll never forget, "Susan, I don't mean this to be hateful or hurtful, but I have people visit me every single weekend. I get mail every day. Stacy has nobody but you. Right now he needs you more than I do." How could I possibly tell her no? So I proceeded to officially remove myself from Deion's list while I cried the entire time.

Then I was hit with a bomb . . . In this state, when you come off one person's list, you have to undergo a twelve-month waiting period before getting on another person's visiting list. *What???* TDOC was serious about this too; no loopholes whatsoever. Believe me, I checked! My heart was broken. Here I was not able to visit two important people in my life, but all I could do was wait it out and jump through TDOC's hoops.

Finally, in September 2011, I was approved to be on Stacy's list. Upon our first-ever face-to-face meeting, it had been almost fifteen months since our first contact. Talk about anticipation, mine was sky high! We were both so nervous. The minute we saw each other, we fell in love all over again. I'll never forget that moment as long as I live; he grabbed me, twirled me around, and in that instant I knew I had made the right decision all along.

Seven months later, in April 2012, Stacy made me the happiest woman on earth when we were married in the prison chapel. Never have I been so proud of someone. I was so honored to be called this man's wife. That day I realized that dreams do come true no matter where you are, the challenges you face, or what obstacles are placed in front of you. The fact that Stacy is serving a LWOP sentence is simply one of those challenges, though I will spend the rest of my life working to bring this innocent man home and hopefully Deion too. Without her, there would be no Mr. and Mrs. Ramsey or this unbelievable once-in-a-lifetime love that we share.

Unfortunately, several people in my life have been unable to overcome the "lock 'em up and throw away the key" mindset I used to share. Even though I did not know Stacy when he was convicted twenty-one years ago, I have been tagged as an unworthy person and ostracized by multiple people as a result of having an open mind and a forgiving spirit. I guess those who now see me as a second-class citizen are too committed to the prosecutor's theory of the case, and the media frenzy that followed, to listen to the truth. They refused to believe Deion and Stacy's charge partner, Walter Smothers, when he confessed on video to forcing Deion and Stacy at gunpoint to participate in his crime, the murder and dismemberment of Dennis Brooks, Jr. In fact, Walter flatly stated that he had intended to eliminate the witnesses (Stacy and Deion) after he killed his victim, but people preferred the lies of the prosecutor and media about what happened on that horrible night in 1993 rather than opening up to another possibility.

A few months ago I was refused car insurance by a nationally known company after revealing that my husband is incarcerated. The telephone sales woman declined my request for a letter explaining the company's refusal to accept my money, but she admitted that the reasoning was related to my revelation of Stacy's imprisonment. Even members of my immediate family and people who had been my close friends for over twenty years dodged talking with me after learning of my relationships with Deion and Stacy, but others have had it much worse.

Thirteen years after her conviction, Deion's parents were in line at a department store when the cashier recognized them. The cashier refused to wait on them. In another incident, Deion's parents were asked to start attending church at another location even though they had worshiped with that congregation for decades. In small towns, just about everyone is related. Many of the people who worshiped with Deion's parents had watched Dennis grow up and graduate from high school shortly before being murdered. These parishioners must have felt great sorrow and horror when remembering their loved one, which is understandable, but Jesus went through a much worse death and still pled for the forgiveness of those who put him on the cross.

How can people who meet regularly to honor and commit themselves to Jesus' teachings refuse to associate with someone because they are related to a person they believe committed a crime? I suspect they excused their actions because their subconscious acceptance of felonism has blinded their minds. Just as I once believed that all adults convicted of a felony should be locked away for countless years, those who used to worship with Deion's parents have been fooled into believing Deion and her parents were unworthy of their community.

Not a day goes by that I don't thank the good Lord for bringing Stacy and I together as well as bringing Deion into my life. The fact that they are both incarcerated makes no difference to me. I would much rather be doing life with them than live a day without them. So remember, whoever you are, wherever you are, don't ever give up hope. Miracles can and do happen to all of us. I am living proof that through God all things are indeed possible.

Commentary on Susan and Stacy's Story

Before any other commentary, we want to recognize the trauma experienced by the family members and friends of Walter Smothers' victim, Dennis Brooks Jr. For Dennis's loved ones, seeing anyone associated with his murder (prosecutors and defense attorneys included) might easily trigger anguish. Anger and a desire for isolation from anyone associated with the gruesome death of a loved one is normal and appropriate. Recognizing the injustices committed in Stacy and Deion's cases in no way diminishes the profound sympathy and compassion owed to Dennis's family and friends. They deserve justice for Dennis's death, and we believe no other people agree with that statement more than Deion, Stacy, and Susan.

William Hawkins (1673–1746) is credited as the originator of felony murder laws. He purposed that anyone who initiated an act with malicious intentions, no matter how minor the act and even if the act was not intended to end someone's life, would be guilty of murder if the act eventually resulted in the death of another human being.[270] Tennessee, like all states with felony murder on the books, is a "common law" state.

That means the state uses old common law from England, which relied on the customs and judicial precedent and in some cases formal written enactments of a legislative authority from the 1700s to judge suspects of crimes. Ironically, England abolished felony murder years ago.[271] This brings us to the question: Why, here in the United States, do we still practice these archaic statutes of common law? Why are we applying laws from the nation our founders fought against? Wasn't the American Revolution fought to make us independent of England's unjust laws?

A felony murder conviction is applied for one of two reasons. The first application is when someone dies as a result of a felony being committed. This segment of the law was used in the case of Philip Workman. The details are in the commentary on Austin's story, but Philip Workman was executed by the state of Tennessee in 2007 because a policeman was killed by a fellow officer's bullet when Mr. Workman robbed a Wendy's restaurant.[272]

The second instance in which a felony murder charge applies is when a defendant is found to be a major participant in a murder or in a felony that resulted in a murder.[273] Most states add the qualifier that the accused showed indifference to human life (i.e., no remorse for the person who died). This was the application used with Stacy and Deion's prosecutions. For some reason, it did not matter that, after begging for protection for herself and her children from her "boyfriend," Deion reported all the details of Dennis's murder to the police when they arrived at her door the next morning. Deion and Stacy wanted to go to the police but Deion had been drugged, they had no car, and both feared for the life of Deion's children and themselves. It seems to us that no mercy and little logic was demonstrated when police and prosecutors assigned more credibility to Mr. Smothers' testimony than to Deion and Stacy's. Why was no credence given to the facts that Stacy and Deion's independent confessions to the police matched each other's (as well as the physical evidence and witness statements) but contradicted Mr. Smothers'?

We believe pressure on prosecutors makes them adjust their methods and ethics as a means of placating public opinion. Other than Mr. Smothers' testimony, little evidence supported his confession. Until Deion offered to tell the police what had happened in exchange for protection from Mr. Smothers, the police did not know who had murdered Dennis.

Even though Deion's confession did not include any type of request for legal absolution, she was depicted as a perpetrator and Mr. Smothers was assigned the role of her victim.

We wonder if the emotional abuse heaped upon Deion is typical in most prosecutions. Deion wept several times during her trial. Most observers would assume she was remorseful regarding Dennis's death, but Mr. Radford, the prosecuting attorney, told the jury that her tears on the outside were a cover-up for the evil that abided inside Deion. If Mr. Radford had presented her tears as sincere, she would have been disqualified from a felony murder conviction. He had no choice but to apply clairvoyant skills to explain Deion's outward signs of contrition and remorse if he wanted to include her felony murder conviction on his resume.

The prosecutor presented Mr. Smothers' account of the murder, and his alleged lack of participation, to be factual even though Mr. Smothers' finger prints were the only ones on the murder weapons, he had an extensive history of violence (this was Stacy and Deion's first arrest), and he had given several different versions of the events surrounding Dennis's murder. It did not seem to matter to Mr. Radford that two witnesses heard Mr. Smothers threaten to kill Stacy if he did not comply with Mr. Smothers' demands.[274]

None of the witnesses were ever called by Stacy or Deion's defense attorneys during the trial, not even the couple who had heard the scene unfold from their porch. If they had been called by the defense attorneys, it would have put holes in the prosecution's theory. Deion's attorney also had access to Dr. Morson, the psychiatrist who examined Deion before the trial. Her testimony could have disputed Mr. Radford's mindreading skills, for she knew Deion had contemplated suicide several times out of remorse for Dennis's senseless death. Another factor that contributed to Deion and Stacy's conviction was that neither was allowed to testify at the other's trial. Surprisingly, the Criminal Court of Appeals did not see this pattern of behavior as ineffective assistance of counsel.

Throughout this case, a great deal of emotion and outrage touched every person related to it, mostly due to the gruesome nature of the offenses against Dennis's body after he was murdered. Dennis was a kind-hearted teenager who stopped to help what must have seemed like a lady in distress. Only Mr. Smothers knew that this would be Dennis's last act of kindness.

In their statements to the police, Stacy and Deion revealed that two bullets from the gun held by Mr. Smothers killed Dennis shortly after he had stopped. The three thought there had been no witnesses, but due to the summer heat, a couple had been sleeping on their porch when they heard Deion yell at Dennis to remain on the ground. She was trying to protect him from Mr. Smothers, but it did not help. The couple heard two shots within minutes of each other as well as Dennis's truck racing off into the night just moments after they heard Mr. Smothers threaten to shoot Stacy if he did not drive the dead man's truck per Mr. Smothers' instructions.

The worst part of this crime occurred when the trio arrived at a secluded part of the countryside where Mr. Smothers planned to dispose of the body. To honor his satanic practices, Mr. Smothers began dismembering Dennis's corpus and forced Stacy and Deion to participate. His most shocking act of mutilation was to remove the heart from Dennis's body and demand that the other two drink its blood. Both Stacy and Deion gave the appearance of complying by holding Dennis's heart to their lips to keep themselves and each other alive. Eventually, Mr. Smothers placed Dennis's body behind the steering wheel, doused it and the truck with accelerants, and set them ablaze. After picking up Deion's children, they walked back to Deion and Stacy's homes, which were across the street from each other. Both Stacy and Deion were horrified, but they felt paralyzed and unable to break away from Mr. Smother's presence. Both were terrified of the possibility that Mr. Smothers would kill them and Deion's children if he were provoked with any type of defiance.

What you have just read is a summary of the narration Stacy and Deion presented to the police while in two separate rooms, unable to hear each other's testimony. After seeing Deion's signed statement, Mr. Smothers presented a far different account in which he claimed Deion was a witch who had cast a spell over him and forced him to commit murder and participate in the desecration of Dennis's corpus. Although there were many discrepancies between the two stories, and within Mr. Smothers' own story, the prosecutor accepted the second one as truth. Eventually Mr. Smothers' account of that night would be the only one depicted in the prosecution's theory and presented in court filings. Even in Stacy and Deion's appeals, summaries of the case followed Mr. Smothers' point of view as if it were factual—without providing readers with the origin of those "facts"—Mr. Smothers—and with very few references given regarding the contradictory testimony and evidence.[275]

Though there was plenty of evidence to convict Mr. Smothers without making a deal, Mr. Radford agreed to reduce his sentence to life without parole (from the death penalty) in exchange for his testimony against Deion and Stacy. While on the stand, Mr. Smothers contradicted himself from his original police statement, but his new statement was more damning against his codefendants.[276] It was unethical for Mr. Radford to allow this and for the defense attorneys to allow these contradictions to go unchallenged, but it happened just the same. According to the American Bar Association, "A prosecutor should not knowingly offer false evidence, whether by documents, tangible evidence, *or the testimony of witnesses*, or fail to seek withdrawal thereof upon discovery of its falsity."[277] (The emphasis is ours.) Did not felonism blind the eyes of the judges who were charged with the duty of making sure such laws were followed?

We can only wonder whether Mr. Radford sincerely believed Mr. Smothers' testimony to be more truthful than Stacy and Deion's, or whether he chose to present it because it would be more damaging to their defenses. Supposing Mr. Radford did believe Mr. Smothers, why did he fail to follow the law and tell the jury of Mr. Smothers' plea agreement? This too was a violation of the law. Supporting Mr. Smothers as a truthful witness may have been a favor to Mr. Smothers' father-in-law. At that time, he was the chief of police in their small town.[278]

About a year after their convictions, Deion received a letter from Mr. Smothers which she used to appeal her conviction. In his 2006 letter to Deion, Mr. Smothers called himself the trigger man and ring leader. He stated that he had no more appeals and had escaped the death penalty, which had been his motivation for testifying against her and Stacy. Mr. Smothers offered to set the record straight, saying he was sorry for testifying against her and offering to help by talking with her attorney and providing the truth.[279] During her appeal, it did not matter that Mr. Smothers had admitted in this letter that he had held a gun to Stacy and contradicted his testimony on several other issues. When they arrived in court, Mr. Smothers told the judge he was kidding about his confession because he wanted a day out of prison. One possible reason for Mr. Smothers' reversal is that between his writing the letter and Deion's hearing with the court of appeals Mr. Smothers learned that he would have been subject to the death penalty if he recanted his original court testimony. If anything had prevented Mr. Smothers from recanting his written confession (such as a brain injury, death, or a moment of rectitude) the outcome would probably have been much different for Deion and Stacey.

Seven years after his apology letter to Deion, Mr. Smothers participated in a television interview for the show "Women Behind Bars." During the interview Mr. Smothers confessed to thinking about killing Deion and Stacy at the end of the night. This was contrary to his testimony at Deion's trial that she had controlled him with an evil curse and forced him to kill Dennis.[280] When Deion filed an appeal pro se (without assistance from an attorney) asking that this video evidence be used to grant her a new trial, the Tennessee Court of Appeals replied that her request was too late. The video had aired on May 4, 2010. Due to Deion's ignorance of the law and being given the wrong address for filing her petition, the Court of Appeals did not receive her request until August of 2011.[281] Asserting that Deion had one year after becoming aware of the video to present this video to the Court of Appeals and that they did not receive her paperwork until fourteen months later, this lapse was assumed to be evidence of Deion's guilt.[282]

This is not a rare occurrence. While no statute of limitation exists for convicting a person for murder, the window of opportunity for defending one's self against a murder conviction is brief, even when new evidence of innocence is discovered. Is that not a demonstration of systemic felonism? It certainly cannot be grounded in a desire for justice.

To some, it may seem that we are nitpicking and overly sympathetic to murderers. But what if Deion and Stacy's stories are true? What if they really were unwilling participants in Dennis's death and tried to correct the situation by cooperating with the police the very next day? How could they prove their lack of guilt for felony murder with such prosecutorial mishandling and time limits for evidence? Stacy and Deion are the first to declare that they should have done something to stop Mr. Smothers. To this day, they both deeply regret giving in to their fears and Mr. Smothers' intimidation. In the end, they did what they could to correct the situation, but now they will remain in prison the rest of their lives unless a Tennessee governor becomes willing to grant them clemency or laws are changed to allow an honest review of their cases.

Mr. Smothers had several convictions and arrests in his past, yet he seemed to get preferential treatment over his codefendants, who had no criminal records. We recognize that this seems to be the opposite of felonism. Since felonism has become a legal replacement for racism and classism, we suspect the differences in the prosecutor and jury's opinions of Deion and Stacy's legitimacy versus that of Mr. Smothers stem from their differences in social classes. Mr. Smothers was raised in an upper-middle-class family and had a family member on the police force while Stacy and Deion's parents were on the lower end of the socioeconomic scale. What logical reason other than felonism/classism explains why Mr. Radford argued before a jury the bizarre idea that Mr. Smothers was the victim of an evil spell cast by Deion?

The application of felonism by Deion's community has fallen on the backs of her family members. Those who believe that Deion is guilty of everything Mr. Smothers stated (that she is a witch and demanded the mutilation of Dennis's body as a form of worship to her "god") might rationalize that Deion's parents, Mr. and Mrs. Smith, bear a great deal of responsibility for Deion's actions. After all, aren't such people obviously unfit if they parented a devil-worshiping teenager? Felonists in their community must have agreed with this line of reasoning when they asked the Smiths to attend a different church, a place of Christian worship that had felt as comfortable as home to the Smiths for decades. If Mr. Smothers' story is correct, and the Smiths did raise their children to be devil worshipers, wouldn't church be the best place for them to learn to turn from their wayward thoughts and actions?

What does it say about the Smiths' community and America as a nation when even churches are willing to turn their backs on the most wounded among us? We understand when people have a hard time following a key principle of the Christian faith, to love our enemy,[283] but the Smiths were never the enemy of those who ostracized them. This is a perfect example of how normally rational people, when confronted with irrational statements and comments, succumb to felonistic practices out of fear, a lack of understanding, and unwillingness to investigate all sides of an issue. Could felonism exist if everyone practiced thinking for themselves rather than listening to the Siren songs of the media and gossip mongers?

Even though Mr. and Mrs. Smith believe Deion and Stacy's versions of Dennis's demise, it is not possible for anyone to be more contrite than they are today, twenty-three years later. They are hardworking "country folks" who have always done what they could to support themselves and help anyone who asks for assistance. They have lived in the same, small community all their lives, but since Deion's arrest, they have suffered greatly at the hands of felonists. Rather than being comforted for the loss of their daughter, they have been shunned. Mr. Smith has lost business at the small repair shop he runs for extra money, and some tried to have him fired from his bus driving job. They have lost friends, and even some family members no longer associate with them as a result of Deion's conviction.

Hardest hit are Deion's children. They were very young at the time of her arrest, far too young to bear any responsibility for Dennis's death, yet they have been ostracized. As if they were demons themselves, they were kept at bay by parents in the community who didn't want their children to play with the "Harris kids." Possibly the most offended by felonists is Deion's son. Family members report that since the very first day he received his driver's license, he has been harassed by law-enforcement officers, frequently stopped despite not having broken any traffic laws. Rather than receiving understanding and guidance from his community, he has received a steady diet of persecution and isolation from city and county leaders.

What possible explanation could there be for twenty-three years of adults discriminating against these children other than felonism? Whether members of this community believe Deion is guilty or not, the shameful treatment of Deion's children hurts everyone. People who see themselves as loving Christians have allowed felonism to separate them from the example of love and forgiveness demonstrated by the God they claim to love, worship, and obey. Perhaps they do not see the hypocrisy of their actions, just as, perhaps, Stacy and Deion did not see that they had other options on that dark night in 1993.

Chapter 16

Terry's Story:
From Outside to Inside and Back

Jail didn't make me find God, He's always been there.
They can lock me up, but my spirit and my love can never be confined to
prison walls.

—Lil Wayne

I f you asked me to identify the time when I first understood the concept of prison, I would tell you it happened about the same time I first
understood the concept of speaking English. My parents' home was
close to Parchman Farm in Mississippi—a prison farm where many of
my friends' parents worked at one time or another.

Plenty of people do not agree with what I'm about to say, but every
word is the truth as I know it. Each phase, each step of my long journey,
has been directed by God, even the darkest parts—and there are plenty
of those. Just so you, the reader, aren't turned away by all my Jesus talk,
I'm gonna tell my story without referring to my understanding of how
God, Jesus, and/or the Holy Spirit were directing my every step, but if
you ever call up and want to know more details, that's what you're gonna
hear. Hold on to your hat, 'cuz here we go.

While I enjoyed growing up in a small Southern town with two loving parents, that's probably pretty boring to most folks, so I'll skip that
part. It is important to know that my upbringing instilled in me a good

work ethic that started before I graduated from high school, followed me into college, and is with me even today. Aside from fighting in Vietnam as a teen, I worked the following jobs before my twenty-seventh birthday—many of them while I was going to college: air traffic controller, book salesman, Sherwin-Williams employee, city and state undercover drug contract agent, intern at the sheriff's office, and correctional officer (CO). I'm leaving out the odd jobs that kids pick up in the summer, but you get the picture. I'm not afraid of work and have worked in some dangerous places.

I considered my life picture perfect. I was married, worked at respectable jobs, went to college, and had my future all planned out. After getting my bachelor's degree in criminal justice, I would move on to become a reputable attorney and support my wife and two children in style. That was *my* plan.

Then one night I came home at 2:00 AM and found a sixteen-year-old "man" inside my house. He had gathered up several of my belongings with the intention of stealing them, and he had raped my wife. That was the end of his good day, and his life. My military training kicked in and my sanity kicked out. After beating the man within an inch of his life, I bound him up, put him in my car, and drove to a bridge where I shot him and disposed of his body by letting him fall into the river. In truth, I'm not sure if shooting him was intentional or an accident. I remember propping him up on the rail with my gun pointed at his torso. Then I looked down the road toward the small community a few hundred yards away, trying to figure out if what I saw were house lights or an approaching vehicle. As I refocused my attention to the man in front of me, the gun fired, and the impact pushed him off the bridge and into the river. By the time I got home that night, a police lieutenant, who happened to be (and still is) a buddy of mine, had responded to my wife's call. Once Mike heard the entire story, he had no choice but to arrest me. I later learned that if I had left the body in the house, or even stayed in my county, the charges would have been much lighter. Instead, I was charged with premeditated murder.

The entire episode was unlike anything I had ever experienced, and to this day, I truly doubt my sanity on that night. Because "innocent by reason of insanity" was my plea, I ended up spending several months— before and after my trial—in what those of us who are not politically correct refer to as an insane asylum. All five of the psychiatrists who examined me came up with different diagnoses. One professional deemed me to be totally sane, but the other four determined that I had some form of paranoia and or various degrees of schizophrenia.

If you ever find yourself tempted to try this line of defense, I suggest you think twice. At the facility where I was evaluated, professional wrestlers worked as assistants to the nurses as a way of supplementing their income. They also seemed to use their jobs to entertain themselves with some pretty sadistic games. When the doctors and nurses left at 5:00 PM, the place became a living nightmare. A favorite pastime of the staff was over medicating a resident and betting on how long it would take them to fall out. I had particular compassion for a guy named Pettaway, who had committed himself into the mental institution (very rare) for help. The night the staff chose to overdose him, they forgot to inject Pettaway with the antidote. When Mr. Pettaway started having seizures, they threw him in the hole and totally forgot about him. He was discovered the next morning by attendants on the day shift. It would be logical to assess that this traumatic experience left Mr. Pettaway in a worse condition than when he admitted himself, but I really don't know the long-term effects of this abuse. I do know that the guilty attendants were never held responsible for their offense toward Mr. Pettaway.

My trial was almost as much of a circus as the asylum had been. I found the man in my house in 1976. At that time, the civil rights movement had finally gained ground in America and there seemed to be some hypersensitivity regarding a white man killing a Black man—regardless of the situation. It seemed like I was in the media every day for weeks before and after the trial. According to the NAACP, I had participated in some big conspiracy with the KKK. Since I had never been a member of the Klan, I have no idea how they arrived at that conclusion. The fact that I had a minor job at the sheriff's office was also used against me to infer accusations of a police cover-up. This is when I began to believe that the statue of Justice wears a blindfold not because she is impartial to both sides of a conflict, but because she is embarrassed by the way America's criminal justice system has become corrupted by people seeking money and power.

As you have probably predicted, I lost my first court battle, was convicted of first-degree murder, and sentenced to life in prison. Since I still claimed insanity, they put me back into the mental institution. The sheriff told my family that he would transport me to Parchman as soon as I called saying I was ready since, during this time, people with mental health issues were not usually housed in prisons.

One day a resident started beating me in the head with part of a broom handle. He wouldn't stop, so I fought back, and for that we were both placed in the hole. My attacker got out pretty quickly, but I was told that the situation was my fault since I was the sane one in the conflict. The staff member supported his opinion by pointing out that I was the only resident in the entire facility who was not taking psychiatric medication. He kept me in the hole until the sheriff came to transport me to Parchman.

It was true that I had no desire to go to Parchman Farm. I had seen firsthand that prisoners committing the smallest infraction would be taken out of their cells that same night, driven to the prison orchard for a lesson in deportment, patched up in the infirmary, and then delivered back to their cells before morning light. While I never witnessed the murder of any prisoners, I'm sure the rumors about dozens of bodies buried in Mississippi cotton fields are absolutely true. Although I didn't want to go to Parchman, days in a small room with a hole in the floor for a toilet, a bare metal slab for a bed, and only a pair of khaki shorts for clothing, with absolutely nothing to do, made a future at Parchman seem appealing. The problem was—residents in the hole had no phone privileges, so my situation was a Catch-22. After thirteen days, I was allowed to call my family. My buddy, Earnest, who had been a CO with me in my "former life" picked me up the next day.

Leaving the asylum caused a small stir because I walked out the front door untethered by handcuffs or shackles. Neither staff members nor residents had ever seen such a display of trust, and it probably hasn't happened since then. As soon as I arrived at Parchman, Earnest escorted me to the warden's office. The room was filled with friends and colleagues I had known for years. The last time I had seen the warden, he had been in college classes with me.

The first order of business was to decide where to put me. When most ex-guards are incarcerated, their lives are in danger as a result of being heavy-handed with prisoners who had no opportunity to fight back. When I was a CO, my job was pretty non-offensive to prisoners because I had one of the most dangerous positions in the institution. I was the CO who handed out mail and medications from behind a counter as the prisoners came in from the fields. I was the only CO in the room as almost 400 men divided up into the two dormitories where they showered and slept. My main strategy for self-preservation was giving people what they needed and keeping to myself.

There had been one night when I saw a prisoner go into the dorm area carrying a long metal pipe. I knew he had bad intentions, so I called for him to bring me the pipe. Of course the man ignored me and disappeared into the crowd. It was one of the few times I called security for assistance—this was before video cameras were installed to watch every angle of the compound. It wasn't long after I'd hung up the phone that two COs from security entered the room with a prisoner we called Herc (short for Hercules). He had earned that name on the fateful night when a highway patrol officer pulled Herc over for a traffic stop. After being hit with two or three bullets from a .357 Magnum, Herc took the .357 from the officer and beat him to death with his own weapon. Just like those old investment banker commercials used to say, "When Herc talks, people listen."

An instant quiet enveloped everyone as Herc entered the room. He stood in the front of the door where the pipe had last been seen and hollered, "I'm ready to fight. Send out that pipe or I will come get it!" Within minutes, not one, but two pipes were tossed out of the dorm. I never knew exactly what the prison staff did to get Herc on their side, but it was worth every penny. It's too bad he wasn't recruited before coming to prison.

The reason I had been taken directly to the Parchman warden's office was two-fold. My friends wanted to let me know they sympathized with my situation, but they also wanted to make a plan for my safety as a prisoner. I don't remember exactly what the plan was, but it worked.

The appeal process in my case was relatively quick. About two years after arriving at Parchman, I won the appeal of my jury trial. Rather than going through a second trial, I accepted a deal. In exchange for pleading guilty to manslaughter, I was granted immediate parole and told to leave the state. By that time, Earnest had become a parole officer (PO), and I reappeared in his life as his parolee. Not knowing how badly I had been and would be damaged by the effects of my conviction, Earnest told me to go on up to Memphis and have a good life. He never sent any paperwork to the parole office in Memphis. When I reported in Memphis, the parole department thought I was crazy (unlike the jury who had convicted me). Even though I was supposed to be on parole for several more years, I never reported again, and the people in Memphis never noticed.

I chose to live in Memphis with my wife and girls because that's where I had worked as an air traffic controller a few years earlier. Returning to Memphis with a felony conviction was an entirely different experience. My wife worked, but during that era women were still being paid a fraction of what men earned. I finally got a job as a bill collector. Although I was competent and became their top collector, the company fired me after three months when they learned of my felony.

To cover my anger and frustration with my new lot in life, I began medicating my emotions with copious doses of alcohol. Needing money to support my family, I started to apply a few of the skills I had learned from the "professionals" in prison. For the first time in my life, I started robbing stores. Not wanting to admit to myself how low I had sunk, I rationalized that this was the only way I could support my family. I opened a bank account, deposited the stolen money, and paid all our family's bills. I only committed armed robbery when the checking account got too low to pay all the bills. For a while, I believed the lie I was telling myself about the appropriateness of this behavior, but I knew deep down that it was wrong.

During that same time, I met a man in a bar, Al, who hooked me up with a job at a construction site. One of my main tasks was to keep up with the time sheets so people were paid correctly. After a few weeks I noticed there seemed to be two invisible employees. I did a little sleuthing and sure enough, two time sheets were being turned in each week for mystery men who never came to work. I went directly to the owner of the company and reported that he was being scammed. For my diligence, I was promptly fired. It was the boss who was padding the books.

When I wasn't working, I was drinking in those days. Since you can't just drink all the time, I would socialize with my bar peers and play a bit of shuffle board—a latent skill I had just discovered. Al also noticed my new talent and pressured me to run a hustle on the man who had just fired me. He was so insistent that we ended up coming to blows over my refusal to take this man's money through trickery. Hustling for free drinks was one thing, but doing it for revenge was not as fun for me. You would think I would have viewed hustling as a more acceptable way to earn money than robbing stores, but for some reason, it just didn't occur to me.

Al and I didn't disagree for long because I got busted for the armed robberies. The police booked me on three charges, but one of them had not been committed by me. Since they hadn't identified several other robberies as my "work," I didn't complain about the false one. Because the prosecutor knew about my Mississippi record, he asked that I be sentenced for three twenty-year terms rather than the three ten-year terms he could have offered. Believing it to be the best deal I could get, I pled guilty. Eleven months after getting out, I was off to prison once again.

Even though my three charges were to be run concurrently (all at the same time), I knew twenty years was too long to expect my wife to wait. I suggested that she divorce me, and she did. Gone was my beautiful support system, but it was my own fault. The prison I went to in 1981 was under construction and out of control. I was shocked the very first day when I saw one prisoner after another disobey and disrespect COs. I just knew a trail of cars would be transporting prisoners to the "orchard" that night, but nothing happened. Herman Davis, the warden at that time, was a hands-on fellow who believed in talking to prisoners face to face. Unfortunately, I mistook his gregarious nature for weakness.

With the prison under renovation, dump trucks entered and exited the prison at all hours of the day. It didn't take me long to identify their schedule and come up with a plan for escaping Fort Pillow. I hitched a ride out of prison by hiding under debris in a dump truck, and a few other guys did the same in other trucks. If a snitch hadn't revealed our actions, eight other prisoners would have left in the same manner. My plan for getting out was better than my plan for staying out, so I found myself having an unpleasant conversation with Warden Davis the very next day. My rewards for being an innovative escapee were ninety days in the hole, an assignment to working in the **long line**, and an extra year added to my sentence. Another consequence was that this could have waylaid me years later, when I was being considered for early release.

Later I got to see a side of Warden Davis that I really didn't like. Prison conditions were terrible, and politicians were continually being elected on the "get tough on crime" ticket. Public sentiment had been focused on the theory that people would not want to return to prison if conditions were bad enough, so the Tennessee Department of Corrections (TDOC) had been underfunded and encouraged to make life in prison as difficult as it could be. It is human nature that people can only be pushed so far, so one day the rubber band snapped. A crowd of prisoners started a sit-down strike. When the long line (composed of men with long prison sentences) was called to assemble, someone yelled out, "We're bucking!" and no one went to their designated areas to prepare for work. A CO continued to call out a few more times for the assigned workers to come forward, but was met with shouts of, "We're not going!"

Eventually, the prison gates were closed and the CO was silent. Along with the outside gates, doors which allowed prisoners to return to their cells were also locked—after men who had refused to go to work that morning were herded from their cells into the recreation area. The men on the **short line** (those with shorter sentences) who had gone into the fields before the strike started were called back into the prison and all prisoners with farming jobs were corralled into a small segment of the yard. Warden Davis fired into the air and told all of us to sit down. When we complied, a group of about forty armed guards in riot gear maneuvered us into a corner of the yard. They strung concertina wire around us to limit our movement.

To meet our sewage needs, we were provided buckets. At meal time, bags of sandwiches were lobbed over the fence. We never knew when COs would start firing above our heads or directly into our group. Some prisoners offered to return to their work in the fields, but Warden Davis declined their offer. Around the third day of being treated like barn yard animals, I witnessed a small group of men wave white flags and move the wire away from the wall. They were shot down by guards. Months later the result of the prison's "investigation" determined that these shootings were righteous because the prisoners were trying to escape. Those must have been some pretty dumb prisoners, trying to escape by moving deeper into the compound, toward guards, and away from the wall that confined them. After four days of living in this pressure-cooker situation, under the boiling summer sun, the protest was over. Life returned to "normal." Nothing had been resolved.

Two years after the sit-in, massive groups of men started a full-blown riot. Prisoners were attacking guards, stealing supplies, destroying property, and fighting among themselves. I later heard that the CO stationed in the library was beaten badly. He was the CO with the most demeaning attitude toward us residents. Prisoners were definitely not angels during this process, but all the captured guards were eventually released and walked out of the compound unaided. Considering the anger built up in some of those men as a result of terrible living conditions, I think it was just about a miracle that no lives were lost that day.

The next morning loud speakers began blaring orders for us to return to our cells. Some of the prisoners' demands had been met, and media coverage gave us hope that things would improve. Almost immediately, men dressed in riot gear walked into the prison and began billy-clubbing every prisoner within reach. As prisoners followed instructions and lay in the hallways of the cell block, they were treated with more hits, kicks, and verbal abuse. The entire prison was on **lock-down** for a long time, but things did get a little better.

The worst part of prison is the constant boredom, so when a fellow prisoner told me he was writing to a lady prisoner, I joined in. With so much in common, like criminal history and life in prison, I quickly developed a relationship of convenience with one particular woman. We weren't in love, but we knew our relationship could benefit both of us in different ways.

We were released from prison within three months of each other. Ms. E (E for Evil) finished her sentence and obtained an apartment in Nashville, so I had a good home and job plan to present when I was evaluated for parole. It didn't take long to realize that Ms. E was a selfish, compassionless, controlling, black-hearted sociopath—but she gave me everything I could ask for and more. In appearance I had a good job at a fertility clinic, but I never went to the office. On the two occasions when my PO called to check up on me, the receptionist, one of Ms. E's associates, reported that I had just stepped out. My PO accepted that as evidence that I was doing the right thing and never visited me at home or work.

Once a week Ms. E bought me an ounce of cocaine. Very talented at stealing credit cards, checks, cars, and anything else she wanted, Ms. E "provided" us with a lavish lifestyle. We had two Lincoln Continentals and several other cars, Rolex watches, and the best of everything our hearts desired. Ms. E and I still didn't really love each other, but she didn't want to live alone, and I didn't want to live in poverty. I especially enjoyed the week when my children came to visit. I was able to say "yes" to their every request without worrying about running out of money.

About nine months into my parole, one of Ms. E's "friends" reported her to the police. We just barely escaped. Shortly after hitting the highway in Tennessee, we heard a news report on the radio that the police had discovered a huge crime hub which included the perpetrators of a credit card ring, a car theft ring, a check fraud ring, and more. Back then, it took six hours to get a search warrant from a judge, so we thought it odd that these discoveries had been made within an hour of us vacating the premises. This fact later allowed Ms. E to appeal her conviction and prevail. The same strategy did not work on my appeal with the same court. With the help of our drug dealer, we got a ride to Alabama where we stole a car. Reaching Atlanta, Ms. E bought an $11,000 Rolex watch for me—as if I needed another one.

I'm not sure where we intended to land, but we were eventually caught in Greenville, Mississippi. I remember being uncomfortable when I was first placed in a cell with thirteen other men and seeing that I was the only white man in the room. Before long the officer came to the cell and said there were warrants out for my arrest in four states and two Secret Service agents waited for me in the conference room. While I hadn't broken any federal laws, the number of credit cards found in our stolen car caused concern regarding national commerce. After our interview, the Secret Service agents left, but my newfound celebrity status with the men in the cell remained until I was extradited back to Tennessee. Mississippi ended up dropping their charges against me in exchange for my new Rolex and the cash and car we had stolen along the way.

Once extradited to Tennessee, I spent two years in a county jail before going to trial for armed robbery. After I jumped that hoop and was back in prison, the parole board held a revocation hearing. Obviously, I wasn't going to be on parole anymore, but they had to make it official. My PO approached me and said she was mystified as to why I would return to a life of crime when I had such a good job in the medical field. I didn't tell her my job was a ruse, so I wonder if she's figured it out yet. When all the lawyers, prosecutors, detectives, and judges were finished talking, I was classified as a **habitual criminal** and given a life sentence—just ten months after leaving Fort Pillow.

A bit of mercy was shown to me in the final combining of my

sentences. Mississippi agreed to parole the original sentence I had with them to the TDOC, and eventually I would have a chance at parole. While waiting for that time, I stayed out of trouble for the most part. By December of 2000, I had worked my way up to becoming the senior counselor aide on the compound. That didn't make me a **trusty shooter** (that practice was abolished by the '80s and never was used in Tennessee), but it did make me the man trusted with ballots when prisoners were asked to vote on particular issues. When the prison installed cable, one issue that came up was which television channels would be broadcast. Why would the prisoners get to vote on this issue? Because they all chipped in to purchase the service and paid for their own televisions.

Still a pretty selfish fellow, I got the two other counselor aides, who each managed five other units, to work with me in rigging the vote. We took the ballots back to our cells and started changing the votes to fit the channels we had agreed to. The unit manager, my boss, walked by and noticed my altering of the ballots. She immediately fired me from my job, moved me out of her unit, and had me sent to solitary confinement. Remembering how tedious the hole is, I grabbed a Bible on my way. It was the only reading material allowed until my release back into the general population.

By the time I got to the hole, I was really upset with myself for throwing away the trust I had built up with the other inmates in my unit. When I emerged from the hole, I had gone from being the top dog to a fifty-three-year-old nobody. I started reading, mostly because there was nothing else to do in the hole, and for the first time I noticed messages in the Bible that related directly to my life. The more I read, the more excited I became. That very night I decided to change my entire approach to life by dedicating my life to God and following the teachings of Jesus. I had a long way to go, but from that night forward, I knew I was accepted and loved by my creator. I also knew that I would be getting out of prison, legally. While I didn't know how it would happen, I knew in my soul that it would.

After being released from the hole, I went directly to the unit manager who had put me there. I'm sure she was expecting a problem from me because she was shocked when I told her I loved her and thanked her for putting me in the hole. That was probably a first for both of us. One year later, eight years before my **RED** (release eligibility date), I was actually released from prison. Although my escape from Fort Pillow disqualified me, I was released as a result of a **safety valve** ruling. Those rulings are tools for the executive branch of the state to allow prisoners who meet certain criteria to leave early when the prisons are overcrowded. In my view, they are tools God uses when He has other plans for a person who has accepted his love and authority.

Even though I've now been out of prison for thirteen years, I can't fix the damage to my family. There is no way to make up for missing my daughters' childhoods. It's my belief that my brother suffered some pretty harsh consequences as a result of my crimes. My infamy was used against him when he got caught up in a banking scandal masterminded by some big fish in Tennessee. Now he too has a felony conviction. One of the deepest regrets I have is knowing that I wasn't there when my mother, father, and sister needed me the most—when they were dying.

One of the many ways I get to give back is by writing letters for men who are eligible for parole. I'm always afraid someone in the parole hearing will recognize me as a parolee and think badly about the person I am trying to support. This concern keeps me from actually attending parole hearings, but I hope that the letters I write for men who have sincerely redeemed themselves will aid in their freedom. I remember years ago when I would look out my cell window during shift change and wonder how it felt to come into a prison and leave at the end of the day. Now I know. It feels *wonderful*, and I hope to share that feeling with many more men and women who are preparing to become contributing members of society.

The good news about my newfound faith, which I've been practicing for the last fifteen years, is that I no longer dwell on negative events, such as missing my parents' funerals. Married to my third wife, a gift from God, we have seven grown children and twelve grandchildren. I do everything I can to support them all and build positive, loving relationships with our grandchildren. When I am not working, I now spend time going back into the very same prison that released me in 2002 to share my truth with the men there. My main message is that God truly blesses those who serve Him; my life is proof of that.

Commentary on Terry's Story

Even though Terry sees himself as winning by the end of his story, his family's suffering could have been reduced if the legal system had focused on justice more than politics. In Mississippi, making an insanity plea required the defendant, Terry, prove he was "laboring under such a defect of reason, from disease of the mind, as not to know the nature and quality of the act he was doing" or, prove that he didn't know what he was doing was wrong."[284] Sanity is assumed in all people unless *the defendant* proves otherwise. Admission of guilt is implied, so it is a tricky defense that rarely benefits the defendant.

The insanity plea was invented by a crafty team of men defending a U.S. congressman. Senator Sickles had publically displayed his mistress, a known prostitute and owner of a bordello, before and after marrying his sixteen-year-old pregnant bride, Teresa Bagioli, when he was thirty-three. On February 27, 1859, the day after Teresa confessed to having an affair with Philip Barton Key II, the son of Francis Scott Key (author of "The Star-Spangled Banner"), Senator Sickles shot and killed Mr. Key in broad daylight and in the presence of several witnesses.

Mr. Sickles' defense team argued that he had become temporarily insane with shame and horror when he learned that his wife of eight years had taken a lover. The local media of the day pronounced the senator a hero for saving the ladies of Washington, D.C., from Mr. Key's roguish activities. The jury agreed that Senator Sickles was not responsible for his actions and acquitted him of first-degree murder.[285] Even though that case set the precedent for an insanity defense, we see a much higher bar was set for Terry's defense.

Because Terry was so successful at working difficult jobs while going to school and raising a family, the prosecutor maintained that his insanity plea couldn't be valid and instead presented him as a cold-blooded, calculating killer.[286] We acknowledge the death of the young man found in Terry's house that night is tragic. It is not our desire to criticize or minimize Mr. Calhoun's life. His alleged rape of Terry's wife did not warrant his murder. It is our desire to hold his life as sacred while acknowledging that few men would have contained themselves if they believed they had come upon a home invader who had raped their wife.

Only Mr. Calhoun, Terry, and Terry's ex-wife know exactly what happened that night, but it seems unreasonable to place Terry in the same category as a person who spent time and resources planning a murder prior to executing it. If Terry had been a U.S. senator at the time he discovered his wife had been raped, we suspect Terry would have been found innocent and his criminal record would be clean today. Eventually, the Mississippi Court of Appeals agreed that Terry had not committed first-degree murder. They reduced the level of his offense, and Terry was immediately paroled. By that time, tremendous damage had been done to Terry's personality, social standing, and career options.

According to the U.S. Department of Justice, the purpose of parole is three-fold: 1) assist returning citizens with residence, employment, finances, and personal problems; 2) protect society and reduce the probability of recidivism by helping establish stability for returning citizens, and 3) prevent needless imprisonment of individuals who have a low probability of reoffending.[287] In Tennessee the BOPP states its mission is "to minimize public risk and promote lawful behavior by the prudent, orderly release of adult offenders."[288] There is another motivation: to encourage positive behavior of eligible prisoners. Men and women who know they will meet the parole board within the next twelve to thirty-six months make extra efforts to stay out of situations that could jeopardize their pending parole.

We know the Tennessee BOPP takes these goals seriously. The 2012–2013 BOPP Annual Report states that over 17,000 parole hearings were conducted in Terry's state, and less than 5,000, or 29 percent, of the eligible inmates were seen as appropriate for parole.[289] Prior to a prisoner being released on parole, they are supposed to have a place of residence and be hired for a job (unless exempt due to disability or age) approved by the BOPP. Policy states that officials from the parole office will physically visit the home (with the exception of approved halfway houses) identified by a prisoner to ensure it is an appropriate setting.[290] This step is very important. A recent California study showed a 42 percent increase in parole success when parolees live in homes or facilities that are within two miles of the services needed by parolees.[291] If the principles in this study are applicable nationwide, there could be forty-two fewer victims for every 100 parolees just by having services close to returning citizens' residences.

Without the benefit of any job or housing assistance from his first PO,

Terry's initial experience with parole may have contributed to his demise and the creation of several victims in Memphis. Had his Mississippi friend/PO notified the Memphis parole office of Terry's presence, a home visit would have been required and, ideally, he would have been given assistance regarding a job. Through a PO's recommendation, he also might have received some much needed anger management and help with finishing his last semester of college. Years later, when Terry was on parole in Nashville, his interaction with his PO was not much more than it had been in Memphis, and the agency did not accomplish its mission.

Yet, as we saw in Bob's story, being a PO is difficult. With the ratio of parolees to POs as high as 110 to 1, even though the goal is 75 to 1 or less, it is nearly impossible for officers to perform regular home checks, face-to-face meetings, and employment confirmations, along with monitoring fee payments and arrest records. They have to cut corners somewhere, so time-consuming home visits are easy to skip. Needless to say, they have no time left over for assisting returning citizens in locating positive employment and housing.

Upon Terry's first arrival to prison in Mississippi, his placement was a serious concern for prison staff. We have seen that when riots occur in prison, it is often the cruelest COs who receive the most abuse, but because of the inhumane treatment of prisoners, all COs, current and former, are vulnerable during any interaction with prisoners. Since Terry had not been a cruel guard, those who put him in the greatest danger were the prisoners he befriended. A citizens' committee established by the Tennessee commissioner of institutions in 1937 found that state prisons were "giving a post graduate course in crime . . ."[292] and the same held true for Terry in Mississippi.

"Classifications" is the department in each prison that decides where newly incarcerated prisoners will live. As Renegade told us in Chapter 12, the objective of classifications is to group prisoners with similar levels of criminal histories and needs so that less violent prisoners do not become prey to more brutal detainees. One year prior to the disturbance Terry described at Fort Pillow, a class action lawsuit against the TDOC proclaimed that the widespread, consistent, inappropriate grouping of prisoners constituted a violation of the Eighth Amendment. According to the judges, the practice of giving new prisoners the security rating of medium (due to lack of the TDOC having their criminal records when they arrived), and then assigning them to cells based on availability of space rather than security level, caused new prisoners excessive psychological deterioration. Having novice, non-violent prisoners become cell partners with experienced violent prisoners created an environment of violence and terror.[293]

This situation was exacerbated by the fact that all prisons in Tennessee (and throughout the South) were severely overcrowded and in such disrepair that conditions were identified as cruel and unusual punishment.[294] Sewage and water pipes not only leaked severely but connected with each other, creating unsanitary conditions. Medical services were severely underfunded and misappropriated, partly because the TDOC believed they did not need to meet the same standards as medical facilities in the **freeworld**. Fire safety, ventilation, and lighting were so deficient that they were considered a danger to life and limb and violations of the Eighth Amendment.

While many people who have fallen in step with the originators of felonism claim that prison life is too easy, Terry's story is just one example of how cruel conditions inside prison yield more victims and increase crime rates outside prisons (the many people from whom he later stole). Dehumanizing people in hopes that they will learn to conform socially is backward thinking. Men and women who leave such humiliating circumstances often see themselves as having been treated unfairly and therefore feel justified in seeking revenge.

At the time of his first arrest, Terry was a war veteran, college student, and hardworking family man. Admittedly, he took revenge upon the man he found in his house who had allegedly raped his wife. If society had chosen to provide Terry with healing instead of more revenge, untold good could have been accomplished. If this dysfunctional pattern of abuse can distort the thoughts and actions of men such as Terry, what logic is there for clinging to abusive institutions as our primary approach to crime prevention?

Chapter 17

Felonism: What Can We Do?

"In the flush of love's light
we dare be brave
and suddenly we see
that love costs all we are
and will ever be,
yet it is only love
which sets us free

—Maya Angelou

Why We Must Act Now

"**M**onster" is the name we used to identify felonism at the beginning of this book. Now you can see why. It is difficult to know exactly how many people in our society have received felony convictions. In 2013, Bruce Reilly, an activist for returning citizens, wrote a report entitled "Communities, Evictions, and Criminal Convictions" for the Formerly Incarcerated and Convicted Peoples Movement. According to his report, over sixty-five million Americans were eligible to join the aforementioned organization.[295] Assuming each current and previously incarcerated person has two loved ones or family members (that is a very low estimate), over 195 million Americans are directly affected by this invisible force that is degrading and weakening our country. That's over 60 percent of our population! If only 10 percent of people directly touched by felonism have plans to retaliate for being mistreated in a prejudicial manner, we are still sitting on a powder keg simmering just under the surface of America's social structure.

Now that we have identified felonism as systemic oppression, it is time to act before this cancer cannibalizes our nation. Consider what would have happened to America sixty years ago if all white people had insisted on a continuation of institutional, racial oppression and segregation. Between the years 1960 and 2000, over 220 protests and riots took place across our land.[296] Imagine how much more violent and prolific those actions would have been if legislators had tried to maintain the status quo rather than initiate the application of the Constitution to minorities. Would not violence from Black citizens have been justified if our leaders had continued to enforce segregation laws and "separate but equal" policies?

Today we are chasing the same goals articulated by Dr. Martin Luther King Jr. and others. America must pick up where the civil rights movement has stalled. We must continue until every person in America is treated with respect and equality because that is what our Constitution says. The principle of equality gave birth to this great nation. How can we consider America a legitimate government if we do not act to achieve the freedom and equality on which it was founded?

Simple but Difficult

What do we do first? Recognize the problem and affirm our belief that it can be fixed. Thom Rutledge, one of our favorite psychotherapists, likes to tell his clients something like this, "The solution to overcoming your problem is simple but difficult." We believe that statement is also true for eliminating felonism. Granting equal status to every person we encounter, regardless of their criminal status or their closeness with people who have criminal convictions, is a simple concept. Fear makes this a difficult task, especially fear generated by those who want to increase their power and control by oppressing others.

Identifying the intentional and unintentional creators of felonism is just the beginning. We cannot change felonists, for people have to change themselves. What we can change is our reaction to felonists, thus reducing their power. Like turning on the light after hearing a scary sound in the night, exposing felonism allows us to defend ourselves with much less effort and greater efficiency. Now that we have a name for felonism, it will be much simpler to see.

As a social worker, Linda (co-author) learned that people rarely change without going through certain steps. Researchers have various names for each step, but we like to use the term "precontemplation" to identify the first stage.[297] In this stage we are clueless regarding our need for change, and unfortunately, just like alcoholics who tell themselves, "I can quit any time I want to," mainstream Americans has been oblivious to the presence of felonism and the destruction it creates in our nation.

From our own history we know it takes a great deal of emotional and physical suffering to awaken from the precontemplation stage of change. The genocide of the indigenous people was almost complete before America woke up to the fact that the Native Americans of this land are human beings equal to the immigrants (white folks) who invaded their territory. A century later, it took the public viewing of Emmett Till's desecrated body, the broadcasting of the Montgomery Bus Boycott, and nightly news reports of the vicious police attacks upon peaceful protesters for our nation to admit changes had to be made. As we have said, acts by the Abusers of Power, who needed to solidify support from the masses to maintain their power and status, are what caused our nation to remain in the precontemplation stages of bigotry for hundreds of years (and what keeps some individuals and organizations trapped there today).

The contemplation, or second stage of change, begins when people ask themselves whether change is possible. It's when they become honest with themselves about the degraded state of mind and/or body they have descended into. This stage is usually much shorter than the first because it is born from pain. People are kicked into the contemplation stage when their spouses or children leave, when they are arrested for their harmful behaviors, or when they just have too much truth in their environments to continue lying to themselves. Hopefully, becoming aware of felonism's corrosive effects, and understanding that millions of Americans are being played as pawns by felonists, will be enough to move our nation into the next, contemplation, stage.

If you were old enough to watch television in the 1960s, you may have witnessed Dr. King's famous proclamation of his dream that Black and white children would one day be able to play and hold hands together without fear of punishment. That speech brought America to the contemplation stage, a place where we began collectively imagining change. Many people, especially in the South, predicted Dr. King's dream would never be realized, but in many ways, it has been. Although countless aspects of racism have morphed into felonism, we believe progress can be made, for we already see it happening. Some pockets of our country have already moved on to stage three, determination (where we make a plan and commit to changing), and quickly slipped into stage four, action.[298]

The police department in East Haven, Connecticut, recently demonstrated these advanced stages of change in a tangible way. In 2012, violence against Latino citizens had become commonplace. Just as in Ferguson, Missouri, this segment of the population was regularly stopped for minor traffic violations, subjected to aggressive confrontations, and endured excessive force from the police. Father James Manship was arrested for filming these events, and that led to an investigation by the U.S. Justice Department. As a result, huge changes were implemented. The changes were not easy, but they were simple. Members of the police department who insisted on remaining in the precontemplative stage had to go, but the ones that stayed developed personal relationships with Latinos in their community.[299] The compliance report submitted by the East Haven Police Department in 2015 states the rate of traffic stops of Latino drivers (12.1 percent) is now much closer to the Latino population (10.3 percent) in that community.[300] This ratio reflects a huge improvement in just three years.

Another place where action is being taken against felonism is the courtroom of Judge Seth Norman, a Tennessee criminal court judge. From our observations, Judge Norman is proof that change is possible. He looks at each person standing before him as a worthwhile human being. From his bench, we have heard Judge Norman refuse to accept a prosecutor's erroneous statement that "the police don't lie on their arrest reports." He has refused to incarcerate parolees whose only offense was not paying their monthly fees when they were unemployed. But Judge Norman's crowning achievement, which defies the felonistic attitude of many judges, is his creation of our nation's first long-term residential drug treatment program.[301]

Without coddling or enabling, Judge Norman has given thousands of the defendants in his court an opportunity to overcome addiction and make amends for the harm they have caused others, which assists them in becoming contributing members of society. Not only has his program saved millions of tax dollars, it has generated money through the successful employment of people who had been doomed to become wards of the state via prison. The thing we really love about Judge Norman's lack of felonism in his rulings is that, as far as we know, Judge Norman has no agenda to get his own television show or to sell lots of books. He doesn't do this for attention; he just loves people and wants to see them succeed—even if they have made some very bad choices in the past.

Judge Norman is not alone. Due to lower crime rates and financial difficulties, prisons in small towns all over America have been shut down, forcing the communities that depended on prison jobs as their financial underpinning to reinvent themselves. In a September 2015 article by the online magazine *Next City*, Anna Clark reported on several towns who are taking action to overcome the negative psychological effects prisons had in their communities. Towns in Michigan, New York, and North Carolina are transforming and finding positive ways to maintain their income while focusing on healing.[302]

We also see groups emerging into the contemplation, determination, and action phases of change on a large scale. Supporting our contention that not all wealthy people are felonists, Target, Home Depot, and Wal-Mart have instituted policies eliminating the "Have you ever been convicted of a felony?" box on their job applications.[303] The Koch brothers, who employ 60,000 Americans, recently implemented "fair chance hiring." That is the practice of not asking about criminal history in the initial stages of the hiring processes and employing returning citizens when they meet job descriptions.[304] According to the same *USA Today* report, thirteen states have instituted policies that "ban the box" on job applications for all state positions, and six states prohibit "the box" for private companies with state contracts.[305] In hopes of making this a national trend, President Obama signed an executive action to ban the box for all federal jobs. He reasons that the 70 million citizens with felony convictions should be given a chance to prove they are qualified for a position rather than being turned away without an interview.[306] Considering that there are over four million federal employees,[307] this action is significant, but we believe it will have a much greater impact on reducing felonism when Congress joins the trend and requires all businesses with federal contracts to ban the box. These actions represent a reversal in systemic felonism that can springboard America into the last step, change. When that happens, the employment of returning citizens will feel normal to our society. Getting to know an applicant before deciding their eligibility for a position is a simple process, but we understand it will be difficult for many companies to initiate. Please do it anyway. We look forward to the day when our grandchildren wonder aloud about why the employment of returning citizens was ever an issue.

A Mental Health Approach

You might think, "Hiring some ex-felons could be a good thing. Providing treatment instead of punishment for some addicts may be good policy, but what about hardened criminals? What about the people Renegade mentioned who will take advantage of you if you are nice to them?" Most certainly some men and women leave prison with the intention of creating more victims. However, it has been our experience that such people are in the minority when prisoners have the choice between living as contributing citizens with a sustainable income or as criminals. Before focusing on the role prisoners and returning citizens can play in reducing felonism, let's make this personal.

Imagine you hear a radio report that someone is holding hostages inside your local bank. Your initial thought might be to hope snipers will shoot the scoundrel's head off before innocent hostages are harmed. Then the police call and ask you to come to the bank. The person holding the gun is actually your spouse (or some other family member), whom you love very much. While you still don't want harm to come to the hostages, you now want a non-violent resolution. Whether your loved one's actions originated in mental illness, greed, or a severe lapse in judgment, wouldn't you plead with the police to refrain from violence if possible? Wouldn't you request assistance from a mental health expert to find out why your spouse had committed such a desperate act? Wouldn't you want to be part of a system where you were included in finding an immediate yet long-lasting, non-violent solution to this terrible scenario? When felonism is no longer a systemic part of our culture, family members, police, mental health professionals, and people who commit crimes will be able to focus on restoring our broken community rather than guaranteeing further alienation and social decay.

In the above example, your loved one would probably receive the harshest punishment possible unless you are rich, powerful, or well connected. Concern for you and your family would not be taken into consideration, especially if the media followed each step of the process. Your victimhood would not be recognized, and your right to maintain a relationship with your spouse would be severely limited.

Does it really have to be that way? How terrible would it be if your spouse were seen by a mental health specialist as soon as the gun was removed from their hand? Instead of being hit by a mountain of legal books, what if the prosecutor figuratively threw the DSM-5 at your loved one? In case some readers aren't familiar with this perfect bedtime read (it is famous for putting psychology students to sleep), the *Diagnostic and Statistical Manual of Mental Disorders V* is the book used to identify all known mental health ailments. Sure, some criminal acts are unrelated to mental disorders, but many more are caused by mental deterioration. Shouldn't people committing illegal acts as a result of a posttraumatic stress disorder, for example, receive different consequences from those who steal because it's easy or attack others because it's fun to them? With felonists in charge, meeting the needs and special conditions of suspects and their families is rare.

A Physical Health Approach

Did you know some behaviors interpreted as criminal are actually the result of physical ailments, such as brain tumors? In *The Ethical Brain*, Michael Gazzaniga discusses the case of a man who, out of the blue, began to have frequent and inappropriate sexual thoughts, even toward young girls.[308] After performing a magnetic resonance imaging (MRI) scan, a neurologist discovered a tumor pushing on the part of the brain that manages self-control. This unnamed Virginia educator did inappropriately touch a child before his tumor was discovered and removed, but this perverse act was the result of a medical condition he had no control over. What would years of incarceration and adding his name to the Sex Offender Registry accomplish (other than following up one awful event with another)? Should he be considered for a lifetime civil commitment? If felonists have their way, he will. He committed a crime, so they reason, "He must do the time." Since a physical evaluation is not a part of the booking process in America, we will never know how many crimes have been committed as the result of brain tumors or other physical disorders.

While certain medical ailments have the ability to negatively distort reasoning and behavior, we have not found a focus on medical explanations or solutions for criminal behaviors. Some scientists have been studying neurological differences in people with violent and anti-social tendencies. MRI studies have shown a structural difference in the brains of prisoners described as cold-hearted psychopaths.[309] While we never want to see a return to the days when lobotomies were administered to resistant or incapacitated individuals to treat mental illness or aggression,[310] ruling out medical treatment and opting for lifetime imprisonment over medical treatment is a cruel choice. Considering the rapid developments being made in neuroscience, we believe voluntary medical treatment will be a viable option over incarceration in the near future if felonists don't convince the masses that punishment is preferable to healing.

A Social Health Approach

Along with heeding physiological contributors to crime, it is important we recognize that the line between victim and perpetrator is often blurred. Andy (co-author) helped a man called Hopper while he was in prison. Hopper was old and confined to a wheelchair. In his younger days he was an upper middle-class entrepreneur with a beautiful family. His financier, who was also his brother-in-law, stole his inheritance, which was intended to send Hopper's daughter to college. In Hopper's mind, his brother-in-law had manipulated the bankers, community leaders, and his sister into believing Hopper was wrong. Having hired the better lawyer, his brother-in-law won the civil suit and, as Hopper saw it, stole his daughter's inheritance. That day, Hopper told his smiling brother-in-law, "That court decision is your death warrant." If only Hopper's community had embraced him and said, "Let's talk this out and find a resolution that both of you can live with," the outcome would have been different for all concerned.

Andy (co-author) once asked a fellow prisoner, Ed, why he'd killed his best friend and driven around town for days with the man's head in his car. Initially, Ed replied, "Do you think I'm fucking crazy? I had a reason!" After gaining his trust, Ed eventually told Andy the whole story. His victim, we'll call him Max, informed Ed that he was moving out of town. Max was the only person Ed enjoyed being around and drinking with on a daily basis. Max was Ed's only friend. When Ed realized he was unable to convince Max to stay close by, he began telling Max and others at the bar he would kill Max to keep him around. Ed said he had two intentions when he made this announcement: he wanted Max to see how serious he was, and he wanted someone to stop him.

Ed is just one example of hundreds of people who see themselves having to choose between being happy and harming others. It is possible to help such individuals before they make their moves, but only if they are able to seek refuge in emotionally and physically secure environments. Before killing Max, Ed was willing to accept support, but it never came. "If only someone had called the police," you might think, "would that have helped?" It may have helped Max escape, but it probably would not have resulted in support and healing for Ed under our current felonistic mindset.

Ed could easily be the poster child for our proposal that prisons be turned into healing centers. Max can't be helped now, but how many people would be saved if people like Ed were supported? Ed's crime might have been prevented if our nation had practiced a history of healing and learning from past prisoners instead of seeking revenge. What changes could be made to save others simply by talking to people like Ed and discovering how their thought patterns became so skewed? If such facilities had been in place years ago, maybe Max would be alive today, and Ed would have been learned coping techniques other than alcohol for dealing with loss and developing new friendships.

As with Hopper and Ed, criminal behavior often occurs as the result of a person, or group, losing faith in their community or circumstances. Initially, Hopper was a victim, and his community (local law-enforcement officials, judges, and mental health facilities) refused to help him. Then Hopper became the "offender." This pattern of victims becoming offenders is common and will continue until restorative practices become the focus of our "justice" system.

Restorative Practice: A Practical Solution

Under our current judicial system, opportunities for forgiveness, reconciliation, and healing are almost non-existent. We do not mean to belittle the counseling and restitution provided in some areas, but they are not the norm. It is important to point out that most victims never get to ask their oppressors, "Why me?" Victims often wonder about the reason for their victimization. Was it personal? Could they have prevented the crime? Can they prevent a reoccurrence? Even if victims have no desire to forgive, understanding the events that led up to the crimes against them and having the option to ask questions is important for healing.

It is not unusual for victims to transform into perpetrators, as Hopper did, resulting in a community's downward spiral. The common law that guides our criminal "justice" system twists the roles of victims and offenders as soon as police and prosecutors become involved. The state, as represented by the prosecuting attorney, becomes the victim. This practice recognizes the idea that an offense against one is an offense against all. While agreeing with that premise, we believe the practice in its current form causes problems for everyone involved.

The real victim loses a seat at the table when offenses are being identified and consequences are being decided regarding the offender. Victims are allowed some input in some phases of the process, but legally, the government's opinion about how to seek revenge, punishment, restitution, or reconciliation trump those of the victim. The original victim is only allowed to answer specific questions (if called as a witness) and make a statement to the accused during the sentencing part of a trial—in the three percent of cases where there is a trial. During a plea bargaining situation, victims' wishes are often considered regarding the severity of the punishment, but their wishes do not have to be honored.

Historically, victims have been so neglected by the legal system that there are now non-profit groups designed to assist victims in reclaiming their power.[311] We are thrilled to see victims of crime uniting to receive support. Such groups may prevent victims from turning into future offenders. If these groups can remain focused on healing and refrain from adopting felonistic behaviors as a means of achieving feelings of vindication or security, their potential for making our nation a safer place is limitless.

In most courts, no built-in system for mediation exists for cases in which the victim instigates the conflict. One famous example played out when Lorena Bobbitt's ex-husband, John Wayne Bobbitt, could not admit to beating and raping her before she cut off his penis.[312] Because victims cannot admit to their wrong without risking arrest, healing of the relationship is not considered an option by the prosecutor. The person first offended/abused becomes cast as the sole perpetrator, and is doubly offended when they are assigned all the responsibility and punishment for the conflict they did not initiate. (Note: in the Bobbitt case neither party received criminal convictions for their offenses[313]).

Using old common law to assign victim status to the judicial system also creates problems for prosecutors. First of all, it removes their objectivity. By design, their focus cannot be on repairing relationships, as it should be. Prosecutors are expected to be single-minded in their pursuit to make sure someone pays for a wrong that was committed against them (in principle). We believe this greatly contributes to the massive trend of prosecutorial misconduct we discussed in Chapter 13. Because their competencies are judged solely on the number of convictions they achieve, and because felonism is such an ingrained part of the judicial system, prosecutors determined to restore relationships rather than find punitive conclusions to a crime would probably be terminated if they made their mission known to peers.

To overcome felonism in our judicial organizations, we propose that all "justice" systems employ Restorative Practices as the first and foremost remedy to crime. While incarceration will still be necessary in some cases, everyone loses when Restorative Practices are not employed.

Assuming most Americans have never heard of this process, we want to present a brief history. In 1974 a Canadian probation officer, Mark Yantzi, was assigned to work with two troubled teens who had vandalized twenty-two properties while on a drunken spree. Mr. Yantzi took the two boys to each home and had them admit their dastardly deeds, apologize, and listen to each homeowner describe what they wanted to have happen to the two boys. When those meetings were complete, it was determined that each teen would pay $550, with money *they* had to earn, to cover the damages not covered by the homeowners' insurance. Along with eighteen months of probation, they each paid a $200 fine and went on with their lives. Mr. Yantzi's plan was so successful in changing the lives of these two teens that he had trouble finding them twenty-five years later when he wanted to include them in a celebration of the program's anniversary. Unlike most juveniles who get caught up in the legal system, these men decided to become contributing members of society.[314]

From that creative intervention, Mr. Yantzi founded Community Justice Initiatives (CJI), a nonprofit organization. CJI's programs are now implemented in eighty countries around the world. In the US, the program is called International Institute for Restorative Practices (IIRP), and their headquarters is in Pennsylvania. IIRP's goal is to restore relationships that have been harmed as the result of an offense, regardless of the severity or nature of the offense. Rather than doing things "for" a victim or "to" a perpetrator, people following the IIRP model act *with* those involved to accomplish healing for everyone.

Even though the Restorative Practices process is simple, and can be implemented by just about anyone, the IIRP provides a master's degree program for serious practitioners.

One Restorative Practices method that has been effective in criminal cases—even murder cases—has been active in Australia. Police Officer Terry O'Connell begins with having the victim and offender sit in a circle. Each person in the conflict has supporters sitting next to them. Without commenting too often in between, Mr. O'Connell asks the following questions of the offender:

"What happened?"

"What were you thinking about at the time?"

"What have you thought about since the incident?"

"Who do you think has been affected by your actions?"

"How have they been affected?"

These questions are asked in a non-shaming manner so the offender's defensiveness does not overpower the process. Once those questions are answered, Mr. O'Connell asks the victim:

"What was your reaction at the time of the incident?"

"How do you feel about what happened?"

"What has been the hardest thing for you?"

"How did your family and friends react when they heard about the incident?"

His final question asks what the victim would like to see happen as the result of the conference. That response is discussed by the offender and other conference members. The final stage of the conference often results in the formation of a simple contract that is signed by the victim and offender.[315] For cases that could be too emotionally devastating if victims were in the same room as the offender, such as parents confronting the person who murdered their child, Mr. O'Connell has seen wonderful healing occur after victims go through this process with offenders who hurt someone unknown to the victim.

Even in cases where damages cannot be repaired, such as when a person has lost a limb or someone has been killed, meaningful consequences can still be applied. In these severe cases, a great deal of preparation is put into helping each party understand that healing for all concerned is the goal of the meeting. Although these meetings sound simple, they are difficult, but more importantly, they are effective in restoring relationships and reducing future offenses.

At the University of Pennsylvania, Caroline Angel studied the effects of Restorative Practices among robbery victims who acquired posttraumatic stress disorder as a result of being offended, and those who had stolen from them. Her findings indicated a reduction in PTSD symptoms for victims. Six months after Restorative Practice conferences were conducted, participants' symptoms continued to improve. Victims who participated in the study but did not participate in conferences continued to experience mental stress with the questions of, "Why did this happen to me?" continually running through their minds.[316]

One of many successful applications of Restorative Practices in public schools was demonstrated during the 2012–2013 school year in Colorado Springs, Colorado. Ms. Mary Lewis, the assistant director of Student Discipline services, reported a 38 percent decrease in expulsions during one school year even though they had previously led the state in expulsions.[317] As you may know, expelling students from school is the most severe punishment that can be implemented and is usually reserved for offenses related to violence or drug possession on school property.

In 2005, Denver schools reported a reduction in suspensions from about 16,000 per year to 6,400 after one year of implementing Restorative Practices. At the same time, their expulsion rate reduced from about 250 per year to 67.[318] School districts in Loudon, Virginia; Oakland, California; and other cities have experienced similar success.[319] Restorative Practices have a proven track record not only of reducing crime but also of healing victims, strengthening communities, and significantly reducing the probability of recidivism.[320]

If you have doubts about the effectiveness of this process, we strongly urge you to read the full text at *http://is.gd/rB6T9v* where a former police officer, Mr. O'Connell—mentioned above—gives detailed accounts of his success in working with men convicted of murder. Considering the success of Restorative Practices, if the goal of our criminal "justice" system is to prevent repeat offenses and help heal victims, why would we use any other method for addressing criminal acts?

Economic and Governmental Remedies

Institutional prejudice, which greatly benefits a minority while crippling the majority, has been an American tradition since Europeans first sailed upon the American continent. In recent history, the civil rights movement put a dent in that tradition. Many people have turned away from the racist teachings of their childhoods, allowing themselves to participate in relationships with those they were taught to hate. Although we still have a long way to go, society as a whole has grown and advanced in *many* ways as a direct result of the civil rights movement. Today, felonism threatens this progress by eroding the civil rights of all citizens. It is our hope that every American will turn away from this growing trend and accept all people as equals. It is the only way we can continue to grow.

There is nothing wrong with being rich or powerful. In this world, having leaders and followers is natural and cannot be avoided. When given an even playing field, the healthy distribution of power and wealth will imitate the pattern of a bell-shaped curve.[321] What skews this pattern is how the people at either extreme of the curve land in those positions. Did those living in extreme poverty, on the left side—very low income—of the bell, get there by any method other than natural occurrences (lack of ability or desire to get an education, inability to earn a living due to birth defects, mental illness, accidents, etc.)? Did the wealthy reach the far right side of the bell by following natural inclinations guided by a compass of integrity, or did they choose to be Abusers of Power, manipulating government policies and convincing those in the middle class to oppress an identified minority?

We believe felonism is responsible for the skewing of the bell curve over the last forty years. In their 1994 book, *The Bell Curve: Intelligence and Class Structure in American Life*, Robert Herrnstein and Charles Murray correctly identify which populations are at the top and bottom of the economic curves, but they miss the main reasons for the disparity between these groups. While cognitive intelligence and environment do contribute significantly to an individual's ability to earn and accumulate wealth, institutional racism, classism, sexism, and felonism have been key components in debilitating the oppressed and multiplying the income of the rich. We predict that when mainstream Americans educate themselves, realize they do not have to sacrifice their tax dollars, nor civil rights, to be protected from given populations, and extradite themselves from their position of servitude to Abusers of Power, the distribution of wealth will gravitate back to a more equitable distribution.

As Warren Buffett says, our opportunity for wealth is often decided by how much of the "ovarian lottery" we win on the day of our births.[322] We suspect people will always try to get more than their fair share via deception and cruelty, but that does not mean the government should cooperate, nor that others have to comply.

Media Remedies

One of the motivating advantages to Restorative Practices is that life is richer and individuals are happier when striving to develop community and support each other's healing.[323]

Aside from implementing Restorative Practices, providing safe and consistent counseling, allowing returning citizens to obtain jobs that are unrelated to their past criminal behaviors, and training police to engage with citizens in the role of peacekeepers rather than head-knockers—our private media companies need to transform themselves: When people are arrested, nightly news should not pronounce them (implicitly nor explicitly) guilty prior to a trial—not even if the suspects are past offenders. Once suspects are convicted, the media should tell the entire story, not just the sensational parts that leave viewers wondering, "What were they thinking?" Would felonism survive if news anchors reported the number of unsuccessful job applications and efforts at starting their own businesses that returning citizens attempted before relapsing into a life of crime? To maintain credibility, all news organizations should disclose the full story, not just the side that props up the felonists' point of view.

Mainstream media can act against felonism by bluntly highlighting the lies and manipulation of facts politicians use when they're trying to get votes. Recently, two major presidential candidates weighed in on the riots in Baltimore, Maryland, and other cities where residents who see themselves as oppressed by the police and other government officials led large protests and riots. Secretary Hillary Clinton expressed sympathy for the residents and called for the creation of terminology to address this pattern of oppression. She promised to address this oppression if she were elected president. Then one of her opponents, Senator Rand Paul, noted that they were finally on the same page regarding the issue of criminal justice reform. He also pointed out that Secretary Clinton's husband created many of the laws that resulted in this oppression. To maintain an unbiased report, media pundits could have pointed out that President Clinton has made multiple public speeches calling for a repeal of the policies he enacted after having witnessed their unintended and destructive consequences. Senator Paul's omission of this fact, and his linking of Secretary Clinton to her husband's past acts, can only be explained as an effort to manipulate voters.

We agree and disagree with opinions offered by both of these politicians, but our political opinion can only serve to distract from the currently biased reporting of various media outlets. Sure, some commentators present their findings after fact-checking each candidate, but those are rare. It is much more common for news programs to disguise their editorial comments as facts, promote felonism with lopsided reporting, sensationalize and condemn behaviors that are normal responses to severe situations, and use a host of other propaganda techniques to sway their audience. These techniques have become so commonplace that they are rarely recognized by average viewers.

It was refreshing to see a high school journalism class in Bennington, Vermont, perform a "professional integrity audit" on a national news broadcast that showed their community in a prejudicial and negative manner.[324] The students presented detailed breakdowns supporting their analysis that a five-minute Bill O'Reilly/Jesse Watters video was only truthful during 18 percent of the broadcast. We challenge all media outlets to commit to rigorous honesty, and forget about how such reporting will affect profits. Should you need assistance with objectivity, there is a great group of teens in Vermont you may want to hire as consultants. If you have the courage to accept this invitation, we suspect you will be awestruck at the long-term, positive results.

Political / Law Enforcement Remedies

We recognize that not all politicians, lawyers, judges, and law-enforcement officers are felonists, so we call on those individuals to participate in a movement to restore and strengthen all of the Constitution's amendments. Based on what we have witnessed to be the most devastating attacks to our liberty by felonists, we offer the following suggestions:

Require police officers to stop demanding to see identification from citizens who are not under arrest. Until trust is restored between communities and law-enforcement officers, demands for personal information only serves to put citizens on the offensive and give some officers an excuse to accelerate conflict.

Require that no seizures or destruction of property shall ever occur without fair market value paid in return unless solid proof of a crime is discovered in a warranted search.

Stop allowing roadblocks on federal, state, or county highways or interstates for the detection of DUI or other potential violations.

Set limits on all fines for any violation or bail to be no more than five percent of the accused's weekly income, and return bail deposits when citizens are found innocent, are acquitted, or have charges dropped by prosecutors.

As long as law-enforcement officials are allowed to lie to suspects, create a constitutional right permitting citizens to lie to government and law-enforcement officials if they have reason to believe those officials are trying to cause them harm, entrap them, or take away their liberty.

Never allow suspects to be blackmailed or bullied into plea bargain agreements. Until plea bargains are phased out, prosecutors should be banned from stacking charges or enhancing the length of sentences to entice confessions. There is no place for manipulative and dishonest plea bargaining in a judicial system where a jury is supposed to be the deciding factor of guilt or innocence.

No citizen should ever be confined to civil commitment, against their will, for something they *might* do in the future.

Returning citizens should not be subjected to any tactics that will restrict their employment, residency, or social status. They should be free to rejoin the community and become productive citizens without fear of being segregated or of their families being ostracized.

No one should ever be put in jeopardy twice for the same offense, or put into an ex post facto situation, nor should evidence of innocence be overlooked due to rigid timeline restrictions.

All victims should have the right to directly confront their offender while in a safe, supportive environment. If reasonable and safe for all involved, offenders should be given the opportunity to restore their relationship with the person and/or community they have offended.

These ten steps are not the only areas that need to be fixed, but their nationwide implementation would be a great start to the elimination of felonism.

We believe these recommendations are in keeping with a new organization, Law Enforcement Leaders to Reduce Crime and Incarceration. This project of the Brenna Center for Justice at NYU School of Law has a bipartisan membership of 130 leading prosecutors and law enforcement officers calling for reform. Their mission statement includes the following:

"...From experience and through data-driven and innovative practices, we know the country can reduce crime while also reducing unnecessary arrests, prosecutions, and incarcerations. We can also reduce recidivism and strengthen relationship with communities. With the goal of building a smarter, stronger, and fairer criminal justice system, we are joining together to urge a change in laws and practices to reduce incarceration while continuing to keep our communities safe."[325]

We can't help but celebrate the creation of this project and feel excitement for the transformations they will enact to overcome felonism in the near future.

Solutions to Be Enacted by Victims of Felonism

Lest readers judge us as minimizing the rights and value of victims of crime by addressing victims of felonism, please keep reading. To men, women, and children who have been the victims of crime, the extension of our deepest empathy should be evident, but we will say it anyway: We are sincerely sorry you have experienced a devastating event at the hands of another. We know it was not fair, and the choices of the person who offended you are not your fault. If we could have prevented it, we would have. This book is our small effort to do just that. It is our hope that shining a light on paths to healing for those who hurt you will reduce your pain and the likelihood of you or your loved ones being hurt in the future.

Within any conflict, total resolution and healing can only occur when all those involved accept responsibility for their behaviors and emotions, and commit to finding solutions. Even the most innocent of victims must work to overcome the conflict that has entered their lives lest they become perpetrators.

We now want to speak directly to all people who have been suspected or convicted of committing a felony, and the individuals who love them. One major problem with being the *victim* of any situation is that with that identity comes the potential for defining oneself as weak, helpless, and less-than. As a victim of felonism, please know that you are still the wonderful person you were before! Your personhood has not changed as a result of your circumstances, so please do not talk to yourself as if your feelings of guilt, defeat, inadequacy, or weakness are facts about who you are as a person. Feelings are only facts about how you feel, not facts about who you are or how you should react to others. Being overpowered or tricked by another person may cause you to feel weak, but that does not mean you are. Linda (co-author) likes to attend a Twelve Step program (CODA) that uses the acronym "A-FOG" to describe situations like the one you have survived. It stands for "Another Fucking Opportunity of Growth." We apologize to those who are offended by the "F word," but the point is, all situations in your life can be used as a springboard to a better place.

When finding ourselves in tough situations, we may think we can transform it into something better by aligning with powerful people who unite for the purpose of opposing our perceived enemies. It was the natural thing to do in Andy's (co-author's) neighborhood. Believing the propaganda of his family and neighborhood, Andy joined a gang, accepted their code as his guide for making decisions, and identified himself as the person they told him he was. When he was in his late twenties, into his fourth year of a life sentence, Andy realized the truth. There was no "code." There were just rules created by people higher up in the gang. They expected him to follow their "code" (even though some of them did not comply) so they could profit from his loyalty. Andy was not the terrible, violent acts they encouraged him to perform. He was the same, loving, human being his parents had cherished the day he was born. Unfortunately, he had abandoned that part of himself at an early age to please adults in his family and neighborhood. As our friend, Geo Geller, likes to say, "He went along to get along."

The wonderful thing about the moment Andy realized he had given up his power and identity was that it was also the moment he began to reclaim his true self. It was the same moment he decided to stop being a violent person—no matter the consequences. Andy knew there was a possibility that the prison gang he had formed might kill him for betraying them, but that did not matter. Although he was not suicidal, Andy decided that even if it meant death, he would spend at least one day on this earth as his real self, a loving person created by a loving creator. That is what you are too. Andy's change did not happen overnight. He lived in the precontemplative stage for almost thirty years, but it only took a few months to cycle through the remaining stages of change mentioned at the beginning of this chapter. There are still moments when he has to remind himself who he really is, but they never last long.

Every person on this earth has an inner conversation that defines how they see themselves. We know prisoners who have drunk the felonism Kool-Aid and identify themselves as lower-class individuals. Here's an example. While leading a group discussion in prison, Linda (co-author) listened to one man describe the emotional cage he had constructed around himself regarding relationships with women. Derrick wanted to have a loving relationship, but he believed any woman who wanted to be with him was not good enough for him. Derrick also thought women who had the qualities he longed for would never be attracted to him. If Derrick re-defined himself, accepted that the loving essence of his infancy is still his true self, he would escape his self-imposed prison and develop the ability to have healthy relationships with emotionally healthy women.

Words are essential, especially the words we use to describe ourselves. People may have called you a loser, an idiot, a villain, a killer, an offender, a liar, and a host of other terrible things during every memorable day of your life, but that is not who you are. One of Linda's (co-author's) students, who was in state custody, told her he was five years old before he realized his name was not "Mother Fucker" because that is how his parents always addressed him. You can identify yourself as a "convict," an "original gangster," or a "loving person"—the choice is yours, but how do you benefit by choosing negative labels? We don't think you can. If you don't believe us, please consider the words of President Nelson Mandela:

"It is never my custom to use words lightly. If twenty-seven years in prison have done anything to us, it was to use the silence of solitude to make us understand how precious words are and how real speech is in its impact on the way people live and die."[326]

He also said, "As I walked out the door toward the gate that would lead to my freedom, I knew if I didn't leave my bitterness and hatred behind, I'd still be in prison."[327] We seriously doubt President Mandela could have led South Africa to the abolition of apartheid if he had spent his twenty-seven years of incarceration ruminating on revenge, outrage, or self-pity.

As President Mandela implies, words are powerful. Nothing on this earth is created until it is put into words. Although we may step on some toes with the following opinion, we think it is important to share it. To us, choosing our words wisely means women do not call themselves "girls," and Blacks do not call themselves "niggers." Maybe those terms really don't mean anything negative to you, but they do mean something to people who hear you define yourself as a child or as a person who identifies with demeaning terms employed by slave owners. Of course, this is our opinion. But know that your words do influence how you treat yourself as well as how others treat you.

Overcoming the labels collected in our memories is a simple concept, but it is also a difficult task. It does not require the acceptance of any religion. Even people affiliated with no religious belief can see that children who are treated with love naturally return the same. It is when children are neglected and/or abused that they begin to strike out. Let's accept the fact that we were born naturally good and refer to ourselves as such.

Once that hurdle has been crossed, it's important to accept the same truth for all people. That prosecutor who knew you were innocent but convicted you anyway, that CO who beat you for repeatedly requesting much needed toilet paper, that spouse who injured you and then betrayed you—all the people in your life who have ever mistreated you, they too have a core being that is pure and good. Even the worst of the worst felonist has a loving essence. You may hate to admit that, just as they hate to admit that you were born a good, valuable human being, but both statements are true.

Acknowledging the goodness in an oppressor may feel ludicrous because it seems to imply your abuser should get off scot-free despite the misery they have heaped into your life; you remain in debt to society while they increase in power as the result of your incarceration. Try looking at this from a different angle. Accepting the loving parts of ourselves and the people we see as our enemies means we now have a reason to reconcile and start over. Consequences like restitution may still occur, but they don't have to be lifelong for people who remain in touch with their true natures. Healing is within reach for everyone.

You might ask, "What about people who don't accept this information? How do I act from a loving place toward people who still see me as a scumbag?" First of all, don't behave in a way that matches their accusations. Hurling insults or feces at a person who thinks you are an animal only serves to validate their false belief. If there is no way to reason with your abuser, leave their presence. You may not physically be able to leave, but your focus can leave the conversation. You can stop responding to their insults and reframe the discussion by pointing out the goodness in your abuser and yourself.

No matter what abusive people say or do, continue talking to yourself in ways that validate your humanity. Follow up with actions that prove your goodness and the fact that you value yourself. Make sure there is sufficient evidence to convict you if you are ever charged with the "offense" of loving yourself. Take on the simple but difficult task of proactively and lovingly teaching people to recognize your humanity. It worked for President Mandela, and it can work for you.

Do you remember the brave, disciplined Black students who sat down at whites-only lunch counters back in the 1960s? It took time, but those students overcame their oppressors by standing up for themselves and claiming their right to be treated with equality. They did not accept nor respond to the insults, spittle, hot coffee, fists, and other offenses hurled upon them. Those men and women did not behave like victims, even though they had been treated badly, and their response changed our nation.[328] That same power is within you.

It is not possible to force others to change their thinking or their behavior. There are racists and felonists who will hold to their prejudices and claim them to be ordained by God until the day they die. Thankfully, you do not have to change them. Changing your response to your oppressors will create the change you seek. That's how it works.

Consider a baby lying in a crib. They want to see the airplane at the top of their mobile move through the air above them, but the infant can't reach that far. All they have to do is touch the lowest mobile object, the one that is closest to their little fingers, and like magic, the plane at the top will appear to fly. Because we are all connected on some level, that's what will happen when you change the way you value yourself and respond to others. People in your environment will change of their own accord. It won't happen immediately, but it will be magnificent when it does.

Felonism does not have power over our natural desires to be kinder to each other. No one needs permission from felonists to foster healthier relationships between prisoners, prison staff, perceived enemies, and our communities. We predict a time when revenge and punishment will not be tolerated as options for addressing errant behaviors, not even the most egregious. In our vision for the future, healing relationships will be the ultimate goal for intervention in all conflicts. Policemen will end their shifts with cheers each day they are collar-free. They will not have ignored wrongdoing but turned conflicts into solutions that benefit everyone. Although that may sound impossible, maybe even laughable, already some police departments take homeless people to shelters, drug addicts to treatment facilities, and mentally ill citizens to mental health clinics instead of jail.[329]

What All Readers Can Do Today

As we bring this book to a close, we have a few ideas that can be enacted immediately by any reader willing to be part of the solution. First of all, we invite you to begin the discussion and educate yourself. If you hear a television show or news program claim that a certain group has the highest rate of recidivism, find out for yourself. If you don't have access to the Internet, visit a friend who does, go to your local library, or make direct inquiries of your local law-enforcement agencies. When you have documentation that proves the news anchors inaccurate, share it with the station administrator, request retractions, and publicize your findings on social media networks.

Talk about felonism with people in your family, your neighbors, co-workers, church members, and homeless people you meet on the street. Especially talk with your children and their friends about their experiences in this area. Within those discussions, allow yourself and others to be honest regarding instances when felonism has been supported. After all, haven't we all acted like felonists at one time or another? We know we (Linda and Andy) have.

Once you have established personal and private supports for yourself, join public discussions. Because Starbucks' CEO, Howard Schultz, has implemented the "Race Together" program to stimulate positive actions regarding racism in America,[330] we suspect their coffee shops would be a safe place to begin public conversations on felonism. Begin support groups for family members of people charged or convicted of felonies. Develop support groups for children whose parents are incarcerated; create safe places for them to talk about their joys, fears, and other emotions associated with the arrest and incarceration of their parent(s). We also encourage the creation of support groups for returning citizens as well as groups for anyone employed in any part of the criminal "justice" system. Police officers and attorneys need a safe environment to talk about how felonism has negatively influenced their decisions, attitudes, emotions, and family lives. It would be helpful for them to examine the codes by which they live, and determine whether any of their beliefs are motivated by felonists who want to use them to gain power.

If you are currently incarcerated, talk to your **cellie** about the messages you have received and/or accepted from felonists. No matter which side of the razor-wire walls you live on, begin practicing (in your mind or with another person) ways to respond to felonists in a firm yet positive manner. Find ways to reply to the abuses by felonists without becoming like them. Rehearse scenarios in which you accept responsibility for your past while acknowledging that you deserve to be treated like a human being today and in the future.

We firmly believe felonism will not be resolved without cooperation between individual members of the community and government employees whose jobs are related to local, state, and federal judicial systems. Get to know the police in your area as human beings rather than uniforms. Let them know you respect the difficult task they have in responding to gruesome accidents and violent situations, and begin discussions about how you can work together to keep officers safe while they are working to protect everyone in your community.

Hopefully, after doing all that, you will be energized rather than exhausted, and ready to make real systemic, institutional changes. Participate in political discussions, town hall meetings, and open forums about eradicating felonism from our policies and procedures. Demand the restitution of all amendments to the Constitution, especially the First through Eighth Amendments and the elimination of the clause in the Thirteenth Amendment that allows slavery. Elect legislators who will stop forking over mountains of taxpayer money so that private companies can make billions of dollars in profits from tax payers and family members of incarcerated individuals. Eliminating the profit motive will eliminate the abuse.

We invite you to publically and privately express to policymakers, and those with control over public funds, your desire that all returning citizens be allowed access to jobs that pay reasonable wages, to affordable housing, and to appropriate social services. Insist on reestablishing voting rights to all returning citizens and encourage legislators to examine the feasibility of granting suffrage rights to prisoners who are currently incarcerated.

We must come together as one nation; not Black American, Latin American, Native American, Irish American, Asian American ... but Americans. As the great melting pot of the world, we argue and fight amongst ourselves. At times we take advantage of one another, compete with one another. Sometimes we try to hedge our bets and tilt the field in our favor, but such divisive actions should never be manipulated or supported by government officials, judicial findings, or legislation.

Our forefathers created a great document, and said that it was ours to use for as long as we could keep it.[331] At the end of the day, we are Americans, equal in human value. It is up to us to work together, to build on and further the goals of our forefathers and prove that we can hold on to it.

Glossary of Prison Terms

Administrative segregation (*noun*): A special group of cells where prisoners are kept away from the general population for their own protection. Also known as "protective custody" or "PC" or simply "segregation."

Booty bandits (*noun*): Prisoners who brutally rape other prisoners to gain power and status; these prisoners may or may not see themselves as homosexual.

Cellie (*noun*): A person who shares a cell with another prisoner

Correctional officer (CO) (*noun*): A guard in a prison setting

Flatten (*verb*): To completely finish a prison sentence and leave prison without being on probation or parole

Freeworld (*noun*): Any environment outside of jail or prison

Hole (*noun*): Usually a single-person cell with bad ventilation, lighting, and sanitation. If they are lucky, prisoners in the hole get out of their cells one hour per day and are allowed to shower three times per week.

Lock-down (*noun*): A period of time when all prisoners must remain in their cells or designated areas. During these times, prisoners are served food from sacks—usually sandwiches—in their cells and are not allowed to go to work. Lock-downs are often seen by prisoners as punishment for the entire prison population for acts committed by one individual or small group. Administrators usually see them as a method for establishing and/or maintaining security.

Long line (*noun*): A prison job in which prisoners—often chained together at the feet or waist—work together performing menial tasks, such as digging out ditches, breaking rocks, or hoeing weeds in a field. Long lines, which are made up of prisoners with long sentences, are surrounded by guards (often on horseback) armed with rifles.

Off paper (*verb*): Once a sentence is complete, or parole and /or probation is ended, returning citizens are said to be "off paper" or "flattened.

Punk (*noun*): A prisoner who is not gay but makes her/himself available (usually as a result of coercion) for sex in exchange for favors such as protection, drugs, phones, etc.

RED (release eligibility date) (*noun*): The earliest date in which a prisoner is eligible to meet a parole board.

Safety valve (*noun*): A tool for the executive branch of the state which allows prisoners who meet certain criteria to leave early when prisons are overcrowded. Being convicted of a new crime while incarcerated usually results in a permanent disqualification.

Shank (*noun*): Any type of sharpened object used as a weapon to stab someone

(*verb*): The act of stabbing another person

Short line (*noun*): A prison job in which prisoners with shorter sentences do manual labor outside prison walls. They are not usually chained together and are guarded by one person with a revolver.

Snitch (*noun*): A person who reports the guilt of another in order to gain something for him/herself

(*verb*): To reveal to the authorities the name or other details of a person who has committed a crime

Trusty shooter (*noun*): A prisoner who earned the trust of the administration to the extent that they could possess a gun when supervising other prisoners—usually during work in the fields—to prevent other prisoners from escaping. Although we have not monitored all fifty states for compliance, this practice seems to have been eliminated from all Departments of Corrections in the US. If trusty shooters shot prisoners who appeared to be escaping, they were rewarded with the removal of six months (times varied according to prison administration) from their prison sentences. This position parallels slave days when trusted slaves were used to monitor the behavior of the other slaves.

Whole squad rider (*noun*): An armed prison staff member who rides a horse in the field to guard prisoners working outside prison walls

Notes

The following references are provided to assist readers in verifying what we have written and coming up with their own conclusions. Unfortunately, we have no control over the fact that some websites, especially on government sites, are modified on a regular basis with no "forwarding address." Hopefully, we have provided all the information you might need to complete your own searches and expand upon the topic of felonism.

Chapter 1

1. Mintz, S., & McNeil, S. (2015). Juan Ginés de Sepúlveda (1547). *Digital History*. accessed October 24, 2015, http://www.digitalhistory.uh.edu/active_learning/explorations/spain/spain_sepulveda.cfm

2. Dorsey, Professor Bruce. Swarthmore College, History 41: The American Colonies, Spring 1999. Bartoleme de Las Casas, Brief Account of the Devastation of the Indies. (1542). accessed October 24, 2015, http://www.swarthmore.edu/SocSci/bdorsey1/41docs/02-las.html

3. Minster, Christopher," Fray Bartolomé de Las Casas (1484–1566) Part Two: Las Casas' Later Years." About Education. accessed October 24, 2015. http://latinamericanhistory.about.com/od/coloniallatinamerica/p/lascasas2.htm

4. Ibid.

5. Gjohnsit, "The Salves That Time Forgot." *Daily Kos.*" 12/27/2013. http://www.dailykos.com/story/2013/12/27/1265498/-The-slaves-that-time-forgot

6. "Africans Americans at Jamestown," *National Park Service. U. S. Department of Interior*. Last modified 10/13/2015, http://www.nps.gov/jame/learn/historyculture/african-americans-at-jamestown.htm

7.   "Indentured Servitude," *U-S-History.com*, Online Highways. Retrieved
      10/24/2015 LLC http://www.u-s-history.com/pages/h1157.html

8.   "Slavery in Colonial North America: 1600–1860" Retrieved 10/24/2015.
      http://arcofhistory.org/U.S._History/The_Colonies_files/Slavery%20in
      %20Colonial%20North%20America.pdf

9.   Rice, James W., "Bacon's Rebellion (1667–1677)," *Encyclopedia Virginia,* Last
      modified: October 3, 2014, http://www.encyclopediavirginia.org/bacon_s_
      rebellion_1676–1677#start_entry

10.   Fitzhugh, George, "Cannibals All! Or, Slaves Without Masters: Electronic
      Edition," *Documenting the American South*, University of North Carolina at
      Chapel Hill, 1998, http://docsouth.unc.edu/southlit/fitzhughcan/fitzcan
      .html#fitz294, pp. 45–45, 294–298.

11.   Ibid. pp. 316–319.

12.   Child, Lydia Maria. *An Appeal in Favor of That Class of Americans Called Afri-
      cans* (Amherst, University of Massachusetts Press, 1833 & 1996) p 117.

13.   Ibid. pp.180–189.

14.   Barker, H. E., Speeches of John C Calhoun: Delivered in the Congress of the
      United States from 1811 to the Present Time. Lincolniana, 1922 South Hobart
      Boulevard, Los Angeles, CA. p. 225, accessed October 24, 2015, https://archive
      .org/stream/speechesofjohnccooincalh#page/225/mode/1up/search/free

15.   "Ten Facts about Washington and Slavery" *George Washington's Mount * Ver-
      non*, Last update, July 21, 2014. http://www.mountvernon.org/
      george-washington/slavery/ten-facts-about-washington-slavery
          "Thomas Jefferson and Slavery," *Thomas Jefferson Encyclopedia*, accessed
      October 24, 2014. http://www.monticello.org/site/plantation-and-slavery/
      thomas-jefferson-and-slavery

16.   Jefferson, Thomas to John Holmes, *Library of Congress*, Monticello Apr. 22. 20,
      accessed October 24, 2015, http://www.loc.gov/exhibits/jefferson/159.html

17.   "Results from the 1860 Census," *The Civil Rights Home Page,* © 2009, accessed
      October 24, 2015, http://www.civil-war.net/pages/1860_census.html

18.   "Women's Rights, WIC Main Page, "Compton's Interactive Encyclopedia,
      Compton's NewMedia Inc, © 1994, 1995, accessed 24, 2015, http://www
      .wic.org/misc/history.htm

19.   Colossians 3:18 KJV

20.   "Representations and the Battle of Ideology over Woman's Proper Place in
      Society," *American Woman Suffrage: Dueling Images* accessed October 24, 2015.
      http://cjuliansuffrageexhibit.weebly.com/conflicting-views.html

21.   "Anti-Suffrage Movements in the USA South," *Women Suffrage and Beyond,
      Confronting the Democratic Deficit*, February 1, 2012, http://womensuffrage
      .org/?p=570

22. https://www.americanprogress.org/issues/women/news/2013/08/26/72988/
womens-equality-day-celebrating-the-19th-amendments-impact-on-
reproductive-health-and-rights

23. Rieder, Jonathan. *Gospel of Freedom; Letter from Birmingham Jail and the
Struggle that Changed a Nation*, Bloomsbury Press, New York, London, New
Delhi, Sydney. ©2013, p. 173.

24. "THIRTY-EIGHTH CONGRESS. Sess. II. Res. 9, 10, 11, 12. 1965 567;" *The
Library of Congress*, accessed October 24, 2015, http://memory.loc.gov/cgi-bin/
ampage?*collId=llsl&fileName=013/llsl013.db&recNum=596*

25. "20th Century America Prohibition and Depression Era Gangsters, Through
the Lens of Fisk," *Legends of America*. Accessed October 24, 2015, http://www
.legendsofamerica.com/20th-gangsters.html
  "Crime 1920–1940, Issue Summary," *Encyclopedia.com*, accessed October 24, 2015 http://www.encyclopedia.com/article-1G2–3424800018/
crime-1920–1940.html

26. MacDonald, J. Fred, "Programing Trends in the 1960's," *One Nation Under
Television: The Rise and Decline of Network TV* ©2009, accessed October 24,
2015, http://jfredmacdonald.com/onutv/trends.htm

27. "Martin Luther King, Jr. and the Global Freedom Struggle: Hoover, J. Edgar
(1895 – 1972)" *Stanford University, The Martin Luther King, Jr. Research and
Education Institute*, http://mlk-kpp01.stanford.edu/index.php/encyclopedia/
encyclopedia/enc_hoover_j_edgar_1895_1972

28. May, Gary, "A Revolution of Values: Martin Luther King Jr. and the Poor
People's Campaign," *Moyers & Company*, January 18, 2015 http://billmoyers
.com/2015/01/18/revolution-values

29. Lehren, Andrew W., "Jazz and the FBI: Guilty Until Proven Innocent,"
JazzTimes, April 2009, accessed October 24, 2015, http://jazztimes.com/
articles/24396-jazz-and-the-fbi

30. Ibid.

31. Mantler, Gordon K., Power to the Poor – 1968 Poor Peoples Campaign video," Heartland Media of Chicago & the Live from the Heartland Radio Show, accessed October 24, 2015, https://www.youtube.com/
watch?v=bwhG7bRJUAU

32. "Martin Luther King, Jr. and the Global Freedom Struggle: Hoover, J. Edgar
(1895 – 1972) Federal Bureau of Investigation (FBI)" *Stanford University, The
Martin Luther King, Jr. Research and Education Institute*, http://kingencyclope-
dia.stanford.edu/encyclopedia/encyclopedia/enc_federal_bureau_of_
investigation_fbi

33. "United States Crime Rate 1960 – 2014," *Rate and Rank of Crime in the United
States 1960 to 2014*, © *1997 – 2014*, accessed October 24, 2015, http://www
.disastercenter.com/crime/uscrime.htm

34. "Incarceration Rate for African-Americans Now Six Times the National Average," *RT Question More*, February 20, 2013, accessed October 24, 2015, http://rt.com/usa/incarceration-african-black-prison-606

35. Gwynne, Kristen, "4 Things You Probably Didn't Know About Crack, America's Most Vilified Drug," *ALERTNET*, August 2, 2013, accessed October 24, 2015, http://www.alternet.org/drugs/4-things-you-probably-didnt-know-about-crack-americas-most-vilified-drug

36. Ibid.

37. Gregory, Ted, "The Black Panther Raid and the Death of Fred Hampton," *Chicago Tribune*, ©2015, accessed October 24, 2015, http://www.chicagotribune.com/news/nationworld/politics/chi-chicagodays-pantherraid-story-story.html

38. http://www.ushistory.org/us/55c.asp

39. "Facts and Case Summary – Gideon v. Wainwright 372 U. S. 335," *United States COURTS*, accessed October 24, 2015, http://is.gd/udRTjM

40. "Legal Information Institute, Miranda v. Arizona 384 U. S. 436," *Cornell University Law School*, accessed October 24, 2015, https://www.law.cornell.edu/supremecourt/text/384/436

41. "Legal Information Institute, Furman v. Georgia 384 U. S. 238," *Cornell University Law School*, accessed October 24, 2015, https://www.law.cornell.edu/supremecourt/text/408/238

42. Zahavi, Gerald, et. Al., "Attica Revisited," *A Talking History Project*, ©2003, accessed October 24, 2015, http://www.talkinghistory.org/attica

43. "U. S. Supreme Court, Wolff v. McDonnell, 418 U. S. 539 (1974)," *JUSTIA US Supreme Court*, accessed October 24, 2015, https://supreme.justia.com/cases/federal/us/418/539

44. "Ethical Considerations for Research Involving Prisoners," *National Academy of Sciences*, ©2007, accessed October 24, 2015, http://www.ncbi.nlm.nih.gov/books/NBK19877

45. "Legal Information Institute, HOWES v. FIELDS 617 F. 3d 813, reversed," *Cornell University Law School*, accessed October 24, 2015, https://www.law.cornell.edu/supremecourt/text/10–680

46. Khan, Huma, "Juvenile Justice: Too Young for Life in Prison?" ABC *NEWS*, July 12, 2010, http://abcnews.go.com/Politics/life-prison-juvenile-offenders-adult-courts/story?id=11129594

47. "Juvenile Life Without Parole," *AMNESTY INTERNATIONAL*, ©2015, accessed October 24, 2015, http://www.amnestyusa.org/our-work/issues/children-s-rights/juvenile-life-without-parole

48. "Facts and Infographics about Life Without Parole for Children," *The*

Campaign for the Fair Sentencing of Youth, accessed October 24, 2015, http://fairsentencingofyouth.org/what-is-jlwop

49.   Impaired Driving: Get the facts," Center for Disease Control and Prevention, updated 11/24/2015, http://www.cdc.gov/motorvehiclesafety/impaired_driving/impaired-drv_factsheet.html

50.   Frenstein, Gregory, "How the World Butchered Benjamin Franklin's Quote on Liberty Vs. Security," TE (blog) February 14, 2014, accessed October 24, 2015, http://techcrunch.com/2014/02/14/how-the-world-butchered-benjamin-franklins-quote-on-liberty-vs-security

51.   Hessick, Carissa and F. Andrew Hessick, "Double Jeopardy as a Limit on Punishment, *Cornell Law Review, Vol. 97, No. 3,* November 3, 2102, http://papers.ssrn.com/sol3/papers.cfm?abstract_id=1776526

52.   "Killed by Police Community," accessed October 24, 2015, http://www.killedbypolice.net

53.   Follman, Mark, "Michael Brown's Mom Laid Flowers Where He was Shot – and Police Crushed Them," *Mother Jones,* August 27, 2014, 6:00AM EDT, http://www.motherjones.com/politics/2014/08/ferguson-st-louis-police-tactics-dogs-michael-brown

54.   Krasny, Michael, "Local Police Forces Becoming Increasingly Militarized," *KQED Radio,* August 15, 2014, 9:00AM, http://www.kqed.org/a/forum/R201408150900

55.   "Investigation of the Ferguson Police Department, United States Department of Justice Civil Rights Division," *as printed in The Washington Post,* March 4, 2015, http://apps.washingtonpost.com/g/documents/national/department-of-justice-report-on-the-ferguson-mo-police-department/1435, p.1.

56.   Rakoff, Jed S., "Why Innocent People Plead Guilty," *The New York Review of Books,* November 20, 2014, http://www.nybooks.com/articles/archives/2014/nov/20/why-innocent-people-plead-guilty/

57.   Ibid.

58.   Shapiro, Joseph, "Supreme Court Ruling Not Enough to Prevent Debtors Prisons," *NPR,* May 21, 2014, http://www.npr.org/2014/05/21/313118629/supreme-court-ruling-not-enough-to-prevent-debtors-prisons

59.   Picchi, Aimee, "Are American's Jaild Used to Punish Poor People?" *CBS Money Watch,* February 11, 2015, 12:47PM, accessed October 24, 2015, http://www.cbsnews.com/news/how-jails-are-warehousing-those-too-poor-to-make-bail/

60.   "George Bush and Willie Horton," *The New York Times, Opinion,* November 4, 1988, accessed October 24, 2015, http://www.nytimes.com/1988/11/04/opinion/george-bush-and-willie-horton.html

61.   "Clinton Terms Anti-Crime Bill His Top Priority," *Los Angeles Times from*

Associated Press, November 28, 1993, http://articles.latimes.com/1993–11-28/
news/mn-61791_1_crime-legislation

62. Mitchell, Josh and Joe Palazzolo, "Pell Grants to be Restored for Prisoners,"
     The Wall Street Journal, July 27, 2015, 7:32 PM, ET, http://www.wsj.com/
     articles/pell-grants-to-be-restored-for-prisoners-1438029241

63. Warren, Robert K., "Evidence-Based Practice to Reduce Recidivism: Impli-
     cations for State Judiciaries," *U. S. Department of Justice, National Institute of
     Corrections*, August 2007, accessed October 24, 2015, static.nicic.gov/
     Library/023358.pdf

64. Mellema, Matt, and Chanakya Sethi, "Sex Offenders Laws Have Gone Too
     Far," *Slate*, AUG. 11 2014 12:20 PM http://www.slate.com/articles/news_and_
     politics/jurisprudence/2014/08/sex_offender_registry_laws_have_our_
     policies_gone_too_far.html

65. Sampson, Robert and John H. Laub, "Life-Course Disasters? Trajecto-
     ries of Crime Among Delinquent Boys Followed to Age 70,"*Criminology
     Volume 41, Issue 3, pages 555–592, August 2003*, http://onlinelibrary.wiley.com/
     doi/10.1111/j.1745–9125.2003.tb00997.x/abstract
         Uggen, Chris and Suzy McElrath, "Six Social Sources of the U. S. Crime
     Drop," *The Society Pages, White Paper*, February 4, 2013, accessed October 25,
     2015, http://thesocietypages.org/papers/crime-drop

66. Stemen, Don, "Reconsidering Incarceration: New Directions for Reduc-
     ing Crime," *Vera Institute of Justice*, January 2007, accessed October 25, 2015,
     http://vera.org/sites/default/files/resources/downloads/veraincarc_vFW2.pdf

67. Serani, D. (2008). If it bleeds, it leads: The clinical implications of
     fear-based programming in news media. *Psychoanalyst & Psychothera-
     py*, 24(4): 240–250.

68. Connor, Tracy, "Hero Ex-Con Bryant Collins was Wayward Baby's Saving
     Grace," *NBC NEWS*, June 17, 2014 2:51PM ET, accessed October 25, 2015,
     http://www.nbcnews.com/news/us-news/hero-ex-con-bryant-collins-
     was-wayward-babys-saving-grace-n133061

69. Cohen, Michael, "How For-profit Prisons have become the biggest lobby no
     one is Talking About," *The Washington Post*, April 28, 2015, accessed October
     25, 2015, http://is.gd/M3jujX

70. "U. S. Court of Appeals Upholds Ciavarella's Conviction and Sentence,"
     Department of Justice, U. S. Attorney's Office, Middle District of Pennsylvania,
     May 24, 2013, accessed October 25, 2015, http://www.justice.gov/usao-mdpa/
     pr/us-*court*-appeals-upholds-ciavarella-s-conviction-and-sentence

71. Lee, Suevon, "By the Numbers: The U.S.'s Growing For-profit Detention
     Industry," *Pro Publica*,, June 20, 2012, accessed October 25, 2015, http://www.
     propublica.org/article/by-the-numbers-the-u.s.s-growing-for-profit-
     detention-industry

Buczynski, Beth, "Shocking Facts About America's For-profit Prison Industry," *TRUTHO-OUT.ORG,* February 6, 2014, accessed October 25, 2015,
http://www.truth-out.org/news/item/21694-shocking-facts-about-
americas-for-profit-prison-industry#

72. Walsh, Ben, "Prisoners Pay Millions to Call Loved Ones Every Year. Now
     This Company Wants Even More," *The Huffington Post,* June 10, 2015, http://
     www.huffingtonpost.com/2015/06/10/prison-phone-profits_n_7552464.html

73. Ibid.

74. Williams, Timothy, "The High Cost of Calling the Imprisoned," *The New
     York Times,* March 30, 2015, http://www.nytimes.com/2015/03/31/us/
     steep-costs-of-inmate-phone-calls-are-under-scrutiny.html?_r=0

75. Schwartz, Ariel, "Here's the Real Story Behind the Apple of Prison Tech,"
     Tech Insider, July 29, 2015, 9:18 AM, accessed October 25, 2015, http://www
     .businessinsider.com/apple-of-prison-techs-real-story-2015-7

76. Ibid.

77. "Prison Phone Justice," © *Prison Legal News,* accessed October 25, 2015,
     https://www.prisonphonejustice.org

78. Wagner, Daniel, "Prison Bankers Cash in on Captive Customers," *The Center
     for Public Integrity,* September 30, 2014, http://www.publicintegrity
     .org/2014/09/30/15761/prison-bankers-cash-captive-customers

79. Kieler, Ashlee, Transferring Funds to Prisoners is Big Business for Some
     Financial Companies, Consumerist, September 30, 2014, accessed October 25,
     2015, http://consumerist.com/2014/09/30/transferring-funds-to-prisoners-
     is-big-business-for-some-financial-companies

80. Schwartz, Ariel, "Here's the Real Story Behind the Apple of Prison Tech,"
     Tech Insider, July 29, 2015, 9:18 AM, accessed October 25, 2015, http://www
     .businessinsider.com/apple-of-prison-techs-real-story-2015-7

81. Walsh, Ben, Walsh, Ben, "Prisoners Pay Millions to Call Loved Ones
     Every Year. Now This Company Wants Even More," *The Huffington Post,*
     June 10, 2015, http://www.huffingtonpost.com/2015/06/10/prison-phone-
     profits_n_7552464.html

82. "Pepsi to Pay $3.13 Million and Made Major Policy Changes to Resolve
     EEOC Finding of Nationwide Hiring Discrimination Against African
     Americans," *U.S. Equal Employment Opportunity Commission Press Release,*
     January 11, 1012, http://www.eeoc.gov/eeoc/newsroom/release/1-11-12a.cfm

83. Love, Julia, "Apple Rescinds Policy Against Hiring Felons for Construction
     Work," *San Jose Mercury News,* posted April 9, 2015, http://www.
     mercurynews.com/business/ci_27881493/apple-rescinds-policy-hiring-felons

84. Ibid.

85. Adams, Susan, "Background Checks on Job Candidates: Be Very Careful," *Forbes/ Leadership,* June 21, 2013, 11:56 AM, accessed October 25, 2015, http://www.forbes.com/sites/susanadams/2013/06/21/background-checks-on-job-candidates-be-very-careful

86. *ONLINE ETYMOLOGY DICTIONARY,* accessed October 25, 2015, http://www.etymonline.com/index.php?term=racist

87. O'Brien, Geoffrey, John Bartlett. *Bartlett's Familiar Quotes,* Douglas, Frederick. Speech at Civil Rights Mass Meeting, Washington, D.C. (1883, October 22) © 2013, Douglass, Little, Brown, and Company, Hachette Book Group

88. Douglas, Frederick, "Narrative of the Life of Frederick Douglass, an American Slave. Written by Himself, 1818–1895," *Documenting the American South,* Academic Affairs Library, University of North Carolina at Chapel Hill, 1999, p. 45, http://www.nps.gov/frde/learn/photosmultimedia/quotations.htm

89. King, Martin Luther, Jr., "Letter from a Birmingham Jail [King, Jr.]," *African Studies Center – University of Pennsylvania,* April 16, 1963, http://www.africa.upenn.edu/Articles_Gen/Letter_Birmingham.html

Chapter 2

90. "U. S. Supreme Court, Wolff v. McDonnell, 418 U. S. 539 (1974)," *JUSTIA US Supreme Court,* accessed October 24, 2015, https://supreme.justia.com/cases/federal/us/418/539

91. Brown, Julie K., "After Inmate Deaths, Department of Justice to Probe Florida Prison System," *Miami Herold,* December 13, 2014, http://www.miamiherald.com/news/special-reports/florida-prisons/article4457578.html

92. Casella, Jean and James Ridgeway, "Supreme Court Takes the Radical Stance that Prisoners are Human Beings," *Solitary Watch,* accessed October 26, 2015, http://solitarywatch.com/2011/05/31/supreme-court-strikes-a-blow-for-the-human-rights-of-prisoners

Chapter 3

93. "Children's Defense Fund," February 19, 2009, accessed October 27, 2015, http://www.childrensdefense.org/library/data/cradle-prison-pipeline-summary-report.pdf

94. Mince-Didier, Ave, "Tactics Police Use to Get a Confession," *Criminal Defense Lawyer, accessed October 26, 2015,* http://www.criminaldefenselawyer.com/resources/criminal-defense/defendants-rights/tactics-police-use-get-a-confession
    "Obstruction of Justice," *Legal Information Institute: Cornell University Law School, accessed October 26, 2015, https://www.law.cornell.edu/wex/obstruction_of_justice*

95. Berkowitz, Bill, "The Blue Wall of Silence Among Police Enables Cop Brutality," *Truthout NEWS.* March 5, 2015, accessed October 26, 2015, http://is.gd/WimS3H

96. Stout, Samantha, The Detrimental Effects of Aging out of Foster Care and Knoxville's Representativeness of Appropriate Services," *University of Tennessee Honors Thesis Projects,* 2013, http://trace.tennessee.edu/cgi/viewcontent.cgi?article=2660&context=utk_chanhonoproj

97. Ibid.

98. "Chapter Five: Race and Juvenile Justice System," *The Leadership Conference,* accessed October 26, 2015, http://is.gd/fDeZxY

99. Toro, PhD, Paul and Amy Dworsky, PhD, "Homeless Youth in the United States: Recent Research Findings and Intervention Approaches," 2007 National Symposium on Homelessness Research, p. 6, http://aspe.hhs.gov/hsp/homelessness/symposium07/toro/report.pdf,

Chapter 4

100. Fitzhugh, George, "Cannibals All! Or, Slaves Without Masters: Electronic Edition," *Documenting the American South,* University of North Carolina at Chapel Hill, 1998, http://docsouth.unc.edu/southlit/fitzhughcan/fitzcan.html#fitz294, p. 107.

101. Mathews, Kevin, "5 Ways Prosecutors Have Too Much Power," Care2.org, October 8, 2014, 11:30 AM, http://www.care2.com/causes/5-ways-prosecutors-have-too-much-power.html

102. Locker, Richard, "Workman Brother, Pastor Cry ,Injustice, Didn't Kill Officer During 1981 Robbery, They Claim," *Memphis Commercial Appeal,* May 12, 2007, http://www.clarkprosecutor.org/html/death/US/workman1075.htm

103. Liptak, Adam, „Serving Life for Providing Car to Killers, "The *New York Times,* December 4, 2007, http://www.nytimes.com/2007/12/04/us/04felony.html?pagewanted=all&_r=0

104. Ibid.

105. Segura, Liliana, "With 2.3 Million People Incarcerated in the US, Prisons are Big Business," *The Nation Instigating Progress Daily,* October 1, 2013, http://www.thenation.com/prison-profiteers

106. "Preliminary Semiannual Uniform Crime Report, January – June 2013," *The Federal Bureau of Investigation*http://www.fbi.gov/about-us/cjis/ucr/crime-in-the-u.s/2013/preliminary-semiannual-uniform-crime-report-january-june-2013

107. Snyder, Ph.D., Howard N., "Arrest in the United States, 1990 – 2010," *U.*

S. *Department of Justice, Office of Justice Programs, Bureau of Justice Statistics,* October 2012, http://www.bjs.gov/content/pub/pdf/aus9010.pdf

108. "Annual Report Pursuant to Section 13 or 15(d) of the Securities Exchange Act of 1934, Corrections Corporation of America," *United States Securities and Exchange,* December 31, 2005, p 22, http://www.sec.gov/Archives/edgar/data/1070985/000095014406001892/g99938e10vk.htm#114

109. Ibid. pp. 21–23.

110. Hodai, Beau, Corporate Con Game," *In These Times with Liberty and Justice for All,* June 21, 2010, http://inthesetimes.com/article/6084/corporate_con_game

111. Sullivan, Laura, "Shaping State Laws with Little Scrutiny," *National Public Radio,* October 29, 2010, http://www.npr.org/2010/10/29/130891396/shaping-state-laws-with-little-scrutiny

112. "From Clearing House to Think Tank," *American Legislative Exchange Council,* ©2015 http://www.alec.org/about-alec/history

113. Sullivan, Laura, "Prison Economics Help Drive Ariz. Immigration Law," *National Public Radio, October 28, 2010,* http://www.npr.org/2010/10/28/130833741/prison-economics-help-drive-ariz-immigration-law

114. "Immigration and Job Displacement (2010)," *Federation for American Immigration Reform,* updated 2010, http://www.fairus.org/issue/immigration-and-job-displacement

115. Pethokousik, James, "How Does Immigration Affect US Wages and Jobs?" *American Enterprise Institute,* January 29, 2013, http://www.aei-ideas.org/2013/01/how-does-immigration-affect-us-wages-and-jobs
      Novak, Viveca, "Does Immigration Cost Jobs?" *FactCheck.org, A Project of the Annenberg Public Policy Center,* May 13, 2010, http://www.factcheck.org/2010/05/does-immigration-cost-jobs

116. Hodai, Beau, "A Case Study on CCA's Web of Influence in Arizona: Mark Brnovich," *The Center for Media and Democracy's PR* Watch September 23, 2013, http://www.prwatch.org/news/2013/09/12251/case-study-cca%E2%80%99s-web-influence-arizona-mark-brnovich

117. Ibid.

118. Ibid.

119. National Immigration Forum Staff, "The Math of Immigration Detention: Executive Summary," *National Immigration Reform, Policy Paper,* August 22, 2013, https://immigrationforum.org/blog/themathofimmigrationdetention/#_ftn40

120. Capeloto, Alexa, "Let's Bring Sunshine Into Private Prisons," The Crime Report, January 29, 2015, http://www.thecrimereport.org/viewpoints/2015-01-lets-bring-sunshine-into-private-prisons

Chapter 5

121.   "U. S. Supreme Court, Richardson v Ramirez, 418 U. S. 24 (1974), *Felon Voting ProCon.org,* October 18, 2006, p. 42, http://felonvoting.procon.org/sourcefiles/ RichardsonvRamirez.pdf,

122.   Petersillia, J. "Probation and Parole FAQs # 14," *Probation in the United States Part II, Perspectives,* 22 (3), 42–49, ©2009, http://www.appa-net.org/eweb/ DynamicPage.aspx?WebCode=VB_FAQ#14

123.   Malcolm, John, Criminal Justice Reform: Suggested Changes for Tennessee, *The Heritage Foundation,* September 16, 2014, http://www.heritage.org/ research/testimony/2014/10/criminal-justice-reform-for-tennessee#_ftn50

Chapter 6

124.   "Who are the Victims?" *Rape, Abuse & Incest National Network,* ©2009, accessed October 28, 2015, https://www.rainn.org/get-information/statistics/ sexual-assault-victims

125.   "U. S. Constitution, Article I, Section 9, Clause 3," *Cornell University Law School,* accessed October 28, 2015, https://www.law.cornell.edu/constitution/ articlei#section9

126.   "Kansas v Hendricks, 521 U. S. 346 (1997), October Term, 1996," *Justia US Supreme Court,* https://supreme.justia.com/cases/federal/us/521/346, p. 347 # 2.
        Austin, Jared, "Michigan Court of Appeals: Sex Offender Registry is Not Punishment," *Austin Legal Services, PLC, posted November 24, 2014,* http:// www.austin-legal.net/2014/11/michigan-court-appeals-sex-offender-registry-punishment

127.   Grose, Charles, "South Carolina's Sex Offender Registry Has Turned into Punishment," *The Grose Law Firm, LLC,* July 12, 2013, 8:30 AM, http:// groselawfirm.com/2013/07/blog/south-carolinas-sex-offender-registry-has-turned-into-punishment
        Evans, Alexis, "Is Sex Offender Registration a Cruel and Unusual Punishment?" *Law Street, Lewis and Clark Law School,* March 17, 2015, http:// lawstreetmedia.com/news/is-sex-offender-registration-a-cruel-and-unusual-punishment

128.   Allred, Gloria, "Dangers of Teen Sexting?" *Lawyers.com,* accessed October 28, 2015, http://criminal.lawyers.com/juvenile-law/gloria-allred-dangers-of-teen-sexting.html

129.   Neyfakh, Leon, "Can Juries Tame Prosecutors Gone Wild?" *The Boston Globe,* February 3, 2013, https://www.bostonglobe.com/ideas/2013/02/03/can-juries-tame-prosecutors-gone-wild-can-juries-tame-prosecutors-gone-wild/yAvVOZPmpm408lskfiMe3M/story.html

130.   McKay, Hollie, "June Shannon: Relationship with Another Man on Sex Offender Registry," *FOX 411,* October 28, 2014, http://is.gd/vfOQNT

131. Marcus, Stephanie, "Police Report Details How Mama June's Ex Abused her Daughter Anna Cardwell," *Huffington Post*, October, 2014, 2:59 PM EDT, http://www.huffingtonpost.com/2014/10/28/police-report-anna-shannon-abuse_n_6061758.html

132. McKay, Hollie, "June Shannon: Relationship with Another Man on Sex Offender Registry," *FOX 411*, October 28, 2014, http://is.gd/vfOQNT

133. "PDF of Survivor Eligibility Requirements," accessed October 28, 2015, http://special.krem.com/splash/survivorcastingcall/2011/forms/survivor_eligibility_requirements.pdf
      "PDF of Participant Application & Release, Extreme Weight Loss (the 'PROGRAM') – Season 5," accessed October 28, 2015, http://www.extreme-weightlosscasting.com/uploads/documents/app.pdf, p. 1
      "Eligibility Requirements # 9 and 14," *The Bachelor,* accessed October 28, 2015, https://casting.bachelor.warnerbros.com/web/eligibility.jsp

134. Durose, Matthew and Alexia D. Cooper, Ph.D., "Recidivism of Prisoners Released in 30 States in 2005: Patterns from 2005 to 2010," *U. S. Department of Justice, Office of Justice Programs, Bureau of Justice Statistics* March 27, 2013, http://www.bjs.gov/content/pub/ascii/rprts05p0510.txt

135. Greenfeld, Lawrence, "Sex Offenses and Offenders," *U. S. Department of Justice Office of Justice Programs, Bureau of Justice Statistics,* February 1997, p. 34, NCJ-163392, http://www.bjs.gov/content/pub/pdf/SOO.PDF,

136. Tweksbury, Ph.D., Richard and Wesley G. Jennings, Ph.D., "Final Report on Sex Offenders: Recidivism and Collateral Consequences," *Sex Offenders: Recidivism & Collateral Consequences,* September 30, 2011, p. 57, https://www.ncjrs.gov/pdffiles1/nij/grants/238060.pdf,

137. "Section 3: Common Characteristics of Sex Offenders," *Center for Sex Offender Management, A Project of the Office of Justice Programs, U. S. Department of Justice,* accessed October 28, 2015, http://www.csom.org/train/etiology/3/3_1.htm#backtrack15, slide 4.

138. Ibid.

139. Chammah, Maurice, Barred from Church," *The Marshall Project,* March 11, 2015, https://www.themarshallproject.org/2015/03/11/barred-from-church

Chapter 7

140. Douglas, Frederick, "Narrative of the Life of Frederick Douglass, an American Slave. Written by Himself, 1818–1895," *Documenting the American South,* Academic Affairs Library, University of North Carolina at Chapel Hill, 1999, pp. 81–82, http://www.nps.gov/frde/learn/photosmultimedia/quotations.htm

141. "Megan's Law Website," *Pennsylvania State Police,* ©2003–2008, http://www.pameganslaw.state.pa.us/History.aspx?dt=

142. "Statement of the American Psychological Association Regarding Pedophilia and the Diagnostic and Statistical Manual of Mental Disorders (DSM-5)," *American Psychological Association,* October 31, 2013, http://www.apa.org/news/press/releases/2013/10/pedophilia-mental.aspx

143. "Mandatory Reporters of Child Abuse and Neglect," *Child Welfare Information Gateway,* 2013, accessed October 28, 2015, https://www.childwelfare.gov/pubPDFs/manda.pdf

144. Goldstein, Sasha, "Conn. Man Arrested After Asking Cops to Stop Him from Harming Schoolchildren," *Daily* NEWS, November 26, 2013, 5:42 PM, http://www.nydailynews.com/news/crime/conn-man-arrested-cops-stop-harming-schoolchildren-article-1.1530218

145. Sun, Fairfield, "Police Praise Man for Reporting His Own Thoughts of Hurting Children," *Fairfield.sun.com,* November 27, 2013, http://www.fairfield-sun.com/18570/police-praise-man-who-reported-thoughts-of-hurting-children

146. Public Charter 461, Section 1 Tennessee Code Annotated, Title 40, Chapter 39,(a), (5), accessed October 28, 2015, http://www.tn.gov/sos/acts/100/pub/Pubc0461.HTM, section 1(a)(5).

147. "Summary of the HIPPA Privacy Rule, What Information is Protected," *U. S. Department of Health & Human Services,* accessed October 28, 2015, http://www.hhs.gov/ocr/privacy/hipaa/understanding/summary

148. "HIPPA Violation and Enforcement," *American Medical Association,* ©1995–2015, http://www.ama-assn.org/ama/pub/physician-resources/solutions-managing-your-practice/coding-billing-insurance/hipaahealth-insurance-portability-accountability-act/hipaa-violations-enforcement.page?

149. Ridgeway, James, "How 'Civil Commitment' Enables Indefinite Detention of Sex Offenders," *The Guardian,* September 26, 2013, http://www.theguardian.com/commentisfree/2013/sep/26/civil-commitment-sex-offenders

150. "Legal Information Institute, Fifth Amendment," *Cornell University Law School, accessed October 28, 2015,* https://www.law.cornell.edu/wex/fifth_amendment

151. "Branding Slaves," *Encyclopedia.com,* © January 2008, *accessed October 28, 2015,* http://www.encyclopedia.com/article-1G2-3057200206/branding-slaves.html

152. Mangino, Matt, "The Cautionary Instruction: Tracking Sex Offenders for Life," *Communityvoice.com,* November 2, 2012, 6:00 AM, http://communityvoices.post-gazette.com/news/ipso-facto/34776-the-cautionary-instruction-tracking-sex-offenders-for-life

153. Zgoba, Ph.D., Kristen and Philip Witt, Ph.D., "Megan's Law: Assessing the Practical and Monetary Efficacy," *U. S. Department of Justice document 225370,* December 2008, p. 6, https://www.ncjrs.gov/pdffiles1/nij/grants/225370.pdf

154. Ibid, p. 39

155. Wildeboer, Rob, "Chicago Police Fail to Register Sex Offenders 601 Time in Just Three Months," *WBEZ91.5,* May 29, 2014, http://www.wbez.org/news/chicago-police-fail-register-sex-offenders-601-times-just-three-months-110236

156. Ibid.

157. Lo, Puck, "Sex-offender Laws Are Ineffective and Unfair, Critics Say," *Aljazeera America,* October 17, 2014, http://america.aljazeera.com/articles/2014/10/17/challenges-to-sexoffenderregistries.html#

158. Allen, Greg, "Sex Offenders Forced to Live Under Miami Bridge," *National Public Radio,* May 20 2009, http://www.npr.org/templates/story/story.php?storyId=104150499

159. Silverstrini, Elaine, "Sex Offender Had Only One Place to Live: A Parking Lot," *The Tampa Tribune,* February 14, 2015, http://californiarsol.org/2015/02/fl-sex-offender-had-only-one-place-to-live-a-parking-lot

160. Rhodes, Ph.D., William and Ryan Kling, M.A., "Federal Sentencing Disparity: 2005–2012," *Bureau of Justice Statistics Working Paper Series,* October 22, 2015, pp. 32 & 40, http://www.bjs.gov/content/pub/pdf/fsd0512.pdf

161. "Civil Commitment of Sexually Violent Predators," *Association for the Treatment of Sexual Abusers,* August 17, 2010, http://www.atsa.com/civil-commitment-sexually-violent-predators

162. "Kansas v. Hendricks, 521 U. S. 346 (1997)," *Justia U. S. Supreme Court,* October term 1996, https://supreme.justia.com/cases/federal/us/521/346/case.html http://criminal.findlaw.com/criminal-charges/civil-commitment.html

163. "Tennessee Code Annotated, §39-17-436," *Tennessee Bureau of Investigation, accessed October 29, 2015,* https://apps.tn.gov/methor
      "Meth Offender Registry," *Bureau of Criminal Apprehension, a Division of the Minnesota Department of Public Safety,* ©2015, https://dps.mn.gov/divisions/bca/Pages/meth-offender-registry.aspx
      Jackson, Angie, "With 500 Convicted Killers on the Streets, Does Michigan Need a Murderer Registry?" *M Live, Michigan,* March 22, 2015, 5:29 AM, http://www.mlive.com/news/grandrapids/index.ssf/2015/03/with_500_convicted_killers_on.html
      "Child Support Enforcement," accessed October 29, 2015, *Office of Inspector General, U.S. Department of Health & Human Services,* https://oig.hhs.gov/fraud/child-support-enforcement

164. Marine, Frank J., "A Manual for Federal Prosecutors, Fifth Revised Edition," *Criminal RICO: 18 U. S. C. §§ 1961–1968,* October 2009, http://www.justice.gov/sites/default/files/usam/legacy/2014/10/17/rico.pdf

165. Stillman, Sarah, "Taken," *The New Yorker, August 12, 2013,* http://www.newyorker.com/magazine/2013/08/12/taken

166. Potter, Dena, "Some Va. Sex Offenders Held Long After Sentence Up,"

Huffington Post, Politics, November 19, 2011, 2:11 PM EST, http://www
.huffingtonpost.com/huff-wires/20111119/us-sexual-predators-long-wait

167. Ibid.

Chapter 8

168. Mosely, E., "Incarcerated – Children of Parents in Prison Impacted," *Texas Department of Criminal Justice,* July 6–12, 2008, www.tdcj.state.tx.us/gokids/gokids_articles_children_impacted.html

169. Ibid.

170. "Little Children, Big Challenges: Incarceration," *123 Sesame Street,* accessed October 29, 2015, http://www.sesamestreet.org/parents/topicsandactivities/toolkits/incarceration

171. "Title I-Reasonable Efforts and Safety Requirements for Foster Care and Adoption Placement, H. R. 867–2, Section 101. (c) TRANSITION RULES" *One Hundred Fifth Congress of the United States of America at the First Session,* January 7, 1997, http://www.pbs.org/wgbh/pages/frontline/shows/fostercare/inside/asfa.html

172. Durose, Matthew R. and Patrick A. Langan, Ph.D., "National Judicial Reporting Program Felony Sentences in State Courts, 2004," *U. S. Department of Justice, Office of Justice Programs, Bureau of Justice Statistics Bulletin,* July 2007, NCJ 215646, http://www.bjs.gov/content/pub/ascii/fssc04.txt

173. Waul, Michelle and Jeremy Travis, "Background Paper: The Effect of Incarceration and Reentry on Children, Families, and Communities," *URBAN Institute,* January 30, 2002, pp. xi–xvi, http://www.urban.org/research/publication/background-paper-effect-incarceration-and-reentry-children-families-and-communities/view/full_report,

174. Sanders, Emily and Rachel Dunifon, "Children of Incarcerated Parents," *Cornell University, College of Human Ecology,* ©2011, p. 3, http://www.human.cornell.edu/pam/outreach/parenting/parents/upload/Children-of-Incarcerated-Parents.pdf,

175. Ibid.

176. "Visitation, G, 2, b," *Administrative Policies and Procedures, State of Tennessee Department of Corrections,* April 1, 2014, p. 8, http://www.tn.gov/assets/entities/correction/attachments/507-01.pdf,

177. Travis, Jeremy, and Michelle Waul, "The Effects of Parental Incarceration on Children: Perspectives, Promises, and Policies," *Parke, Ross D, and Alison Clarke-Stewart, Prisoners Once Removed. Ed.* © 2003, The Urban Institute Press, 2100 M Street, Washington, D.C. 20037, pp. 198–232, http://is.gd/qejaVQ

178. Newby, Gretchen, "Children of Incarcerated Parents: A Bill of Rights," *San Francisco Children of Incarcerated Parents Partnership*, revised summer 2005, http://www.sfcipp.org/images/brochure.pdf

Chapter 9

179. Cagir, MD, Burt, "Lower Gastrointestinal Bleeding Clinical Presentation," *Medscape*, updated December 31, 2014, http://emedicine.medscape.com/article/188478-clinical

180. Ford-Martin, Paula, "Halfway House," *Encyclopedia.com*, ©2001, The Gale Group Inc., http://www.encyclopedia.com/topic/Halfway_House.aspx

181. "Inmate Statistics, Offenses," *Federal Bureau of Prisons*, updated September 26, 2015, http://www.bop.gov/about/statistics/statistics_inmate_offenses.jsp

182. Pollack, Harold, "Alcohol Linked to More Homicides in US Than any Other Substance," *New Haven Register*, August 20, 2014, http://www.nhregister.com/general-news/20140820/alcohol-linked-to-more-homicides-in-us-than-any-other-substance

183. Lambert, Dr., Steven, "Signs of Spiritual Abuse," *Charismatic Captivation*, November 15, 2008, http://www.charismatic-captivation.com/the-signs-of-spiritual-abuse

184. "United States Supreme Court, Shelley V. Kraemer, No. 72," *FindLaw® For Legal Professionals*, Decided May 3, 1949, http://caselaw.findlaw.com/us-supreme-court/334/1.html

185. "Bush Whacked," *Snopes.com*, updated November 28, 2007, accessed November 2, 2015, http:www.snopes.com/inboxer/outrage/bush.asp

186. "Anti-Drug Abuse Act of 1988," *Public Law 100–690, 100th Congress*, November 18, 1988, http://www.legisworks.org/GPO/STATUTE-102-Pg4181.pdf

187. Ibid.

188. Gartner, Nancy and Judith Resnik," Keeping Female Prisoners Close to Family," *The Boston Globe*, September 3, 2013, http://www.bostonglobe.com/opinion/2013/09/03/keep-female-prisoners-close-family/eQf4dCawmOGmQ41Ap53GxL/story.html

189. Holt, Norman and D. Miller, " NCJ 00249, 1972, California State Department of Corrections, https://www.ncjrs.gov/App/Publications/abstract.aspx?ID=2459

190. Latessa, Edward and Christopher Lowenkamp," What Works in Reducing Recidivism? The Principles of Effective Intervention," *University of St. Thomas Law Journal*, Vol. 3:3, 2006, http://ojj.la.gov/ojj/files/What_Works_STLJ.pdf, pp. 521–522

191. Ibid.

192. Ibid., pp. 528–533.

193. Bruns, Chrissy and Lauren McFall, "Great Expectations? An Investigation of Teacher Expectation Research," *EDP 603: Theories of Learning*, December 6, 2000, http://www.users.miamioh.edu/shermalw/edp603_group2-foo.html

194. Mathews, Kevin, "Go to Jail for Free Health Care? 5 Desperate People Who Tried," *Care2*.com March 4, 2013, 6:00 AM, http://www.care2.com/causes/go-to-jail-for-free-health-care-5-desperate-people-who-tried.html

195. Wilper, MD, Andrew P. and Steffie Woolhandler, MD, "The Health and Health Care of US Prisoners: Results of a Nationwide Survey, *American Journal of Public Health*, April 2009; 99(4):666–672, http://www.ncbi.nlm.nih.gov/pmc/articles/PMC2661478

196. Delgado, Melvin and Denise Humm-Delgado, "Health and Health Care in the Nation's Prisons," *Rowman & Littlefield Publishers, Inc.*, Lanham, UK, © 2009, http://www.heart-intl.org/Mort/113010/Healthcareintodaysprison.pdf, p. 169.

197. Ibid., p. 57.

198. Faber, Bernard, "Civil Liability for Inadequate Prisoner Medical Care – An Introduction " *AELE Monthly Law Journal, Jail and Prison Law Section,*-September 2007, http://www.aele.org/law/2007JBSEP/2007–09MLJ301.pdf

Chapter 10

199. Staff writer, "Nashville Police Chief Shares Message, Responds to Questions," *The Tennessean*, January 1, 2015, 2:32 PM, http://www.tennessean.com/story/news/local/davidson/2014/12/26/nashville-police-chief-shares-message-responds-to-questions/20914171

200. "Statement of Laura Moskowitz, Staff Attorney, National Employment Law Project's Second Chance Labor Project," *U. S. Equal Employment Opportunity Commission*, November 20, 2008, http://www.eeoc.gov/eeoc/meetings/11–20-08/moskowitz.cfm

201. Lowenstein, John, "US: Drug Arrests Skewed by Race, National Data on 1980–2007 Cases Show Huge Disparities" *Human Rights Watch*, March 2, 2009, http://www.hrw.org/news/2009/03/02/us-drug-arrests-skewed-race

202. Harris, Alexes and Katherine Beckett, "Racial Disparities in Criminal Justice," *Presentation at University of Washington*, accessed November 2, 2015, http://www.law.washington.edu/about/racetaskforce/Harris_Becket_Sup_Ct.pdf

203. Kansal, Tushar, "Racial Disparities in Sentencing: A Review of the Literature," *The Sentencing Project*, Washington D.C, January 2005, http://www.sentencingproject.org/doc/publications/rd_sentencing_review.pdf

204. "Race, Ethnicity, and the Criminal Justice System, *American Sociological As*-

sociation – Department of Research and Development, ©September 2007, p. 21, http://www.asanet.org/images/press/docs/pdf/ASARaceCrime.pdf

205. "Pepsi to Pay $3.13 Million and Made Major Policy Changes t resolve EEOC Finding of Nationwide Hiring Discrimination Against African Americans, *U. S. Equal Employment Opportunity Commission,* press release January 11, 2012, http://www.eeoc.gov/eeoc/newsroom/release/1-11-12a.cfm

206. "Consideration of Arrest and Conviction Records in Employment Decisions Under Title VII of the Civil Rights Act of 1964, *EEOC Enforcement Guidance Number 915.002,* April 25, 2012, http://www.eeoc.gov/laws/guidance/arrest_conviction.cfm#VB4

207. Kurlychek, Megan and Shawn D. Bushway, "Scarlet Letters and Recidivism: Does and Old Criminal Record Predict Future Offending?" *Criminology & Public Policy, Vol. 5, Issue 3,* September 13, 2006, pp. 483–504, http://www.albany.edu/bushway_research/publications/Kurlychek_et_al_2006.pdf

208. Pager, Devah, and Bruce Western, "Identifying Discrimination at Work: The Use of Field Experiments," *Journal of Social Issues, June: 68 (2), pp. 231–237, http://www.ncbi.nlm.nih.gov/pmc/articles/PMC3807133/*

209. "Written Testimony of Stephen Salzburg, Professor George Washington University Law School, EEOC to Examine Arrest and Conviction Records as a Hiring Barrier," *U. S. Equal Employment Opportunity Commission,* July 26, 2011, http://www.eeoc.gov/eeoc/meetings/7-26-11/saltzburg.cfm

210. Ibid.

211. Laird, Lorelei, "Exo-offenders Face Tens of Thousands of Legal Restrictions, Bias and Limits on Their Rights," ABA *Journal,* June 1, 2013, 10:00 AM, http://www.abajournal.com/magazine/article/ex-offenders_face_tens_of_thousands_of_legal_restrictions

212. "The Attorney General's Report on Criminal History Background Checks," *U. S. Department of Justice,* June 2006, p. 3, http://www.bjs.gov/content/pub/pdf/ag_bgchecks_report.pdf

Chapter 11

213. Brown, Julie K., "Staff at a Miami-Dade Prison Tormented, Abused Mentally Ill Inmates, Former Worker Says," *Miami Herald,* May 19, 2014, http://www.miamiherald.com/news/local/community/miami-dade/article1964709.html

214. Brown, Julie K., "Inmate's Gassing Death Detailed in Florida DOC Whistle-Blower Complaint," *Miami Herald,* July 7, 2014, http://www.miamiherald.com/news/local/community/miami-dade/article1974526.html

215. Brown, Julie K., "After Florida Inmate's Lethal Gassing, Claims of Cover-up," *Miami Herald,* August 30, 2014, http://www.miamiherald.com/news/politics-government/article1985286.html

216. Brown, Julie, "Florida Prison Boss Fires 32 Over Inmate Death," *Miami Herald,* September 1, 2014, http://www.miamiherald.com/news/local/crime/article2176191.html

217. Jones, Secretary, Julie L., "Inmate Mortality with Redacted Case Summary," *Florida Department of Corrections,* accessed November 3, 2015, http://www.dc.state.fl.us/pub/mortality/summary.html

218. Hunter, Frances, "Frances Hunter's American Heroes Blog," October 8, 2009, https://franceshunter.wordpress.com/2009/10/08/murder-and-madness-in-the-lewis-family

219. Douglass, Frederick, "Narrative of the Life of Frederick Douglass," *SparkNotes, Literature Study Guide,"* accessed November 4, 2015, http://www.sparknotes.com/lit/narrative/section3/page/2

220. "Impact of *Uncle Tom's Cabin,* Slavery, and the Civil War, *"Harriet Beecher Stowe Center,* accessed November 4, 2015, http://www.harrietbeecherstowecenter.org/utc/impact.shtml

221. "Thirty-eighth Congress, Sess. II Res. 9–12, Article XIII, 1965, *The Library of Congress, p. 567,* http://memory.loc.gov/cgi-bin/ampage?collId=llsl&fileName=013/llsl013.db&recNum=596

222. Steiner, Ph.D., Benjamin and Benjamin Meade, Ph.D., "Assessing the Relationship Between Exposure to Violence and Inmate Maladjustment Within and Across State Correctional Facilities," *The National Institute of Justice Office of Justice Programs,* September 30, 2013, https://www.ncjrs.gov/pdffiles1/nij/grants/243901.pdf

223. Denhof, Ph.D., Michael and Caterina G. Spinaris, Ph. D, "Depression, PTSD, and Comorbidity in United States Corrections Professionals: Prevalence and Impact on Health and Functioning," *Desert Waters Correctional Outreach,* August 5, 2011, http://desertwaters.com/wp-content/uploads/2013/09/Comorbidity_Study_09-03-131.pdf

224. Finley, Bruce, "Prison Horrors Haunt Guards' Private Lives, *The Denver Post,* March 24, 2007, 01:00 AM, http://www.denverpost.com/ci_5510659

225. Spitz, Rene A., "Emotional Deprivation in Infancy Study," *I Aim Australia,* 1952, accessed November 4, 2015, https://vimeo.com/99876904

226. Breslow, Jason M, "What Does Solitary Confinement Do to Your Mind?" NPT *Frontline,* April 22, 2014, 9:44 PM. ET, http://www.pbs.org/wgbh/pages/frontline/criminal-justice/locked-up-in-america/what-does-solitary-confinement-do-to-your-mind

227. "U. S. Constitution, Eighth Amendment," *Cornell University Law School's Legal Information Institute,* accessed November 4, 2015, https://www.law.cornell.edu/constitution/eighth_amendment

228. Casella, Jean and James Ridgeway, "How Many Prisoners are in Solitary

Confinement in the United States?," *Solitary Watch,* accessed November 4, 2015, 4http://solitarywatch.com/2012/02/01/how-many-prisoners-are-in-solitary-confinement-in-the-united-states/

229. Finley, Bruce, "Prison Horrors Haunt Guards' Private Lives," *The Denver Post,* March 24, 2007 1:00 AM, http://www.denverpost.com/ci_5510659

230. Ibid.

231. *Bartlett's Familiar Black Quotations.* Retha Powers. Redral Edition, Little, Brown, and Company, Hachette Book Group, 237 Park Avenue, NY, NY 10017 © 2013, p. 9.

232. Fuchs, Erin, "America's Prison Guards are the 'Ugly Stepchildren' of the Criminal Justice System," *Business Insider,* May 2, 2013, 9:19 AM, http://www.businessinsider.com/whats-wrong-with-american-prison-guards-2013–4
   "Federal Prison and the Corrupt Partnership Between Inmates and Prison Guards," *HubPages,* updated April 18, 2014, http://klw1157.hubpages.com/hub/Federal-Inmates-are-resourceful
   Winerip, Michael and Michael Schwirtz, "New York's Top Jail Investigator Resigns After Inquiry on rikers Brutality," *The New York Times,* August 22, 2014, http://is.gd/X0b6CP

233. CNN Library, "Iraq Prison Abuse Scandal Fast Facts," *CNN, updated March 27, 2015, 5:31 PM ET,* http://www.cnn.com/2013/10/30/world/meast/iraq-prison-abuse-scandal-fast-facts

234. Montopoli, Brian, "Army Officer Reprimanded Over Abu Ghraib," *CBSNEWS,* August 29, 2007, 8:50 AM, http://www.cbsnews.com/news/army-officer-reprimanded-over-abu-ghraib

235. Dishneau, David, "Charles Graner Released: Abu Ghraib Abuse Ringleader Set Free from Kansas Prison," *The World Post,* October 6, 2011, 2:24 PM EDT, http://www.huffingtonpost.com/2011/08/06/charles-graner-released-_n_920210.html

Chapter 12

236. "Frank Sinatra Quotes," *Brainy Quote,* accessed February 19, 2015, http://www.brainyquote.com/quotes/quotes/f/franksinat379942.html

237. "Staff/Inmate Relationships," *State of Alabama Department of Corrections,* January 14, 2005, http://www.doc.state.al.us/docs/AdminRegs/AR318.pdf
   Reid, Tom, "State Department of Corrections Web-Based Policy and Procedure Manuals (May 2015), *NIC Information Center,* May 23, 2012, 10:04 AM, https://nic.zendesk.com/entries/21457491-State-Departments-of-Corrections-Web-Based-Policy-and-Procedure-Manuals

238. Robbins, Tom, "Attica's Prosecutors Show Their Hand," *The Marshall Project,* March 5, 2015, 2:53 PM, https://www.themarshallproject.org/2015/03/05/attica-s-prosecutors-show-their-hand

239. Ibid.

240. Ibid.

241. Lopez, Oscar, "Prison Officers Need Help, But They Won't Ask for It," *Newsweek*, May 27, 2014, 5:27, http://www.newsweek.com/2014/06/06/prison-officers-need-help-they-wont-ask-it-252439.html

Chapter 13

242. Simon, Mallory, "More Than 2,000 Wrongfully Convicted People Exonerated in 23 Years, Researchers Say," *CNN NEWS*, May 21, 2012, 10:36 AM ET, http://news.blogs.cnn.com/2012/05/21/more-than-2000-wrongfully-convicted-people-exonerated-in-23-years-researchers-say

243. "The Registry, Exonerations and False Convictions," *The National Registry of Exonerations, A Project of the University of Michigan Law School*, ©2015, accessed November 4, 2015, https://www.law.umich.edu/special/exoneration/Pages/learnmore.aspx

244. "An Epidemic of Prosecutor Misconduct," *Center for Prosecutor Integrity*, ©2013, accessed November 4, 2015, p. 5, http://www.prosecutorintegrity.org/wp-content/uploads/EpidemicofProsecutorMisconduct.pdf,

245. Ibid., pp. 13–14.

246. O'Brien, Tim, "Prosecutorial Misconduct," *Religion & Ethics*, July 13, 2012, http://www.pbs.org/wnet/religionandethics/2012/07/13/july-13–2012-prosecutorial-misconduct/11821

247. Davis, Angela, "The Legal Professions' Failure to Discipline Unethical Prosecutors," *Hofstra Law Review, Vol. 36:275*, p. 277, http://law.hofstra.edu/pdf/academics/journals/lawreview/lrv_issues_v36n02_cc3.davis.36.2.pdf

248. Rehavi, M. Marit and Sonja B. Starr, "Racial Disparity in Federal Criminal Sentences," *Journal of Political Economy, 2014, vol. 122, no. 6*, p. 1320, http://econ.sites.olt.ubc.ca/files/2015/01/pdf_paper_marit-rehavi-racial_disparity.pdf

249. Michaelson, Jay, "95% of Prosecutors Are White and They Treat Blacks Worse," *The Daily Beast*, August 17, 2015, 1:12 AM ET, http://www.thedailybeast.com/articles/2015/08/17/95-of-prosecutors-are-white-and-they-treat-blacks-worse.html

250. Rehavi, M. Marit and Sonja B. Starr, "Racial Disparity in Federal Criminal Sentences," *Journal of Political Economy, 2014, vol. 122, no. 6*, pp. 1349–1350, http://econ.sites.olt.ubc.ca/files/2015/01/pdf_paper_marit-rehavi-racial_disparity.pdf

251. Ibid., p. 1349.

Chapter 14

252. Gnaticov, Cristian, "New Jersey Police Destroys BMW Searching for Nonexistent Weed," *INAUTONEWS*, December 30, 2011, http://www.inautonews.com/new-jersey-police-destroys-bmw-searching-for-nonexistent-weed

253. Segal, David, "Mugged by a Mug Shot," *The New York Times, Business Day*, October 5, 2013, http://www.nytimes.com/2013/10/06/business/mugged-by-a-mug-shot-online.html?_r=0

254. Daly, Michael, "The Day Ferguson Cops Were Caught in a Bloody Lie," *The Daily Beast*, August 15, 2014, 5:55 AM ET, http://www.thedailybeast.com/articles/2014/08/15/the-day-ferguson-cops-were-caught-in-a-bloody-lie.html

255. "Voluntary Agreement to Resign from Judicial Office in Lieu of Disciplinary Action, In Re: Honorable Elizabeth E. Coker," *The State of Texas State commission on Judicial Conduct*, October 21, 2013, http://is.gd/sLTdFt

256. "'Texting Judge' Elizabeth Coker Announces District Attorney Run Two Days After Resigning from Bench," *Opposing View*, December 16, 2013, http://www.opposingviews.com/i/society/texting-judge-elizabeth-coker-announces-district-attorney-run-two-days-after-resigning#

257. "Elizabeth E. Coker," *BallotPedia, The Encyclopedia of American Politics*, accessed November 4, 2015, accessed November 4, 2015, http://ballotpedia.org/Elizabeth_E._Coker

258. Hill, Gerald N. and Kathleen T. Hill, "Presumption of Innocence," *The Free Dictionary by* Farlex, ©1981–2005, http://legal-dictionary.thefreedictionary.com/Innocent+until+proven+guilty

259. "U. S. Code § 863—Drug Paraphernalia," *Cornell University Law School*, accessed November 4, 2015, https://www.law.cornell.edu/uscode/text/21/863

260. "Can Passengers Drink Alcohol in a Car?" *Findlaw.com*, ©2013, accessed November 4, 2015, http://dui.findlaw.com/dui-charges/can-a-passenger-drink-in-a-car-.html

261. "Morgan v. DeRobertis, 582m F. Supp. 271 (N. D. ILL. 1984," April 6, 1984, https://www.courtlistener.com/opinion/1759863/morgan-v-derobertis

262. "Tennessee Code Annotated, Section 39–16–201, *Senate Bill 1254 by Gardenhire, accessed November 4, 2015,* http://www.capitol.tn.gov/Bills/108/Bill/SB1254.pdf

263. Ginder, Scott, and Margaret Noonan, "Mortality in Local Jails and State Prisons, 2000–2011 – Statistical Tables, *Office of Justice Programs, Bureau of Justice*, August 13, 2013, p. 25, http://www.bjs.gov/index.cfm?ty=pbdetail&iid=4757

264. Ibid., 35–40.

265. Owens, Michael Leo, "2.7 Million Children Under the Age of 18 Have a Parent in Prison or Jail—We Need Criminal Justice Reform Now," *ALTERNET,*

August 19, 2013, http://www.alternet.org/civil-liberties/27-million-children-under-age-18-have-parent-prison-or-jail

266. Irwin, Ph.D., John and Vincent Schiraldi, "America's One Million Nonviolent Prisoners," *Justice Policy Institute,* March 1999, accessed November 4, 2015, http://www.justicepolicy.org/images/upload/99–03_REP_OneMillionNonviolentPrisoners_AC.pdf

267. Straub, Steve, "James Madison, Speech at the Virginia Convention to Ratify the Federal Constitution," *The Federalist Paper Project,* accessed 12/18/2015, http://is.gd/1jbvn9

268. Biograpy.com Editors, "James Madison Biography," *The Biography.com,* November 4, 2015, http://www.biography.com/people/james-madison-9394965

269. Specter, Michael, "Getting a Fix," *The New Yorker,* October 17, 2011, http://www.newyorker.com/magazine/2011/10/17/getting-a-fix

Chapter 15

270. Binder, Guyora, "Making the Best of Felony Murder," *Boston University Law Review,* Vol. 91: 403, 2011, p. 414, https://www.bu.edu/law/central/jd/organizations/journals/bulr/documents/BINDER.pdf,
    "Homicide Act 1957, Chapter 11 5 and 6 Eliz 2," *Delivered by The National Archives, Legislation.gov.uk,* accessed November 4, 2015, http://www.legislation.gov.uk/ukpga/Eliz2/5–6/11

271. "Homicide Act 1957, Chapter 11 5 and 6 Eliz 2," *The National Archives,* March 21, 1957, http://www.legislation.gov.uk/ukpga/Eliz2/5–6/11

272. Fantz, Ashley, "Tennessee Case Twists and Turns Toward Death, *CNN.com,* May 4, 2007, 11:51 AM, http://www.cnn.com/2007/US/05/02/workman.sidebar/

273. Broadbent, Joseph, "What is Felony Murder?" *Criminal Defense Lawyer published by NOLO,* ©2015 NOLO, http://www.criminaldefenselawyer.com/resources/felony-murder.htm

274. Farber, Ph.D., Seth, "Tennessee Justice—The Scapegoating of Teresa Deion Harris," *The Official Teresa Deion Harris Website,* accessed November 4, 2015, http://www.freedeionharris.com/TN_Justice_-_Scapegoating.html

275. McGinley, Judge, Charles, "Teresa Deion Smith Harris v. State of Tennessee, *In the Court of Criminal Appeals of Tennessee at Jackson,* August 15, 2012, https://www.tba.org/sites/default/files/harrist_081512.pdf
    Guinn, Judge, Gulian P., "District Appeal from the Circuit Court for Carroll County, Stacey Dewayne Ramsey v. State of Tennessee, *In the Court of Criminal Appeals of Tennessee at Jackson,* October 2, 2007, http://www.tba2.org/tba_files/TCCA/2008/ramseys_090808.pdf

276. Farber, Ph.D., Seth, "Tennessee Justice—The Scapegoating of Teresa Deion

Harris," *The Official Teresa Deion Harris Website*, accessed November 4, 2015, http://www.freedeionharris.com/TN_Justice_-_Scapegoating.html

277. "Prosecution Function, Part I. General Standards," *American Bar Association*, ©2015 ABA, accessed November 4, 2015, http://www.americanbar.org/publications/criminal_justice_section_archive/crimjust_standards_pfunc_blkold.html

    McGinley, Judge, Charles C., Appeal from the Circuit Court for Henry County, Teresa Deion Smith Harris v. State of Tennessee, *In the Court of Criminal Appeals of Tennessee at Jackson, August 15, 2012*, https://www.tba.org/sites/default/files/harrist_081512.pdf

278. "Case Corruption, Little Known Facts Surrounding the Case," *The Official Teresa Deion Harris Website, accessed November 4, 2015*, http://www.freedeionharris.com/Case_Corruption.html

279. "Letter to Deion from Walter, 06/22/06," *The Official Teresa Deion Harris Website*, accessed November 4, 2015, http://www.freedeionharris.com/Letter_from_Walter.html

280. Farber, Ph.D., Seth, "Tennessee Justice—The Scapegoating of Teresa Deion Harris," *The Official Teresa Deion Harris Website*, accessed November 4, 2015, http://www.freedeionharris.com/TN_Justice_-_Scapegoating.html

281. McGinley, Judge, Charles, "Teresa Deion Smith Harris v. State of Tennessee, *In the Court of Criminal Appeals of Tennessee at Jackson*, August 15, 2012, https://www.tba.org/sites/default/files/harrist_081512.pdf

282. Ibid., p. 2.

283. Matthew 5:44 NIV

Chapter 16

284. "Insanity Defense," *Cornell University Law School*, access November 4, 2015, http://www.law.cornell.edu/wex/insanity_defense

285. "Teresa Bagioli Sickles," *MationMaster.com, Encyclopedia*, accessed November 4, 2015, http://www.statemaster.com/encyclopedia/Teresa-Bagioli-Sickles#_note-9

286. "Law Enforcement Student Convicted of Black's Death," *Florence Times—Tri Cities Daily*, March 5, 1977, http://is.gd/iACezI

287. "What is Parole?" *The United States department of Justice*, September 29, 2015, http://www.justice.gov/uspc/frequently-asked-questions#q1

288. "Mission Statement," *TN Board of Parole*, accessed November 4, 2015, http://www.tn.gov/bop/article/mission-statement

289. Montgomery, Ricard, "Annual Report 2014–2015, *Board of Parole, State of Tennessee*, October 1, 2015, pp. 3 & 15 http://www.tn.gov/assets/entities/bop/

attachments/2014–15_BOP_Annual_Report.pdf

290. Ibid., p. 12.

291. Hipp, John and Joan Petersilia, "Parolee Recidivism in California: The Effect of Neighborhood Context and Social Service Agency Characteristics, *Criminology,* Vol. 48, Issue 4, pp. 947–979, November 2010, http://onlinelibrary .wiley.com/doi/10.1111/j.1745–9125.2010.00209.x/abstract

292. "Prisons, Reformatories and Penal Institutions in Tennessee," (1937), Ex. No. 8914, at 53, p. 1064, https://casetext.com/case/grubbs-v-bradley (note, you must be a member of casetext to access this url)

293. Ibid., p. 78.

294. Ibid., pp. 76–80.

Chapter 17

295. "Public Housing and Disparate Impact: A Model Policy," *Formerly Incarcerated & Convicted People's Movement,* 2013, p. 2, accessed November 4, 2015, https://ficpmovement.files.wordpress.com/2013/04/communities-evictions-criminal-convictions.pdf

296. "List of Incidents of Civil Unrest in the United States," *Wikipedia,* last modified October 29, 2015, 20:06, http://en.wikipedia.org/wiki/List_of_incidents_ of_civil_unrest_in_the_United_States

297. Gold, MD, Mark S., "Stages of Change," *PsychCentral,* October 4, 2006, http://psychcentral.com/lib/stages-of-change/000265

298. Ibid.

299. Reid, Paula, "Can a Connecticut City be a Model for Reforming the Ferguson Police Force?" *CBS NEWS,* April 2, 2015, 6:00 AM, http://www.cbsnews .com/news/can-east-haven-ct-be-a-model-for-reforming-the-ferguson-police-force

300. Emerman, David and Edward R. Lennon, Jr., "East Haven Police Department Two-Year Compliance Report," *East Haven Department of Police Services,* January 20, 2015, http://www.easthavenpolice.com/files/5614/2204/4621/ East_Haven_Police_-_Two_Year_Compliance_Report_January_2015.pdf

301. "Overview," *Drug Court Metropolitan Nashville & Davidson County,* accessed November 4, 2015, http://drugcourt.nashville.gov/overview

302. Clark, Anna, "Redesigning a Prison Town," *NEXT CITY,* September 4, 2015, http://nextcity.org/daily/entry/closing-prison-towns-economy-jobs-redesign

303. Zillman, Claire, "Apple's Refusal to Hire Felons to Construct Its Headquarters Points to a Deeper Problem," *Fortune, April 8, 2015,* http://fortune .com/2015/04/08/apple-criminal-background-checks-hiring

304. Schouten, Fredreka, "Koch Industries Drops Criminal-History Question from Job Applications," *USA TODAY,* April 27, 2015, http://www.usatoday.com/story/ news/2015/04/27/koch-industries-criminal-justice-job-applications/26325929

305. Ibid.

306. Fang, Marina, "Obama to Announce Executive Action to 'Ban the Box'," *The Huffington Post,* November 2, 2015, http://www.huffingtonpost.com/entry/ barack-obama-ban-the-box_5636aee8e4b00aa54a4e8c9d

307. "Historical Federal Workforce Tables," *U.S. Office of Personnel Management,* accessed November 6, 2015, https://www.opm.gov/policy-data-oversight/ data-analysis-documentation/federal-employment-reports/historical-tables/ total-government-employment-since-1962/

308. Thompson, Nicholas, "My Brain Made Me Do It," *legalaffairs,* January/February 2006, accessed November 4, 2015, http://www.legalaffairs.org/issues/ January-February-2006/feature_thompson_janfeb06.msp

309. Wood, Janice, "Scans Show Psychopaths have Brain Abnormalities," *Psych- Central,* May 11, 2012, http://psychcentral.com/news/2012/05/11/scans-show- psychopaths-have-brain-abnormalities/38540.html

310. Freeman, Shanna, "How Lobotomies Work," *How Stuff Works.com,* October 27, 2008, updated November 4, 2015, http://science.howstuffworks.com/life/ inside-the-mind/human-brain/lobotomy4.htm

311. "NOVA, National Organization for Victim Assistance," http://www.trynova.org "The National Center for Victims of Crime," https://www. victimsofcrime.org

312. Biography.com editors, "Lorena Bobbitt Biography," *The Biograpy.com,* November 4, 2015, http://www.biography.com/people/lorena-bobbitt-235414

313. Ibid

314. Wachtel, Ted, "Defining Restorative, History, *International Institute for Restorative Practices, A Graduate School,*©2012, accessed November 4, 2015, http:// www.iirp.edu/what-is-restorative-practices.php

315. *O'Connell, Terry, "Restorative Justice Pioneer Terry O'Connell Awarded Honorary Doctorate, International Institute for Restorative Practices, October 10, 2008* http://www.iirp.edu/article_detail.php?article_id=NjI1

316. Caroline, Angel, "Crime Victims Meet Their Offenders: Testing the Impact of Restorative Justice Conferences on Victim's Post-Traumatic Stress Symptoms," *Dissertations available from ProQuest.* Paper AAI3165634, January 1, 2005, http://repository.upenn.edu/dissertations/AAI3165634

317. Stanley, I. Adrian, "A Teachable Moment, *Colorado Springs Independent,* May 20, 2015, http://www.csindy.com/coloradosprings/d-11-invests-in-restorative- justice/Content?oid=3077790

318. Ibid.

319. Wachtel, Joshua, "May 2015 Restorative Practices News Roundup, Schools," *Restorative Works Learning Network,* May 28, 2015, http://restorativeworks. net/2015/05/may-2015-restorative-practices-news-roundup

320. Latimer, Jeff and Craig Dowden, "The Effectiveness of Restorative Justice Practices: A Meta-Analysis," *The Prison Journal, Vol. 85 No. 2,* June 2005, pp. 127–144, ©2005 Sage Publications, http://www.d.umn.edu/~jmaahs/ Correctional%20Assessment/rj_meta%20analysis.pdf
      Porter, Abbey, "Restorative Practices in Schools: Research Reveals Power of Restorative Approach, Part II, *International Institute for Restorative Practices,* June 6, 2007, http://www.iirp.edu/article_detail.php?article_id=NTUz

321. M. Carl, "The Origins of the Bell Curve—The Real Secret of the Super Rich, Part 2, blog posted, December 25, 2009, http://paidtoberich.blogspot .com/2009/12/origins-of-bell-curve-real-secret-of.html

322. Weisenthal, Joe, "We Love What Warren Buffett Says About Life, Luck, and Winning the 'Ovarian Lottery'," *Business Insider,* December 14, 2013, 4:48 PM http://www.businessinsider.com/warren-buffett-on-the- ovarian-lottery-2013–12

323. "The Fundamental Premise," *International Institute for Restorative Practices,* accessed November 4, 2015, http://www.iirp.edu/restorative-successes.php

324. NC, Mark, "Bill O'Reilly, FOX News, Jesse Watters, blog posted by *General, Propaganda, Wankery,* January 22, 2015, Fhttp://www.newscorpse.com/ ncWP/?p=24736

325. "Our Mission," *Law Enforcement Leaders to Reduce Crime & Incarceration,* accessed November 4, 2015, www.lawenforcementleaders.org

326. *"In His Own Words, Nelson Mandela's Most Inspiring Quotes," The Daily Beast,* December 5, 2013, 5:00 PM ET, *www.thedailybeast.com/articles/2013/12/05/ nelson-mandela-s-most-inspiring-quotes.html*

327. "Nelson Mandela>Quotes," *goodreads,* accessed November 4, 2015, https:// www.goodreads.com/author/quotes/367338.Nelson_Mandela

328. "54d. The Sit-In Movement," *U.S. History,* accessed November 4, 2015, http:// www.ushistory.org/us/54d.asp

329. Driscoll, Matt, "The City's New Gambit to End Homelessness," *Seattle Weekly,* June 3, 2013, 11:45 AM, http://www.seattleweekly.com/home/947558–129/ seattle-cci-says-downtown-street-homeless
      Kruse, Brandi, "Homeless in Seattle: How One Young Man Ended Up on the City's Streets," Q13 FOX News This Morning, March 31, 2015, http://q13fox .com/2015/03/31/homeless-in-seattle-how-one-man-ended-up-on-the-citys- streets
      "Homeless Outreach Team," *City of Wichita, Kansas,* accessed November

      4, 2015, http://www.wichita.gov/Government/Departments/WPD/FieldSer-
      vices/HOTTeam/Pages/default.aspx

330. "Race Together: Conversation has the Power to Change Hearts and Minds,"
      Starbucks Newsroom, March 17, 2015, https://news.starbucks.com/news/
      race-together-conversation-has-the-power-to-change-hearts-and-minds

331. Burnett, Micha, "Quotes by This Author, Benjamin Franklin" *Our Republic,*
      accessed November 4, 2015, http://www.ourrepubliconline.com/Author/21

82125071R00187